To ı

For his sharp-eyed skill as my
first copyeditor despite having no
professional background as such.
It must be in the genes.
Sadly, so was cancer.

Introduction

I thought long and hard about some way to organize this stuff, but I finally realized it would be impossible. Despite this, I think I can deliver to you a fair amount of entertainment, along with a lot of eyeball-rolling, and perhaps even some education – that is, if you're willing to admit, as I do, that no one can know everything about the English language. But let me begin by telling you about SOTS.

SOTS? What the heck is SOTS?

The idea of SOTS – the **S**ave **O**ur **T**ongue Society – came to me one night in January 1974 as I sat idly wondering what to put on the front page of the mimeographed February issue of *Mensagenda*, the local-chapter newsletter of Minnesota Mensa, of which I was editor at the time. (Using artwork of any kind on mimeograph called for talents I did not possess, so I had no choice but to fill that front page with text.) Hmm, I wondered … what can I talk about? … must be something ...

I then remembered that as I was having my supper earlier that evening I had been watching the *CBS Evening News* with Walter Cronkite, known to a sizeable segment of the populace at the time as "the most trusted man in America." In one respect, however, I was not among them, because I clearly heard "Uncle Walter" pronounce the second month of the year as "Feb-yoo-wary" – indeed I did. It's not that I was a language purist: I had to have something to write about, and Mr. Cronkite's gaffe was better than anything else I could think of. I dared not pass it up.

Remember, now, that this is 1974, I was still a bit wet behind the editorial ears, and it was dashed off somewhat in haste. This is what I wrote on what for me turned out to be a rather memorable occasion:

FEBUARY?

The Annual Meeting of the Save Our Tongue Society (SOTS) will now come to order! Each year at this time, we assemble to discuss the serious deterioration of the English language. As you can all see above [pardon the bad grammar], the month we are now in is spelled the way most television and radio mush-mouths pronounce the word. Many articulate and supposedly knowledgeable (?) etymologists have written at length about the evolution (read "change") in language structure as societies change. Spellings and pronunciations alter gradually over periods of time. Be it hereby resolved that sometimes THINGS GET OUT OF HAND!

Is the oyster crop to be reduced by half this month? Are calendar makers soon to succumb to total confusion, perhaps leaving the month out entirely to avoid all arguments? Feb-yoo-ary? Maybe if we change the first month to "Janruary" typesetters paid by the letter will not be made to suffer financial hardship. How about if we add the missing letter at the end of the year? Would Decemberr turn colder?

SOTS must dedicate itself to bringing this terrible practice to a halt. It has been suggested that we begin by lobbying for legislation setting forth drastic penalties for the crime. First offenders would be required to write "February" 28 times (29 in leap years), have the paper notarized and sent to the appropriate governmental body. Those who transgress twice would be subject to recording the word on audio tape the same number of times and sending it to Joe Garagiola. Three-time losers would be fined $28 (or $29) and subpoenaed to appear live on the Johnny Carson show and try to stump the band with "January, Febuary, June or July." Ten points on the laugh meter would double the fine. It is the feeling of SOTS that no punishment would be too severe.

It has been moved and seconded that members resolve to devote themselves to continuing study of further measures to keep our language intact. We will meet again in 1975 for the same high purpose. A July meeting will be announced at which we will take up discussion of "wut" (what), "wear" (where) and "witch" (which). "Why" and "when" are considered to be lost causes. All in favor? Meeting adjourned!

At the time, I of course looked upon it as just so much silliness, but for whatever reasons, the thing took on a life of its own. The response from member readers was immediate, enthusiastic, and, as you might guess, varied. Some said I was spitting into the wind; most applauded and offered numerous suggestions for future attention. The majority of them were fairly generic, things heard and seen by unnamed offenders. It was at that point that I decided to limit SOTS's targets to *professional* (usually meaning well-paid) writers and broadcasters in the *public* media – TV, radio, newspapers, magazines, etc.

I would omit church bulletins; club and other organizational newsletters; business, political, and academic memoranda, etc., all of which are ordinarily created by people not specifically paid for doing so. I would also avoid books, mainly because I didn't consider books to be public enough. Nor would I include ad-libbing by talk show hosts or politicians, even though they really should know better. (We all know that Eisenhower, Carter, and Bush II couldn't handle "nuclear.")

SOTS does aim at advertising agencies, even though individual writers are invariably anonymous. News magazines catch the heat with a vengeance, but newspapers – especially those small-town ones without copyeditors – are prime sources. (Is that unfair? I think not.)

By the way, just so you know: Generally speaking, a copyeditor (one word) is a person who primarily fixes spelling, punctuation, and grammar errors, performing what is known as *mechanical* editing, while a copy editor (two words) can be a staff member of a publishing organization (book, newspaper, magazine, etc.) who makes changes in columns and articles written by staff writers or reporters, or in the works of book authors, sometimes even rewriting when needed. This is known as *substantive* or *heavy* editing. There are those who will dispute my distinction, and dictionaries are of no help, but I don't care. I have functioned in both capacities at one time or another, and the latter position is the more difficult of the two. In this book I concentrate on the former, and continue to consider myself a copyeditor.

So how is SOTS different from the writings of William Safire, Edwin Newman, Wm. F. Buckley, Jr., et al.? These esteemed compadres are generalists who take a broad linguistic view, whereas SOTS takes the narrow view that media folks should take the time to double-check their work by using reliable sources for reference, especially dictionaries and the Internet, although it is often necessary to look at several sites to arrive at a consensus. Oh, sure, they'll agree, it's something everyone should do, but let's be realistic. Who has the time? We're on deadline!

I am often asked about the differences between myself as "SOTSmaster" and the aforementioned much-esteemed linguiphiles, and my answer is usually boiled down to the essence of simplicity. It's somewhat like the difference between comments exchanged at a baseball game. Whereas one spectator might say to his neighbor, "I really do think that runner was safe," there is another who becomes one with the entire assembly by standing up and delivering a hearty "Kill the Umpire!" It's all a matter of getting attention. So far, I seem to have succeeded.

Let me also point out that I do not steal material from things like Jay Leno's "Headlines," nor do I lift anything from other published works. Everything you see here has either been found by others and sent to me, or I have found it myself.

As should come as no surprise, I have regularly received clippings of the writings of others, such as George Will, James J. Kilpatrick, Buckley, et al., always with the suggestion that I might "be interested in reading" whatever it is. In each case, I appreciate the thought, and I do find most of the material worth reading, but I am very careful not to let the writings of others influence my own.

In those beginning days I received letters from several Mensa members, many from chapters in other parts of the country, and some from our national officers. One of the latter, Marvin Grosswirth, had been a columnist in the national Mensa magazine, the *Mensa Bulletin*. On occasion, he would write about English, including the time he said we should remove the distinction between "who" and "whom." I included reference to this in my newsletter just to twit him in fun. He loved it, and even went so far as to say that "I'm proud, happy & honored to be a member of SOTS. Hang in there, Gordon, don't give up now. ..."

Another writer, whose name I lost, gave me this: "CBS Radio network news announcers Jim Kilpatrick and Maria McLaughlin (who was actually in Caracas with Pat Nixon at the time) both pronounced Venezuela as 'Ven-zoo-way-la' and Lowell Thomas (of all people) first did the same, then corrected himself. ..."

And in another envelope was a report of a recorded radio commercial in which a man comes home, and his wife calls out, "Is that you, George?" Man: "Yes, but I wish it **wasn't**." (I wish I had more specifics, even though the product or service is irrelevant. In advertising, colloquial is the thing. Grammatically, it should be **weren't**.)

Also in the mix were several comments such as "You can't keep a language from changing." When I printed them, others responded that whenever a language becomes corrupted, subtle nuances of expression are lost. No one disagreed with that assertion.

So the pet peeves poured in prodigiously, and I began to think I had created something I could not control. After all, those peeved folks deserved to have their say right along with mine. It carried its own force of motion. One writer said that I had "curdled her brains" and she thanked me for it. She had been a latent SOTS member all along, but didn't know what to call herself. Now she knew.

Meta Neuberger, at the time editor of a Los Angeles area Mensa newsletter, bragged, "I belonged to SOTS before you were born!" High praise.

Then there were those who reacted to my comment about the *Random House Dictionary of the English Language* (1966, 1967) being run by Bennett Cerf, who was not the greatest advocate of proper speech. His dictionary reflected it, with such nonsense as "nauseous" and "nauseated" being interchangeable, and "Feb-yoo-ary" being as acceptable as the original. Today, I own seven dictionaries, and consult them all to keep from going off half-cocked. Two of them, *Webster's Second International Unabridged*, and *Merriam Webster's Third New International Unabridged*, were donated to me, the first by Leo Falardeau, a member in Duluth who was a teacher of French and English, and the second by Lee Orcutt, a contributor to our newsletter who decided I could get better use from it than she could. (She wrote very well, I might add.)

I never got around to making SOTS an official organization, with membership cards and what-not. It looked like just too much trouble, and I'm glad I didn't promise anything but my writings. This was shown to be a wise decision, especially when I was about to take over as editor of the *Mensa Bulletin*. All I said was that anyone who was sympathetic to the aims of SOTS was automatically a member, and that seemed to satisfy everyone.

But until then, on it went, month after month, with my little local newsletter never lacking in material. One contributor called to my attention a television commercial for the Big Wheel Auto Stores that listed disadvantages of a bad muffler, ending with the statement that, above all, leakage of carbon monoxide could be "seriously fatal!" And a very popular radio personality at the time, Howard Viken on WCCO-AM, had heard "junta" pronounced in various ways and added his own Norwegian version of "yoon-ta."

(Viken, by the way, was also heard delivering a commercial for Freeman's Lighting Concepts, in which he proclaimed, "Believe me, they've got it all – and lots of it!" I'm still chuckling.)

When I called the next SOTS convention in print, I had by then (1976) been appointed editor of the national magazine *Mensa Bulletin*, and I held that position for the better part of two years until I burned out. (It has since become a paid job, and rightfully so. It was taking all of my spare time, and some that wasn't spare. I did, however, earn two life memberships.)

SOTS was introduced to the 20,000+ national membership in the March 1976 issue thusly:

> Order! Order! This meeting will come to order!

> Thank you. The Annual Convention of the **Save Our Tongue Society** is hereby declared in session. We assemble today to discuss the serious deterioration of the English language in the

public communications media. First, I have an announcement. The expulsion proceedings against Walter Cronkite, initiated because of his refusal to pronounce "February" correctly, have now been concluded. The adjudication panel has determined that he shall forthwith be branded on the tongue with a large letter "R" so that it will then be impossible for him to say "Feb-yoo-ary" without exposing both Rs. (APPLAUSE, HOOTS, & YELLS.) Thank you; the panel wishes to express its appreciation for the standing ovation.

John Chancellor's motion to censure Harry Reasoner for the same offense has been withdrawn. In a closed meeting, Harry stated that he *knows* the difference, confesses to occasional infractions, and promises to be consistent in the future. John has recommended that Harry be given a vote of confidence. The panel decided to adopt a wait-and-see position.

Now then, for those of you who are new to the group, it is necessary to point out that SOTS is in earnest, despite the air of frivolity of the foregoing. SOTS was founded in 1974, during the month of February, as a direct result of the Cronkite violation. SOTS has not sought formal recognition from any governing body and has no such intention, since membership is open to all and administration of a formal organization is cumbersome and requires assignment of responsibilities. Therefore, if you desire membership, you are automatically enrolled in our ranks. Your obligations as a member are few but vital. You are simply required to be alert for transgressors and report violations to the editor of this publication, but must do so only when you are sufficiently provoked.

It is now important to explain that the target of SOTS is quite specific. When Hubert Humphrey says he "bleeves" something, never mind. When Gerry Ford blows the pronunciation of the Chinese premier's name, no matter. Or when your brother-in-law asks, "Wut's the tem-percher?" let it go. But when a network newscaster speaks of our "new-kew-lar" capability, as he reads from his script, nail him to the wall! When you see a

TV commercial for the Mazda "Mizer" [Miser], groan might-
ily. And when the magazine ad says, "If it wasn't for Winston, I
wouldn't smoke," tear out the page and stomp on it. OK, you've
gotten the idea.

People who are responsible for damage to our language are
very often well-paid professional (so-called) writers. They are
a disgrace to their chosen craft. Where words, phrases, and
sentences are put to paper, either to be read or spoken [and
I caught deserved heat for that], there can be no excuse for
improper usage, whether the infractions are for spelling, pronunciation, or grammar. (SOTS normally does not nit-pick on
punctuation, but does take note of errors that glare.)

No professional announcer, commentator, or narrator is to be
excused for incorrectly pronouncing *February*, for example,
unless he or she is willing to admit either to a psychiatric block
or to a physical speech impediment. SOTS does not expect
absolute perfection [yes, I know], but it cannot condone out-
right assault on that which has heretofore been acceptable to
the great majority of users of the English language. A funda-
mental tenet of SOTS states that "sloppy is sloppy."

See what you think of this one: A radio commercial described
a particular product as "the most unique new innovation ever!"
Friends, they are merciless.

Perhaps, in truth, it may be asking too much for us to expect
even the most respected and renowned communicators to hit
the mark every time. Obviously, no one can write or speak
with total precision in every effort. The English language *is*
the most difficult to learn, *is* the most confusing, and contains
more inconsistencies than any other (for example, homographs
such as *like, lead, read, fair, too, can*, a monumental list). Further,
learning English as a second language is more difficult than
learning any other.

It is not unreasonable, however, to expect those who speak or write to us *professionally* to educate themselves in the use of English to a reasonable degree of proficiency. These people undoubtedly exert the greatest influence on our children's learning and use of our language, greater even than teachers, dictionaries, encyclopedias, and other books. The professional media communicators are, to all intents and purposes, custodians of our language and bear a responsibility not to be taken lightly.

Let it be the pledge of SOTS, therefore, that we shall not allow the pernicious rot of carelessness, over-cleverness, or deliberate obfuscation to deteriorate and eventually destroy the only true method we have for understanding each other. The threat is more serious than many of us are willing to believe, and the conflict lies to a great extent within ourselves. We find it easier, sometimes more fun, and most often "the *in* thing," to play games with words. We are more "with it" when we adopt the jargon of "today." Just as millions of little girls in the thirties *had* to emulate Shirley Temple in dress and hair style, and millions of teenagers today emulate rock and rap stars in similar fashion, so do the masses now fall victim to the gibberish that began with the "beat" generation of the fifties. [In truth, it went back much before that.]

Strangely and horrifyingly, we have come to the point where we are deemed knowledgeable because of the way we deliberately express ourselves *poorly* and sometimes not at all. Y'know, like, I mean …

We must say what we mean and mean what we say. We must agree on terms and definitions, lest we invite misunderstanding and its worst consequence, *intentional disagreement*. It is bad enough that we so often say the *wrong* things to each other. It becomes a cultural crime when we say the *right* things, are *misinterpreted* because we are not properly understood, and find ourselves enmeshed in totally unnecessary conflict because of it. Pardon the polemic, but as the fella says, "We've got enough trouble as it is."

Certainly, we need not ignore the reality, nor even the desir-
ability, of change. Buggy whips are gone and so are many of
the obsolete elements of our language. As the world changes,
and as people change, so must our speech and writing. But
let us not dispose of that which is good and useful even as we
adopt new terminologies of our times. The keys to communication are consistency and comprehension. They are essential to
understanding. When we introduce a new word or phrase in
our writings, let us ask ourselves if it is intelligible to those who
will read it; and we can neither make wishful assumptions nor
adopt an attitude that says, "Too bad for them if they don't get
it." It could be too bad for *us*! Remember the sentry who didn't
know the password? He shot the sergeant of the guard.

ENOUGH! Let us gird for battle. Take heed, poisoners of our
prose – you shall not befuddle us. We shall expose you for the
blatherers you are and let the English-speaking world know
that we stand firm for lucidity, clarity, precision, and plainness
of speech. Beware, you tongue-tainters, SOTS lives!

Some introduction, eh? A bit heavy, perhaps, for a regular column that
would take a lighter approach as it progressed, but again the response was
immediate and almost all positive and supportive. I can recall only one
reader who chastised me for attacking people who were "just trying to
earn a living." I'm guessing he was one of them, but I never found out for
sure.

As of this writing, there followed 44 more columns in the *Mensa Bulletin*,
most after I left the editorship, and much of their content appears in this
book, along with a lot of material I've collected since. In the 30 years of
accumulating this stuff, I thus far have a 36-inch file drawer completely
full, as well as a couple of boxes and a card table stacked with the newly
acquired. My piano bench holds three more piles. (Someday I may play
that piano again, but not until this book is finished.) There is, of course,
a lot of duplication in those files and stacks, but I have carefully kept a
catalog of uses so as to minimize repetition, not only here but in my other
writings and speeches, as well.

In case you wonder whether anyone objected to the acronym SOTS, yes, some did, but those who wrote to express the view can be counted on the fingers of one hand. One fellow applauded my venture whole-heartedly, but added, "My god, you've *got* to change the name. People will think we're a bunch of drunks!" In truth, he was the only one who offered that opinion so explicitly, and the few others who had reservations along the same line eventually came around when they noticed that they were in a rather small minority. So, in case you questioned it, the name's effect has been fully positive – and, I still think it contains a touch of fun.

(One wag suggested that people would think that the Save Our Tongue Society was organized to promote the sale of self-adhesive stamps. Let 'em.)

Truth to tell, I considered several other possibilities – Preserve (POTS), Rescue (ROTS), Honor (HOTS), Defend (DOTS), etc. None struck me the way that SOTS did, and I have never looked back.

So, I'm sure many of you are wondering what qualifies me to do this? I have been in various forms of communications throughout most of my working life. On leaving the U.S. Army in 1953 after service in Korea, I enrolled at Columbia College, a radio and television school in Chicago, where I studied nights to become a TV director. (I also landed a job in the mailroom at WBKB-TV, the Chicago owned-and-operated ABC station [now WLS-TV], and later served as film librarian.) I was never allowed to work at the directing craft, however, because when they found out I could write, they pushed me in that direction. Following a year as assistant continuity director and commercial writer at WNEM-TV in Bay City, Michigan, where I learned to write just about every kind of TV spot, I returned to Minneapolis and briefly joined two advertising agencies, with a year as a small-town newspaper editor in between.

For six-and-one-half years (October 1957 to March 1964) I was direc-tor of continuity and chief writer for WTCN-TV in Minneapolis (now KARE-TV), and later wound up in audio-visual and industrial film pro-duction, eventually operating my own one-man company. Because of my SOTS activity, I have spoken at many Mensa gatherings, to service clubs, and to several social organizations. I was even paid $100 plus lunch to

address the Minnesota Free-Lance Court Reporters Association at their
fall conference, for two hours, which, in effect, technically made *me* a paid
professional. My appearance was billed as "The Fractured English Traveling Road Show." I am also a member of Toastmasters International.

Having left television and calling myself The English Repairman, I
embarked on yet another business venture, which failed, I believe, because
so few were willing to admit that they needed their English repaired. At
the suggestion of a friend, however, I took a test and became a free-lance
copyeditor. West Publishing Co. in St. Paul (the world's largest publisher
of law books) hired free-lancers for their college textbook division, and I
did four books for them. Believe me, college professors need help just like
everyone else, and they took it gratefully.

But note: I am not by any means a true linguist. I do what I do because
no one else has done what I am doing here, at least not in the narrow field
I have chosen. Whatever language skills I have I attribute to good teachers and my sincere desire to learn all I can. Linguistically, I pretty much
fly by the seat of my pants, and so far I've managed to stay aloft. There are
many who know more about our language than I, but I know more than
most.

(I can also modestly boast that during the year 1990 I was the only
copyeditor in the entire 80-year history of a group of suburban weekly
newspapers, the *Sun Post* group of five in our northern suburbs. I would
probably be there yet were it not for a "down-sizing" in which eleven folks
got the axe at the same time in an economy move.)

So while I may not be as well versed in the finer points of English grammar as many others, I continue to press my case by reminding everyone
that you don't have to be a master chef to be able to criticize bad food.
Besides, I have material that no one else has, and it would be a crime not
to use it.

Caveat

The determination of correct usages and other material contained in this
book is based on information found in a variety of dictionaries and other

language references, not all of which may be in agreement. Ultimately, it is my own opinion that is represented, along with those of my contributors. Before any reader goes in search of a high horse to climb upon in order to criticize the contents herein, let him or her be reminded that *no one* has all the answers, not even this writer nor any of those contributing. Feel free, however, to send your comments to the author by way of the publisher. Perhaps you'll appear in my next book.

Second caveat

I am fully aware that certain writers and broadcasters cited herein are no longer where they were when they did what they did. Some have changed jobs, some have retired, and some are dead. They are all, nevertheless, immortalized in this book, which would not have been possible without them. For that I am in their debt, and I thank them for their linguistic transgressions.

The following led off most of my columns in the *Mensa Bulletin*:

Disclaimer

SOTS is the Save Our Tongue Society, an informal, unsanctioned, and unaffiliated organization dedicated to the preservation of the English language in the public communications media. Professional writers and broadcasters who abuse the language are SOTS's primary targets and are subject to public censure and reprimand. All persons sharing the views of SOTS are members automatically without formal enrollment. Members are required to report violations when self-compelled to do so.

Originally, that last said that members were "required to report violations when compelled to do so." As some readers eventually pointed out, I failed to say who was to do the compelling – certainly not I – so I left the sentence off altogether for a while, but later resumed it. I added the "self-" to "compelled" above for use in this book, so as to deflect further criticism.

1

Ready, aim, …

My first contributor, appropriately, was the late Karl Ross, my predecessor as editor of the *Mensa Bulletin*. His comments were in response to my first column:

> There are quite a few instances when the broadcasts on our local [New York City] radio stations make me wince. The flying traffic-reporter Neil Bush, for example, who consistently says, "Try **and** use Riverside Drive"; or that recurrent ad for hair pomade (I believe) saying: "If you are one of today's people who **doesn't feel your** age …" Keep it up!

For any who wonder, the expression is "try to," not "try and." The other should be "… one of today's people who don't feel their age."

Note that I am now adding bold-facing to errors that might not be so obvious to everyone. When I did this in the Mensa publications, some respondents accused me of insulting their intelligence, while others thanked me. As for "try and," does that mean "you'd better do it or else"? Without meaning to insult anyone's intelligence, but rather as a service to those who may not know, I will be correcting errors as I go. (Writers should always make their works easy to read.)

Also, from here on, I'm identifying my contributors by initials and city only; they'll know who they are. Keep in mind too that people move. In all cases, the city is where the contributor lived at the time of submission.

And although most entries in this book do not have publication or broadcast dates (so who's going to look them up?), in case anyone questions an item, explanation, or philosophy in this book, I have everything pertaining to them in my files.

The Walter Cronkite incident led to this from D.R. of Los Angeles:

In 1966 or 1967, Mr. Cronkite announced on his evening
news program that a recently published dictionary had just
sanctioned the dreadful "Febyooary," and commented that this
approval relieved him of the rigorous exercise of trying to say it
right. His face radiated a smug content, which I read as mali-
cious glee ...

I have judiciously pruned D.R.'s letter, sidestepping his comments about
people quaffing of the product of BEWERIES and not spending enough
time in LIBARIES, with perhaps a BISK walk in the bargain. One last
word came from the estimable Ann Landers, who took Cronkite to task
in her syndicated newspaper column as well. She read him the riot act, is
what she did, and he immediately phoned to tell her that dictionaries were
divided as to pronunciation. His own preference was, of course, painfully
obvious. There was simply no talking to the man.

Fair is fair

In early 1991 when most network news anchor types were erroneously
telling us about how the Iraqi Elite Republican Guard had been **deci-
mated**, Walter Cronkite was the only one to point out the misuse, noting
that "devastated," "demolished," or "destroyed" would have served. He correctly noted that to "decimate" is to reduce by one-tenth, which obviously
would not have been enough to knock out Saddam's troops.

Whoops!

I also have some more bad news about a dictionary: In my possession is a
copy of *Webster's New Ideal Dictionary, presented by TIME* (magazine), and
published, regrettably, in 1978 by G. & C. Merriam Co., the same folks
who publish other Merriam-Webster dictionaries, such as the *Third New
International*. In the TIME book, the first pronunciation is Feb-(y)e-we-
ree. I am ashamed to possess this book, but I keep it as proof of what I say.

A friend whom I wish I could have met in person, T. Starr Terrill, of
Carlsbad, Calif., and who had a column similar to mine being published
in the *Omaha World-Herald*, further advised me that another dictionary,
Webster's New Collegiate, also lists the bad way first. Whew! Saved my
money on that one!

Dictionaries, by definition, are books that assist us in selecting words to use, give us the meanings of words, and help us with the pronunciations of words. (A good thesaurus is also handy, with loads of synonyms and ant-onyms, as a further aid in word selection. Note the use of *assist*, *help*, and *aid* in the foregoing.) Also, dictionaries, by their very nature, are reflective of our culture's language, which is why they include all known pronuncia-tions and definitions, even going so far as to identify many uses as *obsolete*, *colloquial*, *archaic*, *idiomatic*, *rare*, etc. Dictionaries do not say, however, that we should help ourselves to those odd forms we find in their pages, nor that we should go ahead and talk funny.

Just because there are supposedly a lot of different ways of pronouncing a word, or even of spelling a word, there is most often a single way of using that word that everyone agrees on. Does it bother *anyone* to hear Febru-ary pronounced Feb-roo-ary? Certainly not anyone I know. So if using the colloquial or common Feb-yoo-ary bothers maybe just a few, why not say it right and **not bother anyone**?

One quick aside about "Febuary": On AOL, the largest Internet service provider, as of this writing in January 2010, there's a pull-down window in the Billing area that asks for the month the subscriber's credit card expires. One of the 12 choices is "**Febuary.**" Is this a legitimate comment by SOTS? Probably not in this book, but I'm adding it here so I don't forget it. Apparently there is no spell-checker at AOL headquarters, and yes, I am a subscriber. Shape up, AOL!

We're listening

Mispronunciations may not bother everyone, but correct pronunciations keep messages flowing smoothly and bother no one. Just as a "clinker" in a musical performance calls attention to itself and detracts from the desired effect and mood, so does an oral deviation interrupt the absorp-tion of a spoken message, by an educated listener. And just as a skilled artisan takes justifiable pride in striving for artistic perfection, so should every professional communicator seek mastery of our language and be proud to reflect that mastery in its use. When there is uncertainty about pronunciation or meaning, professionals should have the sense to look in a dictionary, or at the very least, ask someone. We, their audience, would then find their work completely acceptable, and would then have no reason to figuratively pelt them with rotten fruit.

Language is the major tool of the professional communicator's trade. Just as we would not expect a surgeon to cut into us with a "fairly sharp" scalpel; just as we would not expect a lawyer to represent us by relying on an old set of law books bought at a rummage sale; just as we would not expect the pilot of a 747 to fly by the seat of his pants while looking out the window; so too do we have every right to expect those who are paid to tell us about ourselves and our world to properly use the tools of their trade. Would you go to a psychiatrist who had read no further than the writings of Sigmund Freud? Not I.

Nonstandard grammar is like out-of-focus photography, or a little too much salt in a stew, both of which can be quite noticeable. They usually don't hurt anything, but we would certainly prefer pictures to be sharp and clear, and for our food to be properly seasoned.

An ally

Before I get too far along, I'd like to pay tribute to the aforementioned T. Starr Terrill, who sometimes quoted me in his own newspaper column. His first name was Thomas, and he used the T. Starr only professionally, signing his correspondence "Tom." Tom founded an organization similar to SOTS called SAGE, the Society for the Advancement of Good English, and had membership cards, "goof" cards to mail to offenders, and a newsletter, much like another organization called SPELL (the Society for the Preservation of English in Language and Literature), which as far as I know is still going as of this writing. Anyway, Tom's gone now, but we had a good relationship even though we did not actually join forces. His focus was broader than mine, and he recognized that.

Getting my column about the English language into the *Mensa Bulletin* was easy; I was also editor of the publication during 1976 and most of 1977. Tom Terrill offered his column "to 100 of the nation's top newspapers (with circulations of 100,000 or more). No more than a half dozen replied, one accepted." Newspapers everywhere contain information about sudoku, bridge, personal advice, horoscopes, entertainment of all kinds, sports of every variety, food, gardening, you name it. Our local daily even has a (pardon the expression) real gossip column, remindful to us older folks of Walter Winchell, Hedda Hopper, et al. But newspapers hardly ever deal with two areas that I consider as important as any of those – how to speak and write good standard English, and how to drive a car. Both could be extremely beneficial, but the big wheels in the board room shrug and ignore them. Give the people what they want, they say.

Following a speech by the then editor of the Minneapolis *Star Tribune*, I asked why those two areas were not addressed more frequently. The editor, Tim McGuire, said that there was relatively little interest on the part of the reading public. I then asked about the gossip column, which from the beginning has had a well-known reputation for inaccuracy. His answer was that it was intended to be entertaining and that errors were not uncommon in columns of that nature. Ye gods and little fishes! What has our civilization come to?

Then there is being deliberately sloppy. Broadcasters, and sometimes even writers, often claim that, although they know better, they use informal speech so that their audience will relate to them on more friendly terms. They want viewers and readers to look upon them as being "folksy" or "plain-spoke just like us." That is, if they ever think about it, which I doubt.

And here's something I'll bet hardly anyone has noticed: All of the broadcast and print media are deathly afraid of publishing letters or articles commenting on grammatical, spelling, or other language errors of their own. Only the naïve will believe that such letters and e-mails are not received by the media, but they definitely are. Oh, sure, they'll print or air corrections dealing with proper names, but articles or letters columns are devoid of criticism about language usage. Perhaps it's because they know that opening *that* door a tiny crack by publishing one such letter or article would invite a deluge, so they simply refuse to establish any kind of precedent. In a way, I guess, I can't blame them. But in another, I have to shame them. No guts.

2

The wind is what?

Among those many responses to my first *Bulletin* column was one from J.J. of St. Paul, Minn. He was at the time a student at the Brown Institute of Broadcasting, and had as a teacher one Roy Finden, a weathercaster for local station KSTP-TV.

> Finden would say on the air, "The wind is (or winds are) calm," until I asked him how this could be. Lo and behold, to this very day he will now say, "The air is calm."

I nailed a similar trick during a question-and-answer session following a speech at a Mensa gathering by Paul Douglas, another local weatherman (in 2006) at WCCO-TV. When I offered the definition of *wind* as being the movement of air, along with the fact that if there were no air movement there could be no wind, he agreed. I then asked how it was possible to ascribe any sort of characteristic to something that did not exist. After a moment, he replied, "I'll have to get back to you on that." Subsequently, he, too, adopted an improved terminology. Also, on KSTP-TV, I have never heard chief meteorologist Dave Dahl say it wrong. Either someone got to him, as well, or he learned it by his own observation. I have since likened the gaffe to saying that the thunder is quiet, or the rain is dry, or the lightning is invisible, or some such.

On another TV and radio weather front, I have long listened, with eyeballs rolling, as those wonderful meteorological folks describe temperatures as being warmer, cooler, hotter, and colder? While I am not a physicist, I do know that temperatures are measured in degrees, and degrees can only be *higher* or *lower*, on any scale you can name. Things, including air, can be cooler, hotter, etc. Unfortunately, I am probably spitting into a not-very-calm wind and will have no chance of seeing any change during my lifetime.

And before I leave the subject, at least for now, I have two other observations: One, why does workplace jargon creep into on-air reporting?

No doubt, it's easier and quicker to say "precip" instead of "precipitation" among themselves in their daily work in the weather department, but it's really tacky on the air. And two, what's with this "temp" instead of "temperature"? The cause would appear to be the same, but why on the air? If a summer intern took over a weathercast for a week, would we be getting the temp from a temp? Just asking.

Also, didn't abbreviations used to have periods after them? Or are periods now considered just "clutter"? Perhaps it was the U.S. Postal Service that started things downhill by dropping almost all punctuation from its addressing recommendations, not to mention requirements when it comes to automated/barcoded mail.

Lighten up?

H.H. of Sheridan, Wyo., suggested: "SOTS *can't* mean to take away from me my pleasure in playing with grammar, inappropriate words that are understood, and incomplete sentences, can [it]?" No, of course not, I replied, otherwise we wouldn't be able to enjoy puns, limericks, or shaggy dog stories. Playing with the language is an inalienable right and a great deal of fun, just so long as we make sure we and our children understand the game as well.

I want to point the SOTS finger at specific offenders and name them when I can, but sometimes it just isn't possible. For example, I cannot identify the loan-sharking company behind the radio spot that chirped, "Now you can borrow enough money to get yourself completely out of debt." I swear that's what it said. When I published it in my column, one of the reactions came from R.R. of Bayside, N.Y.:

> I am not a member of SOTS. Thus, I suppose, my criticism will be dismissed as jealousy, peevishness, and/or a natural result of my being a member of SASS (the Steam and Sulk Society).
>
> Nonetheless ... I wish to point out [that] there is a grave danger inherent in preoccupation with the aims and ideals of SOTS that has been unexplored thus far. I refer, for example, to the concluding paragraph in the May '76 [column], which, in

part, is "A radio spot that chirped, 'Now you can borrow enough money to get yourself completely out of debt.'"

When I arrived at this point, an unaccustomed fever pitch regarding grammatical purity, I re-read the foregoing excerpt several times, futilely seeking the foul offender within. I suddenly realized [that] the offender was in the meaning and not the grammar, and I had been nit-picking while the house burned down. There's a message here somewhere (now don't get nasty – or if you do get nasty, you can join SASS). Think it over, SOTS.

Two months later, almost to the day, came this short note:

Strike my previous critical letter regarding SOTS. I now join SOTS with the following:

Leon Lewis, professional interviewer and talk-show host on New York City radio station WMCA, offered [this] cryptic thought: "The complicated man does things for reasons no one can **fanthom**." I can't phanthom it either!

You win some, you lose some, and you get some folks back when the slogging becomes more than they can bear. OK, so maybe that was an ad-lib, but a pro definitely should know better. Besides, it allowed me the pleasure of watching a lemon turn into lemonade. Who could ask for more?

Equal time

M.J.O. of Hallandale, Fla., caught Tom Brokaw on the *NBC Nightly News:*

Reporting on Polaroid's lawsuit against Kodak, Brokaw told us that the suit alleges "ten **violations** of patent infringements." That's enough to get the case thrown out of court.

Surely I don't need to clarify that one. M.S. of New York City sent me this:

A CBS Radio newscaster reported that "the hold-up resulted in an exchange of bullets **among** the hold-up man and the armed guard."

I wonder who got the better part of the trade, and whether the calibers were the same. But "among"? Make it "between." Coming from another direction, S.M. of East Orange, Mass., offers:

> David Brinkley once used the phrase "**Between** the four corners of the country …"

L.W. of Newbury Park, Calif., knows the difference between "between" and "among":

> The *Thousand Oaks Star* had a human interest piece about a family adopting ten children to keep the kids' family together, noting that "The kids have five different biological fathers **between** them." As a public service, I informed the local editor, and I'm sure he needed another annoying letter from me on grammar.

It looks to me as if he needs lots of help, so I hope you keep on giving it to him. Remind him that it's "between" only two, and "among" three or more.

One I heard myself on CBS Radio was an "up-to-the-minute" report in 1999 that said, "The opening round of air strikes against Yugoslavia provided a baptism **under** fire for the controversial U.S. bat-winged B-2 bomber." Since I was a tot I've known that it's baptism "of" fire.

From C.S. of New York City:

> Today I heard writer Sally Quinn say, about interviewing, "If the story is '**revelant**,' I'll write it." The program was *Not For Women Only* on NBC-TV. I frew up.

Make it "relevant." L.S. of Coon Rapids, Minn., heard this one:

> The ad says, " New Raid Solid. Kills bugs dead … up to four months." So what good is it if the stupid bugs don't stay dead? I suspect they're a bit wobbly, though, after four months in suspended animation.

Agreed. And to those who like to say, "Oh, you know what they mean," I reply, "So why don't they say what they mean?" Incidentally, S.C. Johnson

& Son, Inc., the purveyors of Raid, has been using the slogan for so many years that they dare not stop, regardless of what anyone says or thinks. However, their newer products, such as ant and roach killers, say nothing about the four months' effectiveness. Interesting.

Comics?

On the funny pages of some newspapers is a strip called *Funky Winkerbean.* The dialog in one day's offering went like this: "How's the patient doing, Doctor?" "Well, right now he's semi-conscious! All he can think about is trucks!" Drop the hyphen, please.

This brings up another pronunciation problem. Every day you hear some clown on TV or on the radio say ant-eye communism or sem-eye-annual, sometimes even mult-eye-national. Those words are supposed to have the ee sound instead. For example, if you ask a Dodge truck owner, "That thing got a hem-eye?" he'd have your head. "That's hemmy, you moron. What country did you come from?" Also, *semi, anti,* etc., are prefixes. They are not words, they are parts of words. "Multi Housing" is wrong. However, as the shortened form of semitrailer truck (tractor), "sem-eye" has a strong hold on its common usage, and there's nothing to be done for it.

In sharp contrast were the two voices on the Selsyn Blue Shampoo TV spot. The female model said it was "ant-eye dandruff," but the male announcer spoke "ant-ee" correctly. Would that there were more like him.

Dick Chapman, a news announcer on WCCO-AM Radio got a 50 percent rating from SOTS one morning when he reported that a semitrailer truck (semmy, good) was involved in a **multicar** (mult-eye, bad) accident. As just mentioned, semi and multi are prefixes, not words, and are connected to the words they modify or clarify. They are pronounced with the short *i* rather than the long. Oh, sorry. I meant to say "pronounced by those who care, with the …"

A tip of the SOTS hat goes to Best Buy, which had its TV commercial announcer say it right when he told us about a "Mult-ee-media computer program." Unfortunately, today it's a rarity.

I also heard Al Paulson, when he was with KSTP-TV, read a tag for the movie *Semi-Tough*. Paulson pronounced the name correctly, even though the voice on the film spot had it wrong.

Anyway, it was another comic strip that caught the eye of J.K. of St. Petersburg, Fla.:

> In the final panel of a *Prince Valiant* strip: "By the haughty glances they receive [no comma] Val guesses [the governor's guests] regard **he** and his family as infidels."

The cartoonist who drew that strip was not usually so sloppy. I remember it as one of the best-drawn and most intelligibly presented of them all, fanciful though it may have been. I also have a *Wizard of Id* strip from 1992 that has the "padre" character saying, "Let **he** who is without sin cast the first stone." At the time, there were two guys, Brant Parker and Johnny Hart, working on the strip. Funny that neither wondered about the "he/him" question. (Let "him" ...)

Once in a while, though, a ray of sunshine comes through. In Bil Keane's *Family Circus* comic strip, Dad and son Billy are driving down the road in the family car. Little Billy says, "Goin' to Grandma's is a lot **funner** than goin' to school." Dad: "Not FUNNER, Billy. You mean 'Goin' to school is a lot MORE FUN than goin' to school.' Now let's hear you say it correctly." Billy: "Goin' to Grandma's WAS a lot funner but now it seems just like school."

Cause and affect?

W.H. of San Francisco found these in a national magazine ad:

> "On the [new] Subaru, the **thing** most **effected** by inflation **is** the **tires**." It was bad enough that no one (copywriters, editors, agency account executives, even the client's advertising manager, knew the difference between "affected" and "effected," but the tires is a *thing*? In the same publication, another ad, for BMW this time, featured a [big bold] headline reading: "A luxury sedan based on the belief that **all** of the rich **are not** idle." Some of my rich friends resent that. Obviously, what

was intended was "... that not all of the rich are idle." I hope
BMW's craftsmanship is better than its grammar.

Some might claim that "tires" is a collective singular, but I would dispute
it. Start over: Make it "The *things* most *affected* by inflation *are* the tires."
If the "inflation/tires" pun got missed, so be it.

Similarly, R.P. of Tustin, Calif., had reason to lose her appetite after running across this one:

> In the book review [section] of the *Los Angeles Times*, Bob
> Clark writes, "... a number of fine books **is** available about
> deserts."

No, that's not right. *A* number of anything *are* (whatever). *The* number
of anything *is* ... etc. We don't see that error too often, but it glares in its
own light. A couple of readers had trouble with this one and wrote wanting to know what was wrong with "a number of fine books ... **is** available."
Their contention was that "number" is the subject of the sentence, when
it is actually "books" that is, in this case, the subject ("a number of" is the
qualifier). When we write "*The* number of fine books ... ," then we are
talking about the quantity, and "number" definitely becomes the subject of
the sentence, as in "*The* number of fine books *is* now in excess of ten thousand. *A* number of them *are* available to be checked out – especially those
about deserts." If I had said that "a dozen fine books **is** available," I would
have been taken to task for assuming that "dozen" is singular, when in this
usage it is in fact plural. So I didn't. I hope that clears it up for everyone.

Well, maybe not. A postcard from J.S. of Jersey City, N.J., advised me that
"' ... a number ... **is** available' is correct in American English! Are you
British? This isn't the first time your judgment has differed from mine,
but it's starting to bug me!" Oh? And what number would that be? Gee,
I really do hate to bug anyone, but if that's what it takes, that's what it
takes. Another writer even sent me an [incorrect] diagramming of the
term. Unfortunately, that writer made no distinction between "is" and
"are" after the word "number" and at least one other did the same. A third
correspondent said some rather nasty things about my "incompetence"
to serve as a guardian of our speech, labeling me "totally inadequate."

Sometimes I wonder …

J.H. of Brooklyn Center, Minn., adds:

> The ad for Dixies Calhoun restaurant read: "Stone Crab Claws
> **is** comin' to Dixies! Eat them now and on New Year's Eve!"

Aside from the "is/are" booboo, something about that other sentence
bothers me, but I can't figure out what it is. Hmmmm.

3

Smoke?

Several, including the aforementioned W.H., pointed their shaming fingers at:

> "Nobody's lower than Carlton." I shall defend to the death
> the thesis that "nobody" cannot be a "thing," and if Carlton is
> a person, he looks suspiciously like a red-and-white cigarette
> package.

G.B. of St. Louis, Mo. – along with several others – sends up yet another smoke signal:

> How about the billboard on which the entire text is "Winston
> Longs **is** Taste"? They don't *has* taste, you see; they *is* taste.

Well now, when I was trying to quit smoking several years ago, I tried Carlton and quickly discovered why its advertising never used the word "taste." Trust me, it didn't have any. Also, the *is* should have been capitalized; it's the only verb in the sentence, and verbs are always capitalized in titles and headlines, or so they should be, particularly in advertising. (Or did you know that already?)

J.M. of Reading, Pa., was horrified at what he saw:

> There's a billboard near Harrisburg, Pa., advising passing
> motorists to "**Taste** True's **5 mg** of **tar**." Yecchh!

Some of us remember the "Winston tastes good, like a cigarette should" ad campaign, but we may have forgotten the later Winston slogan: "What do you want, good grammar or good taste?" No contest here. Speaking of cigarettes, L.S. of Coon Rapids, Minn., returns with an item he noted when picking up the local paper:

> The *Minneapolis Tribune's* Fixit column recently printed a read-
> er's query about the atrocious grammar used in the Tareyton

cigarette ads. Responding was Daniel A. Conforti, executive
assistant, American Brands, Inc. After stating that "it is done
intentionally," Conforti continues: "The Tareyton campaign is
meant to be light-hearted and humorous. To take liberties with
the English language is a harmless form of humor and humor
can be an effective tool in advertising."

The ad itself proclaimed, "Us Tareyton smokers would rather fight than
switch." My comment following that paragraph in my column was:
"Sure, Dan Baby, but what about some of we adults and most of them kids
what don't know the difference? You are guilty of contributing to a serious breakdown in our ability to communicate effectively, and your offense
is beyond justification. Merely reading your ads could be dangerous to
our health. Suggestion: Use a disclaimer. You'd increase readability and
probably make national heroes of yourselves." Obviously, my words were
ignored.

Et, tu, **Ed?**

I admire Edwin Newman, I truly do. But he is as prone to error as
anyone. (I know I said I wouldn't go after books because they are not
considered public media, but I'm making this one exception.) In *Strictly
Speaking*, Estimable Ed (or his editor[s], which is just as bad) commits
several goofs that should never have happened. I have his Warner Books
paperback, and on page 36 in his very first chapter he discusses talks
intended to halt a strike. In part: "It is a more effective and **healthier**
method than the one so often recommended by irate citizens, locking
them up in a room until they come up with a contract." I do not believe
that a method can be called "healthy," or even "healthier," but describing
one as "healthful" would sit better with more of us.

Mr. Newman mentions **"non-journalists"** and a **"non-interview"** he held
with Yugoslavia's Marshal Tito. Just so we all understand, "non" is not a
word, it is a prefix that is almost always attached without a hyphen
(nonjournalists, etc.), exceptions to the rule being such terms as "non-
Mexican citizens" or "non-native" with the double-letters needing clarification. The same sort of clarification applies to "co-workers," which I
once saw hyphenated as "cow-orkers." The hyphen remedies that.

In chapter 3 Newman should have known better than to say, "That did not make the state **exactly unique** … ," and I have little doubt that each of these has been pointed out to him ad nauseum. However, fame is fame, and pokes in the consciousness are part of the territory.

Viable?

M.O. of Hallandale, Fla., signs in again with:

> According to an article on tourism by writer Don Bedwell in the *Miami Herald*, the advent of gambling will "make the Baha-mas a highly **viable** competitor."

Feasible, maybe – workable, possibly – but viable, no. Not this time. Viable simply means that something is able to live on its own, or existing without outside support. I wouldn't consider an island group as "viable." No sir, not I. Common usage? All too common, unfortunately, but still wrong.

Here's something to ponder: If the English language can change through usage, as it obviously does, isn't it also obvious that change can work in two directions? People change, as do their ways of speaking and writing. Therefore, aren't people generally able to relearn correct English, through the voluntary use of the "change phenomenon" itself? Or are people mostly content with the "sheep following sheep" effect now controlling the "evolution" of English? I see the trend toward more sloppiness rather than less. Fads rule the day, and with so many language innovations in so many areas, it may someday be impossible for us to understand each other except among our generational peers, if that.

C.M. of Mobile, Ala., reads *Science News* and sends us this:

> "In 1960 the average American worker produced nearly twice the value of goods **than** a worker in other advanced nations produced." Should have been "**that**." A typo?

No, I don't think so; the *n* and the *t* are too far apart on the keyboard. C.M. also notes that the *Mobile Register* came up with a news item about a strike that "has **drug** on for more than a month." He says that the writer *should* be – and through the streets yet – perhaps while being pelted with cans and bottles and whatever else is loose.

Speaking of bottles, B.R. of Tulsa, Okla., wonders:

> Many shampoo bottles bear the inscription: "Apply shampoo. Lather. Rinse. Repeat." Is there enough shampoo in the world for one to follow those instructions?

Hype, hype, hooray!

Creative advertising can often be *overly* creative, as suggested by D.S. of Honolulu, Hawai'i:

> 1. Avon: "You never smiled so **good**." ["well"]
> 2. A Pillsbury beverage: "They **squoze** a sugar in half." ["squeezed"]
> 3. "All cotton swabs are not Q-tips." ["not all are"]
> Why is so much bad grammar found in commercials? Perhaps the copywriters are too lazy. Perhaps the mistakes are deliberate so as to catch the attention of consumers. Whatever the reason, the mistakes seem to stand out.

I can't argue with that. As a former advertising copywriter myself, I can recall occasions when I tried to fix a word or a sentence and the client would insist on his "clever" way of pushing his product or service. It mostly depends on who makes out your paycheck. My employers generally backed me up.

R.A. adds fuel to the fire by piggy-backing on #1 in the foregoing:

> On Chicago's Channel 5 [WMAQ-TV] recently, newscaster Ron Hunter said, "There are two Chicago school districts that are not promoting large numbers of their 8th-graders because they can't read **good** enough." I sure hope they can talk good enough.

With that sort of example? I doubt it. R.K. of Jersey City, N.J., piles on with a rather large headline in *The Jersey Journal* that read: "N.J. college freshmen can't read or do math too **good**." No, but they can probably get a job on the *Journal.*

And did you know that Dimetapp Cough Elixir "works as **good** as it tastes"? ("well")

Generally speaking, ad agency types have learned to use interest, appeal, excitement, humor, and sometimes fear, as elements in their concoctions, but seldom is logic or accuracy of major concern. An example is the campaign for Bremer banks here in Minnesota, which has adopted the slogan, "We see banking differently." How's that for being totally vague? No explanation, no specifics, just a claim that can neither be proven nor disproven. I suppose that if a customer of another bank is disaffected by that bank for whatever reason, the Bremer ad might just be enough to tempt that customer into checking on Bremer's "difference."

I do?

Once, a while back, a reader asked what I thought about popular songs that were ungrammatical, such as "I only have eyes for you." (A grammatical improvement would be "I have eyes only for you," or better yet, "I have eyes for you only.") I suggested that the reader look elsewhere for compassion, because I was not about to take on that kind of mess. It's called literary license, and you can't bring back Frank Sinatra to sing about *Love and Marriage,* "it's an **institution** you can't disparage." He, of course, says "**institute**." It's too late. Bob Hope, too, in the movie *Penthouse Serenade* (1938), sang "When We're Alone" with Shirley Ross. The lyrics included "for just you and **I**, etc." There are dozens of others, maybe hundreds, so I'll stop now before it's too late. Give it up; it's a lost cause.

By the way, in the early days of SOTS it received a fair amount of publicity in national publications. Mary Louise Gilman, editor of *The National Shorthand Reporter,* featured SOTS in her October 1976 issue. The publication was read by most of the country's court reporters, as well as by a number of lawyers and judges. I never heard from any of them, but I like to think they may have gotten something out of it.

Pooped?

N.B. of Colorado Springs, Colo., was reading the paper when ... she couldn't believe her eyes!:

> A UPI [United Press International, a news service competing with AP] story in the Colorado Springs *SUN* tells us of the benefits of transcendental meditation, notably that "afternoon meditation **enervated** persons tired from busy workdays."

Then J.P. of Westland, Mich., detected an opposite level of activity:

> Elated by the excitement generated by the young pitching sensation Mark Fidrych, *The Detroit Free Press* assured us that the phones in the Detroit Tiger ticket office were "**literally** jumping off the hook."

"Enervated" should have been "rejuvenated" or "invigorated," and "literally" should have been "figuratively." Using "literally" like that means that it actually happened as described, and, well, you know ... can't be.

R.L. of Milwaukee, Wis., adds this one to the brew:

> A radio ad for a place called Warehouse of Leathers told us of a sale with prices "so low they will **literally** knock you on your ear." I hope they have thick carpeting.

M.W. of El Cajon, Calif., has another variation:

> I literally couldn't believe my "eye" when I read the following in a recent [1977] issue of the *San Diego Evening Tribune*. Rev. W. Lee Truman, writing for the Copley Press, wrote a personal account of a course he took under Dr. Hildreth Cross, the head of the psychology department at Taylor University, Indiana: "Cross was a person of incredible courage who had been almost totally blind for a half-century. She **literally** had only one eye and there were deep scars on the lens of the **other** eye."

If she actually had only one eye, there could not have been an "other" eye. He also failed to tell us which eye was which, especially which had any

remaining sight. It reminds me of what my father sometimes said about a
stubborn person who refused to listen to reason: "He was blind in one eye
and couldn't see out of the other." At any rate, someone somewhere along
the line should have caught it and fixed it and helped the poor Rev. out.

As I said before, I wish I had more detail on some of these treasures, but
I'll take what I can get. Then there was B.W. of Carbondale, Colo., who
glanced at a tabloid, which served him right:

> In a recent *National Enquirer,* an advertisement for a record
> album promises a "Money Back Guarantee if not factory fresh or
> **defective.**" The advertiser was Panhill Inc. of Morgantown, N.C.

Oh, look

J.G. of Trenton, N.J., may or may not have been looking for a new home,
but in *The Beacon and Lambertville Record* of Lambertville, N.J., he saw an
impressive ad for a seventeenth-century house and read the entire description of its attributes, which included a reference to the accompanying
photo: "House is much larger but the foliage **precludes** it." So I suppose
the foliage "occluded" the view of the house, or "precluded" the photographer from taking a better picture of it. "Partially obscures" would have
been my choice And I can tell you that very little of the house could be
seen behind those trees and bushes in the picture.

J.G. also sent me a page from the magazine *New Jersey Outdoors* containing an article about wildlife in New Jersey titled "Raccoons," by Dr.
Dennis Slate. In the middle of a somewhat lengthy paragraph was "Trash
collectors sigh at the sight of tipped-over [garbage] cans along their
routes. Indeed, its ability to frequently capitalize on the activities of man,
its high value as a game animal, and its cute and cuddly appearance have
led to a vocal love/hate relationship (and everything in between) with the
public, **unique to no other** North American wild mammal." My head
hurts just looking at it. To be fair, though, Dr. Slate was probably not a
professional writer (but we don't know, do we?), and the gaffe should have
been detected and fixed by a professional copyeditor. I can't say that often
enough. Every writer, professional or not, needs an editor.

The same J.G., ever alert, spotted an ad in the *Washington Post* that has no advertiser name, so it may well be what is known as a "house ad."

> COMING SOON! FASHION & MODELING with Selena
> Parker, **Well Known** Model & Fashion Columnist. WHO
> SHOULD ATTEND! This seminar is for all women who want a
> chance to improve **her** overall appearance and outlook on life.
> (There is only a phone number.)

All women who want to improve *whose* overall appearance? Selena Parker? Also, "well-known" as an adjectival term needs the hyphen, and "Who should attend?" needs a question mark.

From E.K. of North Miami, Florida, comes:

> In a UPI story in the *Miami Herald*, the lead paragraph begins,
> "The lawyers at ABC and CBS are **pouring** over the 223-page
> court decision ..." Maple syrup, maybe?

Anything to make the news more palatable, I guess. The word is "poring." E.K. has more:

> Staff writer Robert Liss [in the same paper], in an article about
> alligators, says, "... condominium complex, where a grey-green,
> **toothsome** visitor has been lurking all week." Toothsome? An
> alligator?

Hardly. "Toothsome" means pleasant to the taste, palatable, and it can also refer to a good-looking woman, such as a toothsome blonde. The alligator was undoubtedly "toothy," of course. OK, one more from E.K.:

> And in an NBC-TV report on the [1976] Olympics, "A (wres-
> tling) match that saw both men exchange the lead several
> times." Sorry, no name of the perpetrator.

Bullets everywhere

UPI gets it in the neck again, at the hands of C.Z. of McAllen, Texas:

There's no way to know who wrote or edited it, but the UPI story in the McAllen *Monitor* was datelined BROKDORF, West Germany, and dealt with a group of protestors storming the construction site of a new nuclear plant: "They opened up at police with a **fuselage** of gasoline bombs, steel balls propelled by slingshots, and signal flares which they fired at hovering police helicopters ..."

Pretty far off the mark, I'd say. What was meant was "fusillade," but it sailed right past who knows how many eyes, and could have appeared in who knows how many newspapers.

Look who's talking

In a newspaper interview, David Guralnik, editor-in-chief of *Webster's New World Dictionary of the American Language,* is quoted as saying, "Purism in language is absolute nonsense. Its users have a collective wisdom and its glory derives from its flexibility. For example," he continued, "purists are always railing against 'finalize,' but it's no different **than** any of the other '-ize' words and it's survived because nothing else means precisely what it does." The interviewer concluded the piece with, "For Guralnik, language is, in a word, fun."

That, my friends, is trouble. I added when I put it in my column that if people like Guralnik are going to treat [our language] as a plaything, they'll gum us up but good. And how he could use "than" instead of "from" is beyond me.

Compose/Comprise?

This one will knock somebody's socks off – or at least it should. What follows is lifted in its entirety from my Speaking of English column in many of the 26 suburban *Sun* newspapers on October 10, 1990:

"Of course, the Ivy League of today is comprised of Brown, Cornell ... etc." No dictionary or English textbook approves of this usage. The two correct ways are: "... the Ivy League comprises Brown, Cornell ..." or "... the Ivy League is composed of Brown, Cornell ..." Believe it or not, the goof appeared in a newspaper column titled (at least locally) Self Improvement, which is syndicated nationally by the Newhouse News Service. The reason for the astonishment was that the Newhouse column was prepared by the editors of Merriam-Webster's *Ninth New Collegiate Dictionary*, of all people.

It wasn't bold-faced in that column, so I didn't bold-face it here, but the use of "comprised" by such supposedly erudite folks as dictionary makers came as a real shock. Put simply, the whole will *comprise* the parts, and the parts will *compose* the whole. For example, the instruments *compose* the orchestra, while the orchestra *comprises* the instruments. Compose means to bring together or constitute. Comprise means to include or be composed of. Contrary to wide-spread belief, comprise is not just a fancy way of saying compose. The two are opposites, and there is no such term as "comprised of."

Someone should tell that to the fellow in the TV "infomercial" who calls himself the Video Professor. He wants everyone to know "what a computer system is **comprised** of." My, my.

Incidentally, speaking of Speaking of English, my newspaper column that I just referred to, right before my column began running I was interviewed by a *Sun Newspapers* reporter. The article came out quite nicely, and mostly accurately, but whoever created the 24-point headline must have been half-asleep. It read, "**Lanuage** being mangled, claims local watch-dog." That spelling was repeated in the accompanying photo caption as well. Friends, there is no escape.

4

Just advertising?

J.H. of Eugene, Ore., paid attention and heard and saw a lot:

> Would you believe it? I listened carefully to 42 commercials
> during a TV movie and found that nearly one-third were guilty
> of one sort of illiteracy or another. Fab allows one to "**see** the
> clean." Crisco puts "crisp in chicken." Hall's Mentholyptus
> "penetrates **deep**." No-Nonsense Pantyhose is made from yarn
> that is "**stimulating** and soothing." That's some yarn! Mercury
> is "more of a cougar than any cougar before." Then there's the
> one for some detergent that says, "See **them** little green things?
> They **got** bleach."

On listening to the radio myself, I heard Charlie Boone of WCCO in Minneapolis say, "I'd like to recommend you to Baldwin Chevrolet." I said that I
thought it was pretty nice of him, seeing as how we'd never met. Maybe he
knows me by reputation or something. Or maybe it was an ad-lib, in which
case I apologize, but Charlie should have known better anyway.

More of my own finding: If you buy 3M's Precise Plant Food, you can
"**looka them** tomatoes." Also, Gedney Pickles are "packed the way **nature**
intended." So how would that be? And "if Nescafe can please the whole
wide world, **we** can sure please you." I then asked, "Yeah, but who the hell
are you?" Folger's, meanwhile, uses a TV shill to bray, "**Us** outdoor types
just have a knack for finding good coffee." Now if they could find their
language bearings, we might be getting somewhere.

It's not just advertising, either, as L.S. of Coon Rapids, Minn., chimes in
again with this:

> In the Minnesota Statutes of 1974 is this paragraph: "No hotel,
> restaurant, boarding house, or place of refreshment, kitchen or
> dining room used as such shall be used as a sleeping or dress-
> ing room by any employee or **other person**." According to my

reading, you can't change clothes or sleep anywhere outside your own home.

From D.S. of Lisle, Ill., comes a relatively short note that I'm including *in toto*:

Edwin Newman objects to the use of words without regard to meaning. This is dedicated to him.

Bristol-Myers Company advertises and labels its Ban Basic antiperspirant as a "non-aerosol spray," as if such a thing were possible. The weather man might as well predict non-precipitation rain.

The makers of Arrid chime in with advice to "Get rid of the aerosol, keep the spray," or words to that effect.

What they are trying to get across, one assumes, is the absence of chlorofluorocarbons (also known as halomethanes). Why the copywriters assume that "aerosol" means "halomethane" is beyond me. Any ordinary dictionary would tell them that an aerosol is a fog, mist, or smoke. Actually, we should probably blame whoever first decided to call a spray can an aerosol can because it was more impressive. Sincerely, D.S.

Although there is what should be the obvious distinction between a pressurized spray can and the pump type operated by finger pressure, what's implied here is the former. Just so you know.

You can't beat enthusiasm

Despite SOTS's lack of membership cards or not issuing "violation" cards for members to use, those kinds of ideas kept coming, including this from multiple contributor B.R. of Tulsa, Okla.:

The problem is this compulsion; it must have its outlet. [Perhaps] a small SOTS whistle … so that members can "blow the whistle" on all infractions. I find my greatest frustration is when I am alone and can say nothing to the medium [that]

has offended. If I could sound the whistle until the enrage-
ment went away, I feel this would be good therapy. Discretion
would have to be used in public, of course. Besides, one could
become dizzy blowing on that whistle all day. We might even
take to wearing sweat suits and baseball caps while watching
the evening news.

The president of our local Mensa chapter back in the late 1970s liked
the idea so much that she had SOTS T-shirts made, and sold several
of them. I have one and I wouldn't part with it for anything, but one of
my kids may put it up on eBay someday. Sadly, the SOTS whistle never
materialized.

Er, ah, um ...

Much as I would like to go after ad-libs, I have resisted the temptation,
passing by some real doozies. Well, OK, just one: When A.S. of Enfield,
Conn., turned on his radio, he heard a WTIC joker declare that the ten-
nis world was a "disorganized polyglot." A.S., who is a linguist, protested
in writing, accusing the station of taking the name of all disorganized
polyglots in vain. Felt good, right, A.S.? ("Polyglot" refers to multiple
languages and has every right to be disorganized.)

J.H.R. of East Greenwich, R.I., stopped by the drugstore:

> A very large New England cut-rate drug chain, Consumer
> Value Stores of Woonsocket, R.I., markets bottles of green, red,
> and amber **"Oral** Mouthwash." Enclosed is a label.

Now you know what CVS (Pharmacy) stands for. From P.A. of Reston,
Va.:

> Instructions on a package of Nestle's Instant Souptime include
> "3. While pouring water, stir thoroughly and enjoy." Try *that*
> without scalding your nose.

Oh, no, not I – no way, no how. I'd spill it for sure. No doubt it also calls
for boiling water. Forget it.

Here's L.S. of Ringwood, N.J.:

> A nationwide consumer products survey sent to my home
> included the following: "8. Please enter the age, sex, and the
> brand of cigarettes usually smoked by any members of your
> household." Age, maybe, but gender I couldn't guess.

Hang 'em all

Some linguistic disasters are so widespread that it would be unfair of me
to single out any individual. For example, the pronunciation of the word
the. Any dictionary will tell you that when *the* is used before a vowel
sound, it is pronounced with the *long* ē, or *thee*. Before consonants it is
pronounced with the short ĕ, or thuh. So how often do we hear "**Thee**
sheriff said that **thuh** investigation was continuing …"? Or a weather-
person on radio or TV say, "**Thee** wind is out of **thuh** east at 8 miles
per hour"? Some of those "communicators" use the long *e* consistently,
regardless of the sound, such as "**Thee** doctor determined that **thee** cause
of death was **thee** inability of **thee** patient's heart to withstand **thee** rigors
of climbing **thee** mountain."

Credit, of course, is due to all those who use the word correctly, and I
have to give Nelson Benton of CBS News a hand for "**thee** ash," "**thee**
east," "**thee** effect," and "**thee** eruption." He was reporting on the volcanic
Mount St. Helens incident.

Unfortunately, even school children today are being taught that **thuh**
is the correct pronunciation in all cases, with many teachers themselves
totally unaware of the distinction. You'll pardon me, I hope, for not providing a specific example. To single out one broadcaster would hardly be
fair, since there are so many others who are guilty of the infraction. Listen
and you will hear them. Quite often, as can happen, you'll hear a speaker
accidentally use one correctly, and sometimes you'll hear a mixture as he
or she goes blithely along, completely unaware of pronunciations.

Not wishing to tar all teachers with the same brush, but needing, nevertheless, to vent spleen at specific sources of anguish, I offer this short UPI
story datelined LAFAYETTE, La.: It seems that a teacher sent a note to
the local newspaper inquiring as to why substitute teachers receive only

$25.00 a day, and added, "What does the [school] board expect to get for this kind of pay?" Although the question appeared perfectly grammatical, the newspaper revealed shortly thereafter that the teacher's actual letter comprised seven grammatical and spelling errors, with the word *substitute* misspelled twice. It did not offer to show the actual document, which is why it doesn't show up here.

Free money?

Ignorance, they say, is bliss. Who *they* are is anyone's guess, but the ignorance of language bumblers is far from blissful for those of us who have to ingest their dreck. G.W. of Austin, Texas, is next up to prove the point:

> From an item in the *Austin American-Statesman*: "Generally, a lending institution sends you a print-out at the end of the year showing how much taxes were **dispersed** out of your escrow account. Take this to the head of the mortgage service department and say, 'I don't understand this, please explain it.'" No doubt the money was eventually dispersed – *after* it was disbursed.

Talk about throwing your money around. Now try this one on for size. D.K. of Dayton, Ohio, found fertile SOTS ground in the sports pages:

> The *Dayton Daily News* took a backward step in a sports account of newscasters waiting for Rose Bowl crowds to **"disburse."**

This time the word is "disperse," unless, of course, the fans had to pay to get *out*, too. But no, we will not lump all sports types in the same bucket. Most of them know better. The same goes for staffers on what were once called "ladies' magazines," as revealed by P.R. of Berkeley, Calif.:

> *McCall's Magazine* [had] a contest going that announced as its 6th prize: "**You're** Best Friend In The Kitchen: The famous, 624-Page McCall's Cookbook!" The type was set exactly the way you see it; an incredible gaffe.

How many errors? Let me count the ways: (1) "Your," obviously, (2) the first "The" (before "Kitchen") should not be capitalized, (3) "famous" should be capitalized, (4) "page" should not, and (5) the name of the book should be in italics. The cleaning lady could probably have done better.

Also poorly handled was what L.K. of Hot Springs Village, Ark., found in another magazine:

> An ad in *Modern Bride* [showed] two models, with the heading: "Bridal gown created by Mona, **bridesmaid designed** by Doreen."

That one escaped through sheer carelessness. Making it "bridesmaids'," assuming there were more than one, would have saved the day. "Bridesmaids' gowns (or dresses)" would have been even better.

Got grammar?

For those who think that "**Got Milk?**" was the first of its kind, I have news: As far back as 1977 there was an ad on TV for the Volkswagen Rabbit that had singers singing, an announcer announcing, and the screen reading, "You **Got** to Drive It to Believe It." When I included the item in my column, I added, "There should be a clearly legible notice on every TV commercial break that says, 'WARNING: TV commercial-watching is dangerous to your children's education.'" Isn't it funny how nothing changes?

Nowadays, we hear "Got this?" or "Got that?" incessantly. I'm guessing that the gaffe goes back even further than '77; no doubt I'll hear about it.

The Tortilla Factory in Scottsdale, Ariz., advertises in the America West inflight magazine that it offers outdoor dining with: "GOT STARS? WE DO. EVERY NIGHT." I just hate the idea, but it looks as if we have another contribution to the Department of Lost Causes. Sickening thought.

Even the 3M Company, otherwise a valued long-time member of our local business community in nearby St. Paul, had a coupon in the Sunday paper, accompanied by "**Got Lint?** Pick Up a 3M Lint Roller today!" A fine product, no doubt, but the "got" got to me. Also, why is "Up" capitalized and not "today"? Another unknown high-powered ad agency running on reduced wattage, methinks.

Daughter Judy notes that Musicland stores, later named Sam Goody, once used the slogan "We Got What's Hot!" Technically, in one sense, that usage is correct, particularly when it means "We *obtained* what's hot." But if it means "We *have* what's hot," it's not. Think of the baseball player going for a pop-up who hollers, "I **got** it!" Before he catches it – and he could just as easily drop it – he really should say, "I'm going to get it," or "I've as good as got it," or "It's mine!" although after he catches it he can say that he got it, but you'll never hear it said under those circumstances because any fool can plainly see that he did indeed "get" it. However, I suppose "I got it" *is* the shortest way to warn his teammates off and prevent a collision. No one ever said that this language game is easy.

Ain't ain't no good

We have no way of knowing how long it lasted, but another ad campaign bugged B.W. of Somers, Conn., in 1982:

> Those Wendy's TV commercials are really bad. After the jingle, "Ain't no reason to go anyplace else," two (supposed) 8th-grade English teachers "correct" the grammar by saying, "It should be *isn't* no reason."

One double-negative is as good or bad as another, I guess, but we can be thankful that the ads ran their course. They did, didn't they?

A bad spell of whether?

Some things are awful enough to make one struggle to stifle a scream. For example, here's one from N.E. of Midland, Texas:

> On the front page of the *Midland Reporter-Telegram*, a photo caption includes "Hundreds of motorists, stranded by the **incli-mate** weather, took shelter in National Guard armories."

Could this be a case of "inclement" speech? It reminded me of the time in 1993 when CNN News announced that "This big storm [on the East Coast in March 1993] happened on the 100th anniversary of the killer storm of 1888." I missed the "expert's" name, but G.K. of Mill Valley, Calif., nailed his particular quarry fair and square (or fairly and squarely, if you insist) thusly:

Peter Giddings, our beloved San Francisco television weather-man, described West Virginia's 174 inches of snow as "**breaking a new record.**" Since it's a new record, it must have wiped itself out.

I scratched my head thinking that this was more than likely an ad-lib, but decided to publish it in my column because it was just too good to pass up. Not an ad-lib, however, was this blunder found by L.F. of Cincinnati, Ohio:

> Headline in the Feb. 17, 1977, *Cincinnati Inquirer*: "Cauthen **Topples** New Mark." Contained in the text was: "Young Steve Cauthen shattered another thoroughbred racing record … breaking the mark … set by Johnny Longden in 1952." Obviously not a new mark.

A previous record, yes, but a new one? No. Same goes for the one before it. P.S. of Tempe, Ariz., put this one in the mail:

> From the *Phoenix Gazette*: "Mountain Flurries Expected."

Look out! One flake could kill you! Oh, sure, we know what the head-line-writer meant, but surely there was a better way to say that snow flurries were expected in the mountains. How about "Flurries Expected in Mountains"? One problem, and I know from experience, is that headlines are rarely edited, which explains why so many of them go awry. If I had had the opportunity to change that headline, I may have been told that my version was too long to fit. This is almost never the case; dropping the type size a point or two can often solve that problem easily.

World's greatest newspaper?

Here's more newspaper stuff, this time a foursome from R.A. of Naperville, Ill.:

> Recently the *Chicago Tribune* supplied more than its share of atrocities. To wit: "… the day-to-day heart-**rendering** torture of soap operas," "… legal **council** was never far from [John] DeLorean's side," and "… one shot blew Mrs. Spencer's wig

off, and they [the gunmen] apparently thought they had blown her head off. She just **laid** there and **pretended to play** dead until they left." Also, an Associated Press item datelined **BUF-FALO** [N.Y.] noted that "Reserve goaltender Al Smith failed to show up for a Sabres' practice Monday ... His whereabouts **are** unknown."

In short: "heart-rending," legal "counsel," "lay" there, "pretended to *be* dead" or "played dead," and whereabouts "is" unknown, which is singular, believe it or not, even though some dictionaries allow the plural use. I'll break the tie and stick with the singular, my reason being that a person's whereabouts cannot be more than one place at a time. If, on the other hand, we want to know all the places a person has been in a given time period, but which places are as yet not known, I'll go along with the plural.

OK, then, so how is soap made? By "rendering" the fat from animal meat by boiling it in a vat, no doubt including hearts, none of which has anything to do with soap operas. And Mr. DeLorean could afford a whole team of lawyers, so "council" may not have been too far wrong. If it was a "hen" that had just "laid" there and was trying to fool the fox, "lay" wouldn't fit. Take your pick.

All that from the self-described "World's Greatest Newspaper." My, my, wouldn't Colonel McCormick be dreadfully embarrassed?

* * * *

Readers: Allow me to make a suggestion. It can be numbing to try digesting too much of this stuff at a single sitting or over long stretches, so I recommend having another book handy as a breather. You will, of course, now have even more difficulty reading *anything* else without looking for errors, but good literature published by reputable houses should be fairly safe. (If, however, you can't resist finding out what's next, by all means, press on.)

5

Less or fewer?

T.C. of Kennesaw, Ga., was watching the tube one evening, and … :

> In a variety of TV commercials, Lite Beer (from Miller) claims
> it has **less** calories.

It was, unfortunately, just one of a long parade of similar goofs. So many retail stores – grocery, etc. – have checkout-counter signs for 10 or 15 items "or **less**." The establishments with any kind of class will have those changed to read "fewer," and several have done so. The rule is that if you can count whatever it is, even theoretically, *fewer* is the word. Anything as a mass, however, will be *less*. Less snow, fewer flakes; less sand, fewer grains; less cloudy, fewer clouds; less lightning, fewer strikes; less thunder, fewer rumbles (but less rumbling), etc.

One of the high-end grocers near where I live is Byerly's, and it was with some amazement that I saw a sign on the #1 checkout lane reading "10 items or **less**," and another sign on lane #2 reading "10 items or fewer." I asked the clerk what was happening, and was told that they were in the process of changing. As of today in 2005 they all say "fewer." The same goes for Target stores. Who could ask for anything more?

Another beer, in a rather puzzling full-page color newspaper ad, claims in the largest type: "New Michelob ULTRA has fewer carbs and fewer calories." In smaller type below is "With less carbs, less calories … Lose the carbs. Not the taste." Can't you just hear the arguing in the ad agency conference room? "Let's say it *both* ways. Maybe we'll keep more people happy." Sorry, can't swallow your beer ad, Michelob agency folks, and Michelob folks too. It needs fixing, so hop to it!

My personal favorite appeared in the comic strip *Frank & Ernest*, by Bob Thaves. In a single panel, a man approaches a checkout counter, over which are two signs: On the first is "10 items or less," and below it, "For English Majors: 10 items or fewer." Thaves is one of us, I think.

And so is Jeff MacNelly, creator of *Shoe*, the strip with well-shod birds running a newspaper. On one particular Sunday, Shoe, the strip's namesake, sees "Express Lane: 9 items or **less**" on a sign over a checkout counter. He climbs up on the counter, whips out a marking pen, and changes "less" to "fewer," causing the checkout clerk to silently say, "Everyone's an editor."

Zippy the Pinhead is a comic strip by Bill Griffith, and D.N. of Minneapolis, Minn., handed me a clipping of it in which Zippy stands outside a darkened window calling, "Pat? Are you in there, Pat?" The second panel reveals that it is "**Pats** Diner," and when Pat answers from within, "Yeh what is it?" Zippy replies, "Pat, you left out th' apostrophe on your diner sign!" As Pat screams obscenities at being awakened in the middle of the night, Zippy walks away remarking, "If I can't bring peace to the Middle East, I can at least bring an apostrophe to Pat's!" Every little bit helps, Zippy.

Oxen gored?

I think it would be only fair, at this point, to give voice to those who didn't like the entire idea of SOTS. The following is extracted verbatim from the Letters to the Editor column in the November 1977 issue of the *Mensa Bulletin;* again, initials and city only:

> [To the Editor] Each month the back cover of the *Bulletin* contains an item that proclaims, "Mensa is an ... organization whose only purpose is to serve as a means of communication and assembly for its members. Mensa itself holds no opinion. ... Special Interest Groups ... provide a basis for ... the sharing of opinions."

> I suggest that SOTS, the Save Our Tongue Society, unsanctioned and unaffiliated as it is, be formed into a SIG [Special Interest Group], with its own newsletter containing its derogatory opinions, rather than appearing in the official organ of Mensa.

> By its own admission, SOTS is dedicated to the censure and reprimand of the media. However, anyone reading the column (including people in the media) and noting the terms "stupid"

and "bubblehead" used to describe members of the same media that members of Mensa are striving to cultivate as friends, must realize that "censure and reprimand" actually mean ridicule and derision.

Insulting the less gifted should be done in closets and dark corners, not in the pages of the *Bulletin*.
                                        –P.S., Kingston, Massachusetts

Hold on, here's another.

[To the Editor] I am a charter member of SOTSOTS (Stamp Out The Save Our Tongue Society) and find myself in agreement with [an earlier letter from a writer who may or may not have been a professional communicator]. Despite the statement that SOTS is concerned with the "misuses of language that carry the potential for misunderstanding," the stuff that gets printed seems to consist of nitpicking and out-of-context distortion, while the main misunderstanding seems to be the deliberate one on the part of the SOTSers.

I must say I enjoy the humor of the July/August issue's "the Oklahoma law which allows 18-year-old women to buy beer, but not 18-year-old men," and the like, but the potential for genuine misunderstanding is quite small.

On the other hand, one of our former members rejoined partly because he liked the SOTS column, so you can't please everyone.
                                        – J.W., El Paso, Texas

(Editor's note: [This is new *Bulletin* editor Meredy Mullen.] *Occupying a dual role as* Bulletin *editor and editor of the "SOTS" column, Gordon K. Andersen chose not to publish any comments on SOTS among the letters to the editor. Now that those two editorial roles have been separated, however, letters to the* Bulletin *editor regarding SOTS will be considered on an equal basis with letters regarding any other* Bulletin *feature.*

The following four letters are selected from among many received by Gordon during his term as Bulletin *editor.)*

Hooray for SOTS! I had thought I was almost alone in believing that improved pronunciation and usage will lead to improved communications and understanding of ideas, feelings, and so forth.

– J.L., Forestville, Md.

I thoroughly enjoy your column, even if you are not a master chef. It also does not take a wine expert to determine that the content of a bottle has turned to vinegar.

– J.H., Charlotte, N.C.

Continuing good fortune to you and your widespread cadre of SOTS-sleuths.

—S.W., El Paso, Texas

It gives me a great sense of gratification to know that I am not alone in my reactions to what is being done to our beautiful, flexible, expressive, and infinitely more than adequate English language.

—L.A., Vidalia, Ga.

Did you notice how J.W.'s tone changed from utter distaste to somewhat tolerant to what I would call high praise? I will also tell you that the two letters from El Paso were from husband and wife. Go figure. I also realize that I was out of line to use the term "bubblehead." Nowadays I would need to use "airhead," and I've recently heard much worse, but I won't go into that here.

By the way, those last four were only a sampling of the great many letters I received that were favorable, most of which included useable contributions. As I learned later, well after I left the editorship, positive mail invariably came to me, while negative stuff went to my successors as editor. I am pleased to report that the former outweighed the latter by several orders of magnitude. Also, because there were no subsequent negative letters published, I have to assume that none were received. Hah!

As the leadoff to my column following those letters, I made these comments:

> [Writer] P.S. ... offers some thoughts that I am having trouble understanding, [implying] that SOTS speaks for Mensa. It does not. We all know that no one, collectively or individually, may express opinions on behalf of Mensa, and the box on the back page [which I wrote while editor] effectively disclaims the possibility. What concerns me even more, however, is the suggestion that criticism of the media may be detrimental to Mensa's publicity efforts by offending potential "friends." ... SOTS has been excerpted in many publications [outside of Mensa] and the few appended comments have been commendatory without exception. My close observation tells me that the media people enjoy playing the game as much as we do.

> Another letter writer [J.W.] ... has me chuckling. [He begins with a jab at SOTS, but ends in SOTS's favor, which is exactly the same thing he did in a separate publication of which he was editor]. I quote: "While I'm definitely not a [SOTS] member, I do realize that the appearance of such things in any reading material is distracting and that the diminished readability reduces the usefulness of a publication, not to mention its attractiveness."

I concluded my remarks by suggesting that the writer relax and enjoy his (non)membership.

You could get such a headache ...

From D.N. of Durham, N.C., comes this TV pair:

> Two classic examples of bad grammar (in television advertising) are: "**All** aspirin **is not** alike (Bayer)" and "**Every** refrigerator **is not** a Frigidaire." Doesn't Frigidaire make refrigerators?

Chemically, if you don't count the buffered or coated kind, all aspirin *is* formulated the same, if not by law, at least by common practice. But to give the idea that each tablet is unique, or completely different from all others, is "kinda stupid," don't you think? The Frigidaire thing goes even farther afield by figuratively putting itself out of business. We had at least one Frigidaire in our house and I can assure you that *some* refrigerators are indeed Frigidaires. My response to the ad would be, so what brand *is* every refrigerator if it's not a Frigidaire? (Do I hear that grumbling in the ad agency board room again?)

However, credit should be given where credit is due. On the radio I heard it said that "Not all funeral homes are alike," on behalf of First Memorial Waterston Chapel.

Jumping back to Bayer for a moment, P.Y. of Petaluma, Calif., reminds us that "Nothing works better than Bayer," so he plans to take nothing, of course. Unless, that is, he finds something that is *better* than nothing. Bayer, as we now know, is not. Are we clear? No? How about if we suggest "No other aspirin works better than Bayer"? (Now they're probably shouting at each other in the ad agency board room.)

Also competing in that category is this from M.B. of Los Angeles, Calif.:

> An otherwise lovely newspaper ad for the May Co. featured "a ruffled peasant or a soft blouson that will light up your evening like the warm glow of candlelight. **Nothing** could be more feminine. ..." So, why not wear *that*? Advertising copywriters should be more careful.

Let me guess – now they're throwing things at each other in the ad agency boardroom. Well, maybe not. "Nothing" is intended to mean "no other thing of similar purpose," which, you'll have to admit, would be hard to fit into an ad campaign. Another possibility would be "There is nothing that could be more feminine," but that doesn't quite have the ring to it that they were looking for either, so, left with few alternatives, obviously "nothing" must do the job. Yes, I know – let it go.

Where to, pal?

Here's one that made me laugh out loud. It's from A.W. of Alleghany, Calif.:

This gem is from the February 14 (1977) issue of *TIME* magazine: "Early in 1979, [the] space-shuttle will open up a new age in space exploration by taking its first **round** trip **around** the Earth and **back**."

Even though we don't know who wrote it, I just had to include it here. My comment at the time was: "Incredible! A triple play, no less." I have, however, since ceased using *incredible*, as well as *unbelievable*. Those two words have become such cliches that they have lost their meaning, and they sort of fall back into being self-descriptive. But when you think about it, so have *fantastic* and several others.

A.M. of Bronx, N.Y., got tired of hearing the radio commercial for the New Jersey Haunted Mansion that said that it had many features to recommend it – "some even **more incredible** than others." A.M. says that so are some commercials. I agree. Many superlatives have totally lost their usefulness, but they will not fall from use.

J.M. of Fairfax, Va., favors us with this one:

In the *Washington Post*, The Hecht Co., a department store, ran a full-page, full-color ad for Helena Rubenstein that offered "our snappy little fold over [*sic*] Rich Brown Bag made of **genuine mock** suede ..."

No better, no worse, is this one from H.K. of Chicago, Ill.:

Walking through several department stores, I saw the same sign on more than one store's counter full of wallets and small purses: "**Genuine Imitation** Leather."

Be sure to ask for the *real* fake, not a cheap imitation.

Twice as bad?

Remember Underalls? They've been off the air for quite a while, but I recall them well, and so did A.W. of Kingston, Mass., back a few years:

That wretched commercial on TV for Underalls drives me frantic. "They make me look **like** I'm **not** wearin' **nothin'**." [And] why can't people say "as if" or "as though" instead of "like"?

My answer was that it would "detract from their cuteness. That copywriter had a hatchet in *both* hands." Among my many regrets is not having the names of all the perpetrators, but it can't be helped. Ad agency people fear exposure, which would put a severe damper on their creativity. Needless to say, the advertising manager for the client, also unknown, was just as culpable as the copywriter, as were all others who had a hand in the atrocity. Shame, shame! A double negative in the bargain, too. Double shame! (Or is that put too strongly? Sorry.)

In strong competition in the double-negative department is the Subway sandwich chain. Recently revived was (or is) the TV spot featuring an overdressed, over-made-up blonde hollering almost off-key musically, "I don't want **no** burger … ," thereby not only giving little kids a chant, but legitimizing the double-negative in their confused but still-developing minds. Also, consider: Which learning source, teachers or TV, makes the stronger impression? We can only hope that their little brains can be rewired before they go off to their eventual job interviews.

When we stop to think about it, the whole business of role-modeling appears to have gone into reverse. We are supposed to be looking to professionals to guide us in the use of our language. Instead we have so-called "professionals" copying the general population, picking up slang, colloquialisms, and sloppiness in general. As so many say nowadays, "What's wrong with this picture?"

The real thing?

B.B. of Elmhurst, Ill., picked up the morning paper and … :

> In the *Wall Street Journal*, March 18, 1977: "**Synthetic natural** gas made from an oil-refining by-product is … more costly than natural gas."

I assume that the writer meant that the synthetic stuff cost more than *natural* natural gas. Contrariwise, though, how else would one describe it?

Real or synthetic, it's still called "natural gas." Calling the synthetic stuff "synthetic gas" without specifically identifying it as the gas used for heating and cooking would likely be confusing to most of the general public. But I have to agree with B.B. that it looks funny, no matter how we say it.

Then, on a different day, in that same "prestigious" daily, I.L. of Michigan City, Ind., spotted this:

> The headline of a rather large ad in the *Wall Street Journal* for Savin copiers says, "Now, 1 out of every 2 copiers we place – **replace** a Xerox." The letters are almost an inch high.

Here we have the old subject-verb disagreement, with "1" being the subject requiring the plural verb "replaces." There were also four other errors in the body of the ad, such as, "less chance for **jam ups**," and "whether you copy **on to** one side or two." Ads like that cost plenty, too, and I can hear more than one high-powered executive facing a deadline saying, "Looks good to me – run it!" (For the record, hyphenate "jam-ups" and put "onto" together.) Anyway, here comes N.B. of Colorado Springs, Colo., again:

> From the *Colorado Springs SUN*: "While such young American people still constitute only a minority of young adults, they are **sufficiently** concentrated **enough** in some parts of the country." [redundancy]

> On another note, a newspaper ad for the Family Fare Sandwich Shop offered Hot Submarines, one choice being "**Vegetation.**" I have no idea what kind, but it does create an image in the mind. ["vegetarian"]

> Wait, there's more: The *Denver Post* headlined a movie review of *Evening at Byzantium*, in which actor Patrick Macnee endured actual pain when fellow actor Harrison Ford was supposed to feign killing Macnee. The secondary headline read: 'Actually, It Was Very, Very Funny. He Had My Head in a **Vice** Grip.' ["vise"] [Single quotation marks are OK in headlines.]

And the *National Enquirer* [how'd that get in here?] article by Rod Gibson about ostriches contained this sentence: "And its toes may be 7 inches long, with thick nails that become such dangerous weapons when the bird is cornered that it can easily **disembowel** a jackal or lion **wide open** with slashing blows."

Stare at it. It'll come to you. Then there's this that K.K. of New York, N.Y., saved from the bottom of the bird cage:

> A column by Daniel Lewis and Milton Leebaw in the New York Times Review of the Week contained the following: "The fifth judge felt that the evidence was **sufficient enough** to hold a formal hearing …" [Why does this have a familiar ring to it?]

Let's listen to what D.H. of Massapequa Park, N.Y., heard on the radio:

> The news director of WGBB (Freeport, N.Y.), in an editorial on the killings of Canadian seals, said, "They literally beat the seals to death, then skin them alive."

Scene: the newsroom. Underling: "Would you like me to give it a quick scan, chief?" News director: "Scram. I ain't stupid, you know. It's OK!" Although imaginary here, that sort of conversation actually does take place. I have heard similar ones more than a few times during my longer-than-10-year career in television and advertising; fortunately, no such conversation involved me. In fact, that sort of resistance to help was the cause of one of my business failures, the ill-fated English Repairman venture I mentioned in the introduction. No matter how carefully one writes, *every writer needs an editor.* Sadly, too many writers are unwilling to admit it, as are editors themselves frequently, when they too do the writing.

Here's another extract from my *Mensa Bulletin* column:

> *Thanks to B.W. of Los Angeles, Calif., we have our first real entry into the ethereal world of advertising agencies, where so much of the damage to the language originates. [He notes:]*

> Some insight into the continuing advertiser-SOTS conflict may be gained from the Annual Report (1976) of Foote, Cone, and Belding Communications, Inc., one of the largest agencies. Discussing telephone surveys, the report states:

"Because the primary purpose is to understand consumers, copywriters and art directors, TV producers and assistant producers, account executives and management supervisors, media and research people manned the phones. Also, the chairman, the president and the general managers of our offices."

It took me three readings to sort out the first part, and I think I know what it's supposed to say. The last part, however, conjures all sorts of images. Agency copywriters, unfortunately, are so immersed in a peculiarly punchy shorthand style of writing that proper sentence structure has been lost to them. A perfect example of this is the "bullet" technique now being used heavily in cigarette advertising, such as, "I'm realistic. I only smoke Facts."

Would it have weakened the ad's impact [no, I don't use the word "impact" that way anymore] *if it had said "I smoke only Facts"? Assuming that someone even thought of the correct form, you can surely bet that the decision was made to say it "the way people talk," and that grammar was given little or no consideration. The selling of any product requires implementation of the "Three A's" — Attention, Acceptance, and Action (or Acquisition) on the part of the consumer. How these three elements are accomplished* [can one accomplish an element?] *is strictly dependent on the impact* [last one] *and effectiveness of the methods used, and grammar, punctuation, and too often spelling, are almost never of any real concern. It is the results, the sales, that are important.*

6

More heat?

Some might think me foolish to give my opposition any ink at all, but I've always believed that if you have confidence in what you are doing, you need not worry. In that spirit, here's another letter to the editor of the *Mensa Bulletin*, exactly as published:

WOTS wrong with SOTS

SOTS looks like a good idea gone wrong. Instead of taking constructive action toward language salvation, it's become a smug little collection of fussiness. Most of the time, contributors to the SOTS page are aiming at the wrong target:

Newspaper headlines. These are deliberately written in cryptic language to: (a) save space; (b) catch a quick, passing eye; and (c) arouse curiosity that will lead to buying the paper. Headlines never claim to be pillars of grammar or syntax.

TV and radio commercials. Also deliberately written in mass-mentality language so a wider audience will identify with them or feel superior to them. Point is to sell the merchandise, and if a catchy but ungrammatical phrase makes the public remember the product and buy it, so be it. Also, commercials are priced by the second and sometimes a less elegant phrase is shorter, punchier, and does the selling job faster.

This is not to excuse their use of imperfect language. It's only to point out that it happens, in most of these cases, not from ignorance or carelessness but from shrewdness. That's a different kettle of fish and beyond the scope of SOTS.

The point of SOTS is, or should be, to keep watch on serious speakers and writers who are in positions of influence. Those most apt to be used as authorities. News commentators.

Politicians. Lecturers. Columnists. Editorial writers. Reporters with by-lines. Authors of books. Writers of articles. (Not
comedians. Not the dialogue in comic strips. No one takes
these seriously.)

And why stop at potshots in the *Bulletin*? The real purpose of
SOTSmanship should be to go beyond the *Bulletin*: to notify
the persons making the errors, suggest better phraseology, and
ask the offenders to sin no more in the future. Without this,
what good are we doing for our language?

As things are now, we're talking to ourselves. Scoffing and
sneering to ourselves. And accomplishing nothing. –M.K., New
York, N.Y.

I suspect that M.K. came in late to the game. My disclaimer clearly lays
out what I do and don't do, and I wish the new editor had offered me
the opportunity to respond in the same issue. M.K. does make one good
point, though, which is that taking the fight right to the offenders would
be a good idea. I agree. However, it would be more work than I wanted
to commit myself to, as I have earlier pointed out. Further, I did respond
in the following issue, thusly:

Much of what [M.K.] wrote about SOTS in the April issue is
true. I would, however, like to change her title, "WOTS wrong
with SOTS," to read, "WOTS incomplete about SOTS." [I
don't know who dropped the question marks.] There can be
no question as to the need to take SOTS beyond the pages of
the *Bulletin*, and it is my plan to eventually do so. Violation
notices to offenders, increased exposure in the media, a book, all
are parts of the SOTS plan of action. Nevertheless, there are
reasons these developments cannot be accomplished as soon as
we would like, the most important of which is shortage of time.
Then there is the necessity of sooner or later divorcing SOTS
from Mensa. Much as I dislike the idea, it will have to be done.
If you think about it for a while, I'm sure you'll understand my
reasoning. To put it briefly, we would want to reduce or eliminate the likelihood that recipients of our criticism would say

such things as "Who do these people think they are?" Opposing opinions, of course, will be welcomed. In all events, I want to assure everyone that [M.] is correct, but, at least for now, a bit premature.

As to [the writer's] other remarks, concerning the excusability of headlines, radio and TV commercials, and comic strips, the incorrectness of many of which [are attributed] to "shrewdness," I cannot, in general, agree. Headlines, of necessity and in form telegraphic, should nevertheless follow standard rules of syntax. Broadcast advertisements (commercials) should also conform to all the basic tenets established for grammar and pronunciation, except where misuse is *clearly and obviously designed for a specific effect.* In any case, straight expository information in commercials deserves a straight treatment, and because there are always some in the audience who don't recognize the "shrewdness" when they see it or hear it, it is up to those of us who do know the difference to point it out to the unaware. By the former tokens, neither are comic strips exempt. Illiterate characters are entitled to follow illiterate form, but characters otherwise depicted as literate are expected to reflect the same without exception. Cartoonists, after all, are quite well paid and have editors and proofreaders available to them in the same manner as do other writers.

[M.K.] says that SOTS should keep watch on "serious speakers and writers who are in positions of influence." I am hard pressed to think of any elements of modern communications that have more influence than do headlines, commercials, and comic strips. [M.K.] has, however, earned our thanks. One out of two is not bad. –Gordon K. Andersen

There were a few letters after that, but they were pretty much repetitious. Most writers applauded, some booed. Either way, one thing is evident: No matter what your cause, someone will come along to help you with it, and someone else will come along to try to trash it. The odds may be against our winning, but that doesn't mean we shouldn't try. At least we're not doing any harm.

More nonsense

J.K. of San Francisco found an unusual place for a grammar goof:

> Postmark message from the Illinois Department of Public
> Health: "Women – Help **Prevent** Cancer – Get a Pap Test."

This was a private postmark authorized by the Postal Service but prepared by someone on the health department staff who should have known better. A Pap test can't "prevent" anything, but it can "detect" the presence of cancer.

Naturally, I love the way R.L. of Walnut Creek, Calif., begins his presentation:

> Whatever happened to the most delightful column *Mensa Bulletin* ever produced? In the *Contra Costa Times*, an unnamed writer penned, "An unseemly furor has finally been stilled in the contented town of Danville. It seems that a couple sought a permit from the still-new city to **covert** a pool house into a little apartment for a live-in nurse. The wife has multiple **cirrhosis** and needs constant nursing care."

OK, so I could have fixed the "covert" typo, but I didn't. Cirrhosis, of course, is a liver disease, and without a second liver the "multiple" cannot factor in. The word is "sclerosis," a far cry from the result shown here.

How much?

A.M. of Decatur, Ala., took the positive step of writing to the perpetrators of these two, for which I gave special thanks in my column:

> In a *Wall Street Journal* article by Bernard Wysocki, Jr., … he referred to a "**hot-water** heater." And on another day in the same publication, the president of a major corporation [not a paid professional communicator] said in a letter to the editor, "Coal gasification plants … release **1,000** percent less pollution into the air than coal-burning electrical generation plants of the same capacity." Isn't 100 percent the maximum?

OK, all together, now: *"Why would you want to heat hot water?"* And yes, 100 percent is tops.

B.W. of Redstone, Colo., tunes in the radio for us:

> On the noon news broadcast from KWSR in Rifle, Colo., the announcer said, relative to the search for an airplane missing in the mountains, "The search has been called off until we have a **100 percent** improvement in the weather."

W.B. of El Toro, Calif., nails an unknown *Los Angeles Herald Examiner* photo-caption writer with: "Its proponents say recycling offers savings up to **several-hundred** percent." No way.

Back to school?

Wouldn't you think that getting a job at a prestigious, high-powered, big-city newspaper would call for a college degree? Or does that not necessarily equate with an education? L.L. of State College, Pa., found this one for us:

> Headline in the Sunday *New York Times,* no less: "Controversy Over Testing **Flairs** again." The article is about scholastic aptitude testing.

If I had my way, I'd have every headline in every paper signed by the writer. *That* would wake 'em up! (The word is "flares.")

Let's take a break for a moment and play a little game. What do you think of this? "There is 4 errers in this sentence." It's not hard to figure out, but take whatever time you need, and no, I'm not going to help. If you think it's a bit sophomoric, humor me – I'm just having a little fun.

Overkill?

Every once in a while I see something that makes me wonder whether I should report on it or just consider it an ad-lib slip of the tongue. Because news anchors are invariably reading from a TelePrompTer, this redundancy sent to me from C.V. of San Jose, Calif., has to qualify as a writer's goof, except that the anchor has to take the heat:

On a local KNTV newscast, anchorwoman Joan Edmondson
reported that "an East San Jose resident was **murdered** to death
last night."

Then there's this one wherein the guilty broadcaster was not named, but I
had to include it anyway. It's from E.S. of Chula Vista, Calif.:

Heard on radio KYXY, San Diego, was "Actor Bob Crane [Col.
Hogan of TV's *Hogan's Heroes*] was murdered as he slept by an
intruder." Not ungrammatical, but a comma after "slept" would
have helped a lot.

Not far away, W.S. of San Mateo, Calif., had to blink twice:

An article in the *San Francisco Examiner* on crime in the Grand
Canyon area included: "Last January, for example, Michael Sherman and his wife, Charlotte, both 27, were found **fatally** dead."

And I found this headline in my local paper, the Minneapolis *Star Tribune*: "Body of man found in St. Paul; he apparently was **fatally** shot."
If he had not been "fatally" shot, he could not have been described as a
"body." Or am I telling you too much?

And yet another case of wandering attention comes from C.O. of Tacoma,
Wash.:

From a story in the *Seattle Post-Intelligencer*: "The clerk of
another North End 7-Eleven store ... was found badly beaten
by police."

No, not inaccurate, but a poor choice of words. And I can't help following
that one with another from P.A. of Reston, Va.:

In the *Washington Star*, Richard Slusser reported that Canon
Mary Simpson, a nun of the Order of St. Helen, "will preach
and lecture ... on the ordination of women and other things."

Yep, that's what he said. OK, so we all know what those writers meant to
say, so where's the harm? Oh, I suppose there's no real harm, but that sort

of thing tends to derail our train of thought, especially among those of us who possess a critical awareness. It also makes us wonder whether there are any other gaffes like it. Some of us will re-read the entire article looking for more foolishness. Anyway ...

From Phoenixville, Pa., J.O. sends his regards along with the following contribution:

> On Channel 10's 11 o'clock news, Larry Kane reported that "the car driven by the woman broke through the guard rail, and, **for some unknown reason,** plunged into the creek." Perhaps he doesn't understand gravity, although Larry may have fallen victim to a "cub" news writer and didn't catch it in time. It's unlikely that the car needed a reason.

Mea Culpa

Once in a while I blow one myself, and I would not be totally honest if I kept it quiet, now would I? Crossing my desk back in the good old days was a contribution from a fellow ignoramus – well, to be fair, it's just that neither of us bothered to check – about a paperback from Ballantine Books titled *"The SEVEN-PER-CENT SOLUTION."* I published it exactly that way in my 17th column in the *Mensa Bulletin*, and thought it bad enough not even to need comment. I was dead wrong and I was immediately upbraided by several readers, including S.C., who was then stationed in Tehran, Iran (before the hostage-taking, of course). As it turned out, that was the way it appeared on and in the book by Nicholas Meyer, which purported to be "reprinted" from the last writings of Dr. Watson, Sherlock Holmes's faithful companion. (Conan Doyle had nothing to do with it.) And yes, I confessed my error in a subsequent column. I have since paid closer attention. Also, I probably deserved to be caught red-faced, since I had deviated from my stated purpose and wandered into books, which are not normally considered fully public and are thus out of my main arena. It was a judgment call that didn't work out very well.

Confession is supposed to be good, etc., so I may as well get one more out of the way. In one of my 1982 columns in the *Mensa Bulletin* I made the statement that: "Mispronunciation by broadcasters is now so bad that ..."

A.V. of Iowa City, Iowa, was the first to catch me, commenting, "Heaven forbid [that] their *pronunciations* ever become so bad." What I originally meant, of course, was that mispronunciation was then so rampant or widespread, etc., and describing it as "bad" was engaging in redundancy. By definition, "mispronunciation" is bad enough to begin with. Caught in my own trap, I was. So now you know, and I can sleep better at night – or in the morning, as is more likely.

Before I doze off, though, let me bare my soul once more: I was softly chastised for mentioning "pierced earrings" in one column, that time by a television advertising copywriter, which I, too, once was. R.W. of Abilene, Texas, the copywriter, called the phrase a stroke of genius that saved time, space, and, no doubt, money too. He said that "earrings for pierced ears" would sound awkward, and I guess I have to agree, but you have to admit that "pierced earrings" can cause one to hesitate, that is, if one is inclined to hesitate at such times, and I am among those who do. It is, of course, not the earrings that are pierced. Could we say "pierced-ear rings"? Or "pierced-ear-rings"? Maybe "pierced-earrings" would work. No? OK, I give up.

Take names, please!

I really hate to let so many things go by just for lack of full attribution. My files are full of items rejected for that particular reason, but a few are included here because I simply cannot resist. Here are two perfect examples, from M.S. of Chula Vista, Calif.:

> From an article in the *San Diego Evening Tribune*: "Christine Baker is surrounded by dolls representing different African tribal **people** she has **created**." And a headline in the same paper: "Competitor **slayed** in fast-food war."

That first one looks as if it's a photo caption, most of which are written by headline writers, or by the photographers themselves. At some papers, captions and headlines are written by a person called a designer. In any event, in both cases a copyeditor was needed. Badly. ("slain")

I don't think we've covered the lay vs. lie question, except for a brief mention a while back. It's about time we tackled it and it was brought to mind by c.l. [lower case by request] of Villa Park, Calif., who blew the whistle on the Lectric Shave people for "Your beard just **lays** there. Prop it up with Lectric Shave!" (lies)

> A person lies – tells an untruth.
>
> A person lies down – reclines, usually horizontally.
>
> A person lay down – reclined earlier.
>
> A person has lain down – and may have done so again.
>
> A person lays a thing somewhere – places it.
>
> A person has laid a thing somewhere – placed it earlier.
>
> A thing was or has been laid somewhere by a person – done earlier.
>
> A thing lies where it was placed.
>
> A thing has lain where a person placed it.

I think that says it.

Wanted!

Is the following item public, in accord with the purpose of SOTS? Yes, of course. Was it someone's specific job as a professional writer? Well, maybe, but I doubt it. It was probably one of those "In addition to your other duties" sort of thing that is so prevalent in the armed services, and it doubtless applies in this case to an employee of the U.S. government. Nevertheless, I'll sit on the fence and conjure the image of J.S. of San Francisco, Calif., stepping into the local post office:

> On an FBI poster: "This deposit slip will bear a fictitious account number and if questioned **will depart** the bank immediately leaving the documents behind."

G.S. of Fort Pierce, Fla., sent me this multimedia offering:

> The *Fort Pierce News Tribune* persists in running a classified ad for "**Part Time** Ladies," and if *Today Show* (NBC-TV) host Tom Brokaw continues prefacing every third sentence with "**Hopefully**," I think I'll cease watching.

All right, all right, so I deviated from my own policy on that one. Classi-fied ads are borderline, even though the phone and counter clerks are paid. Without intending to demean their honest labor, I think we all know that they are probably the lowest-paid employees on any newspaper's staff, and are probably not even subject to copyediting. If they were, there would be fewer gaffes like that one. Therefore, from here on, I'll be very sparing of the classifieds and leave most of that kind of stuff for Jay Leno or whoever else does his "Headlines" gimmick. As for Brokaw, he is no longer on the *Today* show, as of this writing, but he is still fair game as he is still on the air and can therefore continue to serve as the poster boy for "hopefully," a much misused adverb. We can be hopeful that he will reform, and we will be listening hopefully (… hopefully listening doesn't quite do it).

For the record, I did receive mail asking why I objected to "hopefully," which means "it is to be hoped," as in "Hopefully, we will get to the show on time." Surprisingly, that sentence – along with "if all goes well" – is the illustrative example in the aforementioned *Random House Dictionary* of 1966 that allows that particular usage. SOTS begs to differ. In both *Merriam Webster's Second* and *Third Unabridged*, there is no mention of that use at all, but it is included in the same company's *Ninth New Colle-giate*, which is based on the Second Unabridged and was obviously pub-lished at a later date. This is a case where common usage has gotten such a tight grip on our speech that it cannot be dislodged. Nevertheless, there are those among us who will rail against "hopefully" as a sentence starter, yours truly and SOTS included, thank you very much.

Yet another classified? I have to admit that they can be good for laughs, and I didn't promise to drop them altogether. A help-wanted ad in the *Star Tribune* was for a **FART TIME RECEPTIONIST**. Yes, indeed it was.

Sorry, but looking for goofs in classified ads is like eating potato chips; you can't eat just one. R.C. of Berkeley, Calif., has one, perhaps or perhaps not the last, for us:

> The ad is a display ad in the classified section of the San Jose *Mercury-News* and is for a position in sales recruitment. At the top, in large type, is the word "OVERACHIEVERS," and the first sentence reads: "If you're blocked **where your at** and feel your

efforts aren't adequately rewarded it's time you took corrective action." ["where you are"]

That particular locution is nothing new. In the January 11, 1930, *Saturday Evening Post* appeared an article headlined "Where's Vaudeville **At**?" Several improvements come to mind; mine would be "Whither Vaudeville?" (Vaudeville, of course, was in its death throes, unable to survive against the onslaught of radio and talking pictures.)

Considerably larger, courtesy of M. of Fresno, Calif., were the 30 or 40 4-foot by 5-foot signs spaced at about 6-foot intervals all along the approximately three-block length of one side of the Ford agency on Blackstone Avenue, all saying the same thing: "**Your** in Ford country." ["Whadda ya mean, change them? We spent a bundle on those signs."]

7

Geographically challenged?

By now most of the world knows that a pair of ruby slippers used in the filming of *The Wizard of Oz* was stolen from the Judy Garland Museum, which is located in the town of her birth, Grand Rapids, Minnesota. Unfortunately, someone on the staff of *The Tonight Show With Jay Leno* bungled badly. Whether it was a researcher, a writer, a cue-card maker, or Leno himself, he announced that the theft had occurred in Grand Rapids, **Michigan**. If he corrected the information at a later time, I am not aware of it as of this writing in September 2005.

Oh, the pain ...

Appropriate for all occasions, I offer this from a TV ad: "Tylenol Arthritis Pain works as well as prescription Ibuprofen. **Hopefully**, that will give you something to hold **on to**." It may not look as bad as the previous use of "hopefully," but it's still bad. And "on to" should be "onto." Trust me.

In TV advertising, the idea is to get as much information as possible across in as few seconds as possible, so sometimes things get crunched a bit, and sometimes things get crunched far too much (way too much?). I once noted that a TV commercial for Ben-Gay pain-relieving cream said that "We asked **minor** arthritis pain sufferers what they used, etc. ..." The question arises, Are these pain sufferers minors? Not very likely, although the ailment can strike at any age. Would it have been better, though, to say, "We asked sufferers of minor arthritis pain ..."? But then the product wouldn't have wound up here with a free mention, which, of course, does not constitute an endorsement, but neither does it reflect in any way on the product itself.

In a somewhat different vein is this dilly from E.L. of Canon City, Colo.:

> In the June 1977 issue of *Car and Driver* magazine, senior
> editor Brock Yates says, "**Thankfully**, the high-style plas-
> tic nose will meet the U.S. bumper standards without awful
> alternatives."

Describing a plastic nose as being "thankful" endangers editor Yates's credibility, unless, of course, he is no longer editor; he may by now have retired. Fear not, however, there are still plenty of others out there dropping the same ball. "Thankfully" and "hopefully" should not be used in the same manner as such introductory elements as "fortunately," "oddly," etc., because the former indicate characteristics attributable to humans, whereas the latter describe conditions or states of being. People are thankful or hopeful, while situations are fortunate, odd, etc. Let's not lose those distinctions.

Hear that?

Even though no tape was provided, I have to believe the following from R.J. of Los Angeles, Calif.:

> On KFAC [radio], Bill Carlson recently introduced "sixteenth century **anominous** lute music," and not once but twice. ["anonymous"]

Although it was possibly being ad-libbed, it's more likely he was reading from prepared copy. And even though sometimes the ear can play tricks, I don't think that was the case either for Carlson or when J.M. of Arlington, Mass., listened to WEEI as it reported on a project at a Boston hospital. The nameless announcer said, "The program is intended to **decimate** information on teenage pregnancy." J.M. figures that the plan to reduce information by one tenth is unlikely to similarly reduce teen pregnancies. ("disseminate")

R.R. of Miami, Fla., also was listening to the radio, this time to WJOY-FM (107), when the announcement was made that the pope was visiting Spain. Heard was "This was the first **beautification** service ever performed by him outside Rome." The implication that the saint referred to was ugly was uncalled for. (The mispronunciation, which also implied a misspelling, was of the word "beatification.")

Making headway?

Whenever a contributor reported taking positive action against an offender, I made special mention of it in my column. What follows, from J.P. of Atlanta, Ga., is a perfect illustration of that idea:

I wrote to John Chancellor (*NBC Evening News*) to point out his error in saying, **"A million and a half dollars"** ($1,000.000.50) and suggested "one and a half million dollars ($1,500,000)." He kindly responded with "I think you are right (not absolutely certain) and I will try to change the habits of a lifetime."

Here's another with the gumption to speak up, namely, J.C. of Largo, Fla.:

After writing a letter to our local TV station and chiding them for a commercial that said, "Visit one of your Florida Dodge **dealer's** today," I received an answer blaming the advertiser and promising to notify the advertiser. The next time I saw the commercial, it was correct. Another SOTS victory?

Hooray for them both! Over the years I have had many reports just like those, and I cheered them all. It takes a little time and a postage stamp, but there is great satisfaction in having an effect. Try it. You'll like it.

That plural apostrophe, which is not only inappropriate but misplaced (can it be misplaced if it is inappropriate to start with?), is the bane of copyeditors everywhere. Buying a full-page ad in *Time* magazine, investment bankers Morgan Stanley Dean Witter (if that is still their name, they change so often) asked us to "invest with a firm that leads everybody in **IPO's**," has the "most **IPO's** worldwide," and has "lead-managed the largest number of **IPO's** ..." An IPO, by the way, is an initial public offering, meaning that a company is issuing shares of stock to the public for the first time. But couldn't they do it without those dumb apostrophes?

Air talk

We've all listened to the radio while doing other things and been unable either to recall who said what, or to call and get details from the station. This was exactly the case for H.T. of Bronx, N.Y.:

These were all heard on WINS, a news radio station in New York City: "They are open seven days a week, **including Sunday.**" For Pan-Am Airlines: "This $99.00 fare is good anywhere in the continental U.S. Book me, I'm going to the

Bahamas." And for whatever reason: "The results **bespeak** themselves."

On radio, we can't always tell what is extemporaneous and what is scripted, but these were all in advertisements, so ad-libbing is unlikely. H.T. also included a line from a scripted newscast: "A blast destroyed the **premise**." ("premises")

Turnabout

In the interests of fair play, it is only fitting that SOTS recognizes excellence as well as bungling. Frequent contributor P.A. of Reston, Va., recommended that staff writer Bill Gold of *The Washington Post* be named an honorary member of our little unorganized band. Although perhaps unwittingly, Mr. Gold is already a full-fledged member, as he obviously appears to subscribe to our principles. See if I'm not right about that. Here is an excerpt from his The District Line column in 1978:

> With no column to write for a few weeks, I had more time to read my favorite newspaper, and to wonder about some of the things I read.
>
> The word *minuscule* is still being spelled **miniscule**, I regret to report. Twice in one week we wrote **imposter** when we meant *impostor*, and on three occasions *led* or *misled* appeared as **lead** or **mislead**.
>
> *Which* has almost driven *that* out of the language, and there's nothing like a set of commas to confuse the writer who must decide between *who* and *whom*. All too often what emerges is a sentence that says, "Jones, **whom** police believe was involved in the crime, refused to comment."
>
> In two stories, we reported miraculous changes that should have been more fully explained. In one, a man suspected of homicide "turned himself **into** a policeman." In the other, Firestone 500 tires were "turned **into** dealers."
>
> I understand how a criminal could decide to reform and

become a policeman, but those tires that turned themselves into people baffle me.

More recently, several newspapers have installed "readers' representatives," who, in many cases, will 'fess up on behalf of their co-workers and employers. Still, a lot of errors continue to slip by, and that's what provides grist for the SOTS mill. I salute Mr. Gold and others like him. If you're still around, Bill, thanks for the contribution, and feel free to print your own membership card. Incidentally, I have the stub from a General Mills coupon that says, "Use the attached coupon on your next purchase of Raisin Nut Bran and help expose the **imposter** Raisins." There's a story behind it, but it would take much too long to tell. ("actor," "alligator," "motor," "doctor," "impostor")

L.L. piggy-backs on the foregoing with this little morsel:

> From a news item in the Los Angeles *Herald-Examiner*:
> "Arthur Schlesinger Jr. has finally finished his massive study ... and has turned it **into** his editors."

Abracadabra, presto-change-o ... oops! In both cases, "turned in to" is the way to go.

Before we get too far away from **miniscule** and **imposter**, I should mention that I referred to the two misspellings in a 1979 column and was upbraided by a couple of readers who said that those were listed in Merriam-Webster's *Ninth New Collegiate* as being variants of "minuscule" and "impostor," and should therefore not be considered incorrect. I didn't reply to those comments in a later column, but I can do so now:

There are so many words in the English language that are variants of words more commonly accepted as correct that it would be fruitless, in the main, to argue too stridently against those variants. However, in view of their overwhelming acceptance in modern literature, including the academic, as well as in periodicals written and read by the better-educated populace, it is not unfair to call those variants incorrect. No matter how commonly they are used, they are nevertheless interruptive "speed bumps" on the road of effective communication, causing some, if not most, readers to react, however briefly, to their incongruous appearance and, on occasion, to find it necessary to reread the passage, if not the whole sentence or paragraph.

To paraphrase my earlier observation, if one spelling of a word bothers only a few, perhaps little harm is done. But if a better spelling bothers *no one*, why not use it? For my part, I intend to stay away from those variants – except, of course, to report on them.

Now see here!

Using another First Class postage stamp was G.M. of Mesquite, Texas, who wrote to Radio Shack and enclosed in her letter to me one of their catalog pages that bore the 28-point headline: "**PIECE-OF-MIND** SECURITY BEGINS AT THE SHACK." No more than a week after her copy to SOTS arrived, a copy of a letter to her from Paul McVey, national advertising copy director for Radio Shack, landed in my mailbox. I quote in part: "Your letter … is correct and our faces are appropriately red. … Thank you for your interest in our spelling and grammar." Now, there was a fellow who knew the value of even a small bit of image-polishing. You're OK, McVey!

Good health to you!

Here's another can of worms, this one opened by J.M. of Staten Island, N.Y., whom we thank:

> An ad in *National Geographic* for Kellogg's Corn Flakes
> includes the following sentence: "Dr. John felt the need to
> find a lighter, **healthier** food to replace the heavy, **fat-ladened**
> breakfast of the times."

The people who publish national magazines – and newspapers – are reluctant to criticize advertisers, and refuse ads only if they contain what the editors consider to be harmful material, or are libelous or otherwise objectionable. SOTS of course decries the oh-so-common *healthy* replacing the correct word *healthful*. (In this case, the term *healthier* should be *more healthful*.) Dictionaries will frequently waffle on the subject, but will still lean in the direction of *healthy* meaning "in good health," which can apply to humans, animals, plants, and even bank accounts. *Healthful*, conversely, is used to describe things that contribute to good health. The geniuses who dreamed up the brand name Healthy Choice should be taken out back, lined up, and shot, in my less-than-humble opinion.

In that regard, while our local *Star Tribune* newspaper generally accepts either usage, I can happily report that Al Sicherman, in his other incarnation as Mr. Tidbit and editor of the weekly Taste section about food and cooking, has consistently used the correct form, except, we fear, when intercepted by a copyeditor who disagreed. In 1991 he wrote:

> You pick up a package of Le Menu Light Style turkey divan from the supermarket freezer, and the package behind it is Le Menu **Healthy** turkey divan. What's going on? Nothing much, really, except that Campbell has renamed and repackaged its Light Style line. ... We could get *really* excited if one of the new "healthy" foods was labeled "healthful" for a change, but that's too much to ask.

Well, he did what he could, but, alas, to no avail. So, to all the rest who advise us to "eat healthy," I say, take a hike! As far as I know, it's not possible to eat an adjective, although I do have a healthy, and perhaps healthful, respect for most of them.

As for **fat-ladened**, there is simply no such word as ladened. Even my spell-checker agrees.

R.S. of Elizabeth, N.J., invites us to breakfast, healthful or not:

> I'll bet you a penny you don't know how long to cook grits to serve in lieu of mashed potatoes. Well, here it is, according to my box of JIM DANDY QUICK GRITS: "To serve as a substitute for mashed potatoes, cook for two minutes longer than directions." But what if you like your directions rare and your grits well done?

You throw them in with the grits two minutes before the grits are done. What's so hard about that?

8

What's in a name?

OK, as you already know, my local daily is the Minneapolis *Star Tribune*. If you're wondering why "Minneapolis" is not part of the name of the newspaper, it's totally by design. Across the river – *generally* speaking (part of Minneapolis is actually across the Mississippi to the east as well) – is the lovely city of St. Paul. Not only is it our state's capital, it is home to many educational and cultural organizations and institutions, and several large corporations. It also has the state's second-largest newspaper, the *St. Paul Pioneer Press*.

Not satisfied with being the only daily paper in Minneapolis, the *Star Tribune*, or *Strib*, as it is sometimes called even on its own pages, decided that its city name on what's called "the flag" (the paper's name atop the front page in large type) was somewhat limiting. Just below the name the legend now reads, "Newspaper of the Twin Cities." Of course, no one was fooled, but I understand that they did pick up a few readers "over there." Were there enough to make the name change worthwhile? Probably not, but you'll never get them to admit it.

Anyway, aside from that oddity, I have come back to haunt James Lileks, who is already mentioned in my autobiography and who wrote the Backfence column in the *Star Tribune* and now writes, as of 2006, a short column called the Daily Quirk in the same paper. This time, however, I go back to when he was a writer for the Newhouse News Service. He wrote an article about moving into a new neighborhood and having difficulty remembering names; it contained the following: "Maybe practice and long tenure in the neighborhood will increase my **pneumonic** skills." OK, I agree that just because Lileks had his byline on it, there's no proof that someone else down the line, such as a copyeditor, didn't change "mnemonic" to the awful thing that eventually appeared. Also, remember that in order to look up something in a dictionary, one has to have an approximate idea of how to spell it. Obviously, in this case it just didn't happen.

As a result of that item appearing in my *Mensa Bulletin* column, and of Mensa member K.C. of Minneapolis sending a copy of the column to Lileks, an extremely odd thing occurred: I had sent the following to him a few days earlier:

> **From G.K. Andersen:** In the St. Paul phone book, the business section of the white pages lists Montgomery Ward and notes, "See Wards." When you turn to "Wards" it says, " See Montgomery Ward & Co." If I'm not mistaken, there isn't even a Wards retail store anywhere in the metro area anymore, only catalog stores. I found the listings when I wanted to verify the closing of the last MW in the Midway [area of St. Paul], in case it was still open. I wanted to buy some long underwear. I'll try Sears.

The foregoing, along with Lileks's comments about it, was published in the first part of that day's Backfence column and was followed by his reactions to my *Bulletin* column thusly:

> [K.C.] included the Bulletin [newspaper style without the italics], which quotes my 1994 column about memorizing street names. "Maybe practice and long tenure in the neighborhood," I wrote, "will increase my **pneumonic** skills," it said. Yikes. Not mnemonic: pneumonic. Yes, you all remember that bad Keanu Reeves movie about a cybernetically enhanced data courier with a hacking cough: "Johnny Pneumonic." I did *not* write pneumonic. I'm not that stupid. Someone changed it for reasons I can't imagine. But now for all time I'm in the MENSA databanks as Jimmy Pneumonic. Great.

> The article, it goes without saying, was written by a fellow named – Andersen.

> Wait a minute. It's by G.K. Andersen. G.K. Andersen who wrote the letter listed a St. Louis Park address – and this MENSA column author has the exact address. I'll be switched: What are the chances of that? I get one letter from G.K. with a nice Backfence offering; then I get another letter in which the very same individual humiliates me before the eggheads. Sheer

Andersen perfidy! Let's examine *his* letter for errors, give him a taste of his own steel.

Hah! He didn't capitalize "Midway"!

In the war against the Andersens, even the smallest victory counts.

And that is how I became, as of this writing, the only person ever to appear in Lileks's column twice on the same day, and he had been writing it for several years. Funny how things turn out.

My name ...

On the same page as the aforementioned column appeared an ad for Treasure Island Casino with the large-type heading: "Long Before **Schizophrenia**, Bill Dana & Jose Jimenez Were The Same Funny Guy." (Dana was on the casino's entertainment program at the time.) Apparently there are still many, professional copywriters included, who have no idea what schizophrenia is. Implied in the ad is the old "dual-, split-, or multiple-personality" syndrome, and that is a total disconnect from reality, which is what sufferers of the disease endure. Persons afflicted with schizophrenia, technically and medically, have varying degrees of difficulty telling the difference between what is "real" and what is not. Its symptoms are withdrawal from society, confusion, and often dementia, and it has nothing whatever to do with any form of multiple personality. Let's all learn not to use words without knowing their meaning.

I've occasionally heard people say, "Well, what difference does it make?" The difference is that there are people out here who *know* the difference, and there are not just a few of us either. The effectiveness of poor communication with *those who know* is certainly diminished, as is the credibility of those with diminished communication skills; if they miss the mark, it's their own fault and not ours.

Every little letter ...

Just two extra letters can change the whole meaning of a sentence. B. W. of Commerce City, Colo., gives us an excellent example:

From an article in the *Denver Post*: "The **prerequisites** our pampered elected representatives enjoy include plush offices … free medical care, free plants and picture-framing. …" A sub-headline also mentions "free parking spaces, telephones, **stationary**." Do I get to be in SOTS now?

Absolutely. The short form, of course, is prereks, maybe? Maybe not. *Post* newspaper folks no doubt found out that the word is "perquisites," now condensed to "perks." How they got the one they did is anybody's guess. And "station*a*ry," as everyone knows, means unmoving. "Station*e*ry" refers to office supplies.

P.E. of Los Angeles, Calif., sent me a rather expensive full-page magazine ad for the Empire Pencil Co., a division of Hasbro Industries, Inc., that said that their products were "available where **stationary** and school supplies are sold."

Ignorance is rampant in the media, folks. As evidence, check out this from C.E. of San Antonio, Texas:

> On three separate broadcasts, KMOL-TV anchorman David Cruz informed us that a "murdered policeman's **internment** would take place later in the week."

If you have a SOTS whistle, now's the time to blow it. Make that "interment." The deceased was hardly able to work as an intern anywhere.

Looking for a place to eat out was previous contributor C.M. of Mobile, Ala.:

> Tommye Miller's Dining Out column in the *Mobile Register* touts a local restaurant where "Prompt and **courtesy** service is the aim of [the management]." The manager was also quoted as saying, "There are 138 seats … during the two-hour lunch period they are **turned over** three times."

Ahh, *that's* how they remove dawdling customers, not just crumbs. Also, replace "courtesy" with "courteous."

Same contributor, same newspaper, no writer's name: Headline: "Two men rob woman at home." The item's last line read, "They were last seen **walking on foot** from the front of the residence." Beats walking on hands, doesn't it? Faster, too.

Soap opera?

C.G. of San Francisco, Calif., says that she copied the BBD&O ad agency on this one:

> A television commercial for Lifebuoy soap proclaims that: "Lifebuoy is the soap that was **born to clean**."

And M.W. of Longview, Texas, asks:

> And how about the salesman [on TV] who invites everyone to "Try Zest. You'll feel cleaner than **your** soap"?

No, I think maybe my soap feels cleaner than I do. I'll have to ask it. I really am pretty clean. Along those same lines is this from V.B. of Wayne, N.J.:

> Among the precautions on a bottle of Kwell shampoo is: "If irritation or sensitization occurs, **discontinue** the product and consult physician." A bit drastic, no?

First you get a job with the manufacturer, climb the corporate ladder, become the CEO, and *then* you can discontinue the product. It would probably mean closing a plant and putting many employees out on the street, but you'd be able to say, "I was only following instructions!"

＊＊＊＊

Hey, let's take a break here. As previously discussed, there will always be those who criticize, and SOTS has had a few potshots taken at it. I already included some of them in this book, but I particularly enjoyed reading a rebuttal that said some things better than I could.

Championing SOTS

Why are so many *Bulletin* readers suddenly sniping at SOTS?

Do they feel their own license to use English badly in today's climate of contempt for word-communication threatened?

SOTS is surely not so special an interest that it deserves removal from the *Bulletin*. You might as well call puzzles, cooking, and scientific speculation the stuff of arcane [special-interest groups] and remove them, too.

One critic seems to resent the clear and proper pronunciation of February, for God's sake. It's easy if one's jaw isn't lazy. And to disregard a word's clear structure, or its derivation, or its meaning, or its value, is to disregard the glory of language itself. Language is a superb device that has helped us, as humans, to become what we are, to go beyond other species of animals.

As for the brouhaha over who dictates proper English usage, the same old mistake is being made. English usage is a matter of taste, and there is no democracy in taste. Democracy's great as a political concept, but good taste rests in the cultivated sensibilities of those few – alas, always so few – who concern themselves with it. That statement will elicit howls, I know. If good taste were determined by majority preference, the top forty would be the greatest music, cheesy landscapes the greatest art, and appalling TV sitcoms the greatest drama. And slack-jawed, mala-propped speech, plus careless, fuzzy writing, would be the highest standards of English. There's a kind of Gresham's law at work here; bad taste tends to drive out good taste.

Who says what English should be? Guys like Andersen, who concern themselves with it, that's who. And the nurturing of the language by those who love it will not at all freeze or stultify it. It will change, for the better, as vigorous new words, new accents, and new phrases come into it – elements that fulfill needs, and not careless changes made out of ignorance or contempt.

Please keep SOTS, and any other "special interests" that brighten up the *Bulletin*. –W.S., Bellingham, Wash.

My thanks to W.S., wherever he may be. This is as good a time as any to offer three reasons *not* to endorse or approve of changes in our language. They are:

1. When new or different words and expressions are not understandable to the general public.

2. When the words do not accurately convey their true meaning.

3. When the words sound just plain dumb.

The phenomenon of common usage leading to changes in usage is not new. Witness what happens when common perceptions threaten to change history. George Washington is said to have thrown a dollar all the way across the Potomac River. (Insert joke about money going a long way.) In the first place, the Potomac is much too wide, at least where Washington would likely have been. And in the second place, according to the history books, it was the Rappahannock River, not the Potomac. Look it up. But since so many believe it was the Potomac, should we rewrite history to accommodate those widespread and "popular" beliefs?

Hot and cold

Goof-ups are hardly a new phenomenon. P.L. of College Park, Calif., looks back a ways:

> An advertisement in *House & Garden* magazine of June 1927 for Johns-Manville asbestos shingles is headlined: "Each beautiful shingle is a hardy **fire-fighter**." A piece of text says, "Try **an'** burn it." A shingle puts out fires?

Fire *resistant* it may be, but we still need the fire department to fight a fire. Some over-eager advertising copywriter (which I once was, remember) got carried away with his or her own brilliance. Got all fired up, as it were.

Opposite to that is this chiller from S.W. of Orlando, Fla.:

> The wrapper advertises the Eskimo brand Twin Pop as being a **"quiescently** frozen confection." Are they tranquilized when they are not quiescent?

I have no idea how the word applies here, or what the writer meant. "Quietly," maybe? It made me shake my head in wonder when I first saw it some years ago, and I still can't figure it out.

Yuck!

J.H. of Palmdale, Calif., did a double-take on seeing this one:

> In the Los Angeles *Herald Examiner*, an excerpted portion of the novel *The Deep* was accompanied by a photo with the caption: "Gail surfaces after discovering a strange **vile** while diving off Bermuda." As it turned out, it was a vial.

Although not a typo, it may have been transmitted by phone from one department to another, in which case someone was simply not paying attention, or may have been insufficiently educated. It can happen. It is not to be excused, however – caption writers need watching, too.

Not watchful at all was the *Star Tribune* caption writer who looked at an Associated Press photo in December 1990 and composed the following: "Mike Hanson from Chaseburg, Wis., wore an 'Escape **from** Wisconsin' slogan on his back as he waited Sunday in Baghdad's Saddam International airport for a flight out of Iraq. The slogan is a state tourism effort." Effortlessly, however, the photo clearly showed the slogan to read "ESCAPE TO WISCONSIN." Attention to detail is required.

Same paper, on a different day, the caption reveals the subject of the photo: "An old man **weeped** as he prayed in front of the Imperial Palace, where the coffin of Japanese Emperor Hirohito rested." That night, the man went to bed and "sleeped," I suppose. ("wept")

Another photo caption made J.M. of San Rafael, Calif., question his vision:

> In the *San Rafael Independent Journal*, under a picture of Marines in Lebanon sharing a yule-log cake, the caption read: "**Secretarian** fighting erupted Thursday **with** earshot of the Marine garrison at Beirut airport."

"Sectarian" and "within" will fix it, of course. And get a load of this mind-bender that made P.B. of St. Petersburg, Fla., blink more than once:

> An article (sorry, writer not identified) in the *St. Petersburg Times* included the following: "Venereal disease, which can have lifelong manifestations, **including death** ..."

Oxymoron? Non sequitur? Goofy writing? All of those, probably. Some things simply defy description. Death pretty much puts paid to anything "lifelong," doesn't it?

Phew!

Making a case against Smell-a-vision is M.Y. of San Diego, Calif.:

> A commercial for Ship Ahoy, a seafood company, led off with "We catch our fish **fresh**." Is there any other way?

Only if they're belly-up in the net and not moving. Most unlikely, however. Holy haddock, Batman, there's something fishy here.

Unique?

Different things drive different people up different walls, and here's something that does a lot of that driving; it's time we looked at "unique" head-on. Setting the stage with an example that goes back a while is J.R. of East Greenwich, R.I.:

> A good-sized newspaper ad for American Motors bore the heading "We've gone to great **widths** to build you a better car." Also, the text contained the following: "One look tells you that the Pacer Wagon is **unique and unusual**."

We see and hear it over and over, and it drives me and many others to distraction. "Unique" means one-of-a kind, like no other, completely different from anything and everything, not even similar. The prefix *uni* is Latin for *one*, in such words as unicycle (one wheel), uniform (one design), unicameral (one legislative body), etc. It does not mean rare, unusual, distinctive, cute, clever, or anything else, despite what some of the modern dictionaries tell you. The foregoing usage example, then, is redundant. Something unique can also be called unusual, but there is no need. It's either unique or it isn't. It's solitary, alone in its class, unequaled, the only one in existence. Something made by hand is, of course, unique. Anything made in quantity by machine cannot be unique, in spite of what the ads for gift shops want to you believe, unless changes are made by hand. For more definitions, see a dictionary or a thesaurus. So there.

Afterthought: Wells Fargo, where I bank, before it changed its name from Norwest Banks, once advertised to corporations that "Your Business Is **As Unique As** You Are." That, of course, made me ask, How can either I or my business be any more or less unique than any other? ("As," of course, is capitalized unnecessarily.)

By the by, no doubt you noticed the play on words, "We've gone to great **widths** …" in the American Motors ad. Cute. They went to great "lengths" to bring that to us, I'm sure.

Finger-walking?

Not too often do I spend time reading the Yellow Pages of the phone book, but once in a while something jumps out at me and … what can I do? My local one had a display ad under Furniture Designers & Custom Builders classification for a company called Saxman & Morf, Furniture-makers (one word?). The part that caught my eye, however, was "Specializing in **Unique and One-Of-A-Kind** Custom Hand-Crafted Furniture." How's that for a daily double?

J.M. of St. Paul, Minn., enters our linguistic jousting with a report on a network news report on local Channel 9 about a house where furniture is made of newspapers: "It's unusual, it's **unique**, it's probably **one-of-a-kind**." J.M. apologized for failing to note the speaker's name. We accept, with thanks.

We come now to the "unique" capper, and it was delivered right to my door – or maybe it was in the bushes. Regardless, the weekly *St. Louis Park Sun-Sailor* carried a quarter-page ad placed by the Excelsior (Minn.) Area Chamber of Commerce. Excelsior is a small community out by the fabled Lake Minnetonka, and we were being asked to buy a celebratory button. The ad's subheading read: "Buy a 'Lake Minnetonka 4th of July—it's a Blast' button for $5.00 and your button number will automatically be entered into a drawing for **super-unique** Lake Minnetonka prizes." That's one I'd never heard or saw before, and one I hope I never hear or see again. Out! In the back! Against that post! Blindfold, please.

Sweet tooth?

Keeping up with the latest was J.V. of Seattle, Wash.:

> In a *Wall Street Journal* report on women's clothes and those who model them: "One of the new breed of heftier models was shown in a recent Legacy Apparel ad holding a box of **candy being admired** by a handsome man."

"Heftier"? Pardon my curiosity, but doesn't "hefty" relate a bit too closely to a box of candy? You'd think that *someone* on that big-city newspaper would have been smart enough to put the word "and" after "candy." And no, a comma would not have helped much, either.

Another case of comma-lack appeared in the 1990 TV listings of the *Star Tribune*'s Critic's Choice column (with no writer to blame): "Do return to Channel 5 for the late show, Frank Capra's wickedly entertaining 1941 version of *Arsenic and Old Lace* (10:35 P.M.), with Josephine Hull and Jean Adair as the sweet little old ladies who **poison their visitors and Cary Grant** as their nephew." No, they did not poison Cary Grant, as would be evident on a second reading even without my boldfacing, but the educated eye is halted midscan, and the piece is less than efficiently written. Doggone deadlines!

Here's one to chew on, from J.A. of Miami, Fla.:

> The little ad in the paper for BRIMM'S PLASTI-LINER says in big type, "EAT ANYTHING WITH FALSE TEETH." It makes me jump every time I see it.

Quick, step on the breaks!

K.G. of Rosemead, Calif., spotted one that was hard to miss:

> Billboards for Benson & Hedges 100s simply say, "**That's** the breaks."

Oddly, I never got much mail about billboards, but yes, they do qualify as a form of public communication. We can all wonder why the sign didn't say, "Those are the breaks," but one can certainly speculate that some ad manager didn't want it cluttered with an extra word. Had I been there, I would have asked, "What's the breaks?" and no doubt been told to "Shut up!" It would not have been the first time.

Another big billboard, this one for a newly built high-rise apartment building in Minneapolis, displayed the legend "Why give up **a** hour a day? Live at Cedar Square West." It's bad enough to hear people speak that way, but to see it out there waving in the breeze is something else. ("*an* hour," please)

Sometimes things just don't look right, and it takes a while to figure out why. Yet another billboard, this one for Manhattan shirts showing a man presumably wearing one, read: "Don't just look at it, wear it." Long after I drove past it, the lightbulb over my head flashed on: I obviously couldn't wear the shirt on the billboard, and how would I recognize a Manhattan shirt anyway unless it was hanging on the rack at J.C. Penney, for example. In that case, I wouldn't just look at it, I would seriously consider buying and wearing it. (I know. It doesn't make a lot of sense to me either.)

Headline in the *Star Tribune* over a *New York Times*-originated article (no writer's name): "Damage to soil leads Utah town to put **breaks** on off-road riding." Could my writing about it be called "slamming on the breaks"?

Me, myself, and I

S.G. wrote to me from Ardmore, Pa., offering this pair:

> A *Philadelphia Bulletin* story by William J. Storm included the following: "They had captured James Earl Ray about a quarter-mile from where **myself** and several other members of the press

had stood – in darkness …" A headline in the same paper on a different day: "**Who's** job is it?"

The word "myself" should never be used in a sentence or an independent clause that does not include the word "I." For example, "I was interested only in looking out for myself." Or, "Interested only in looking out for myself, I left the scene hurriedly." Usage such as "The boss praised Tom, Larry, and myself for our efforts" is incorrect. "The boss praised … me …" is correct. Unfortunately , the error is one of those that have become so common, even in print and on the air, that they almost seem right, even though we know they are not. As for "who's," please make it "whose." Thank you.

Making matters a bit worse is this from R.K. of Fort Lauderdale, Fla.:

> In the *Fort Lauderdale News/Sun-Sentinel*, "Education Writer" Patricia Sullivan, although not a teacher, took the Florida teacher certification exam. "The test was no breeze. **Myself** and seven other reporters who took the test in Tallahassee Friday, passed the same exam that thousands of would-be teachers will take today."

Why are some people reluctant to say "I and seven other reporters … ," or "seven other reporters and I"? Myself cannot fathom it. Or how about "My self cannot fathom it"? And why is there a comma after Friday? Beats me. Anyway, it's good that she passed the test. Her photo shows a very nice-looking person.

C.M. of Los Gatos, Calif., adds:

> I watch Channel 60, San Mateo, for a couple of hours each morning. I finally got tired of hearing "Dave and **myself** will be right back, so stay with us." I wrote to the station [about it] and in a few days, and after a few misses, they corrected themselves. Now they don't even use "myself" when they properly could.

It's alive!

D.C. of Goleta, Calif., made me chuckle over this find:

From a magazine ad: "Fostoria, the glassware that **lives** like you do." When I'm full of wine, I fall over a lot.

Shades of the "living bra." If glassware were alive ... uh ... forget it.

9

Speak the speech ...

If this book had chapters, no doubt at least one would deal with pronunciation, and this slip heard on the radio by G.V. of Grosse Point Farms, Mich., would definitely be included:

> On WJR, J.P. McCarthy used the term "short-lived" with a short "i." When I called to correct him, he said he wasn't interested in discussing it. However, he hasn't said it that way since, and I am a regular listener.

Hey, good going! There we have another case of changing a bad habit, as well as an obvious case of failure to check. "Short-lived" gets the long "i," as in "having a short life," which makes it easy to remember. Perhaps it's just as well that we don't hear the usage very often, but when it comes out right, it sounds good. Here in my neck of the woods is Minnesota Public Radio, on which I recently heard announcer Michael Barone say "long-lived" as in "dived." To sort it all out fully, that last derives from "life," or sentience. The use of "lived" as in "he has lived there a long time," refers to residency. The difference is not inconsequential.

Nice work!

This is as good a place as any to show the benevolent side of SOTS and pay tribute to some who deserve praise for their excellent enunciation, as well as pronunciation. During 1980 when I was making copious notes there were two who stood out, Jed Duvall of CBS-TV and Reed Collins of *CBS Radio News*. What was remarkable was that they were the only two I heard at the time who knew the difference between PROtest and proTEST. I later heard both Gary Nunn and Bob Schmidt say it right on ABC Radio, and Roger Erickson on local WCCO Radio did likewise. Dan Rather, Bill Plante, and Deborah Potter on CBS Television got it right as well. So did Ed Bradley on CBS's *60 Minutes*. Nowadays, all you hear is "The PROtesters sang as they marched ..." or "The demonstrators PROtested the use of barricades ..." Just for the record, PROtest is a

95

noun, not a verb. A PROtest is organized, lodged, registered, proclaimed, conducted, staged, etc. ProTESTing is what people do, not PROtesting. Think of Shakespeare's *Hamlet*: "The lady doth proTEST too much, methinks." Or your favorite TV attorney imploring, "Your honor. I must PROtest." Nope, that one's wrong.

Putting the accent on the verb's first syllable is ludicrous. The SOTS hat is off to those who say it right, including political comedian Mark Russell. Another is Jan Crawford Greenburg, a *Chicago Tribune* reporter assigned to the U.S. Supreme Court who appears with some regularity on PBS's *News Hour with Jim Lehrer*. Further, although Brits usually speak a different but similar language, BBC reporter Mary Small also got it right.

If proTEST is so difficult, why does no one have a problem with OBject (the noun) and obJECT (the verb)? Or with PROGress (the noun) and proGRESS (the verb). How about "convict" in both uses? Same difference. There are several others.

What's the apostrophe for?

If you haven't read Lynne Truss's book *Eats, Shoots & Leaves* yet, you might want to look for it in your public library; for many of us it was worth buying. The book contains several flaws, but one thing she knows about is the apostrophe, British usage notwithstanding. The little mark's primary purposes are to signify possession, or to indicate missing letters, as in contractions. However, its misuse is so rampant that one almost begins to wonder what is correct and what is not. Contributor J.J. of St. Paul, Minn., took time to examine some of his junk – sorry, advertising – mail and found this:

> A Hanover House catalog allegedly contains "Over 200 fabulous buys for Gifts 'N Home."

Shortening the word *and* to *'n*, *n'*, or *'an*, doesn't cut it. The apostrophe goes where a letter is missing, so *and* could be *'n'*, or *an'*, but nothing else. In my neighborhood there is a Scratch **N'** Dent store, and one of these days I'm going to tell them their fancy sign is wrong. Well, maybe not. Wouldn't want to hurt their feelings, especially since I was unlikely to buy anything. I'm used to adding my own scratches and dents around my house, without any outside help.

On that same subject, there is a restaurant here in the Twin Cities area called the **50's Diner**, big neon sign and everything. If they'd move the apostrophe up front, I might be tempted to sample their food. I've tried to find ways to justify the use, but all I can think of is that some athlete well known for his jersey number has opened a diner and is capitalizing on his fame as "Old #50." It's the best I can do.

Nor is the U.S. Postal Service immune from SOTS's prosecution: In August 2005 the USPS issued a booklet of stamps depicting "**50s Sporty Cars**." That legend does not appear on the stamps themselves, for which we can all be thankful, but is printed on the booklet's cover, as well as on the cover of a packet of postal cards that are already stamped – and at least there is no apostrophe in the wrong place, just a missing one. I have no way of telling where in the long chain of stamp development that that error could have occurred, but someone along the line should have caught it. Was it done by a paid professional? Paid, yes – professional, I'm not so sure. Borderline.

And none other than that crack crew at the *Star Tribune* is responsible for another front-page foul-up: Headlining in big type over an article in the Variety section on women's fashions was: **"60's** turns **90's** upside down." In both cases, I ask, what the heck is the apostrophe for? It's neither for contractions, nor for missing numbers or letters. William Safire was once asked why he favored the apostrophe in 1950's, for example. His reply was that that was the way he was taught and he's been doing it that way ever since. Hey, good reason, no? I don't think so. Simple logic should tell you that just because you've been doing something wrong all your life is not sufficient reason for continuing, once you know you're wrong. I have some good examples of that kind of thinking coming up.

Another revolting development is the total disappearance of the apostrophe as normally used in shortened forms of decades, as in the foregoing. *Jeopardy!*, a Merv Griffin creation, uses it properly, as in "the '90s," while *Wheel of Fortune*, another Merv Griffin product, once moved the apostrophe – the 80's – but is now dropping the apostrophe altogether, as in "the

60s." Naughty, naughty. *Jeopardy!* host Alex Trebek once interviewed a contestant and commented, "You say you do proofreading as well – if we had a lot longer time here we could talk about the positioning of commas and question marks, which we do differently on *Jeopardy!*" Mostly, they do it right, but once in a while, as Trebek said, differently.

Even though it doesn't qualify in the public and professional categories, I have to include what was left on our front doorknob by Le Maids, Inc., a house-cleaning service. It offered "professional maid services for the busy family of the '80's." I hereby declare it a "grand slam" of apostrophes, with one right and the other wrong, but with no chance of getting any worse, because there is simply no place to put another one.

And before we leave that tiny but important mark, we'll hoist *TV Guide* up on the verbal gibbet, and I guarantee that it won't be the only time. We hear from J.S. of Chicago, Ill.:

> In a [*TV Guide*] program CLOSE-UP on *Everybody Loves Raymond*, "Marie accuses Debra of killing Christmas when she suggests that instead of **she**, Ray and the kids spending the entire holiday with the Barones," they make other plans. On the same page, a *Dateline NBC* program note refers to a feature on "a look at **Readers'** Digest sweepstakes."

The "she," of course, should be "her," and while the readership of the magazine may be plural, its name is, singularly, *Reader's Digest*.

Then we have *Wheel of Fortune* again. The puzzle (which is the only reason I watch) turned out to be "Roy **Roger's** horse." (The contestant was then asked to supply the name, which, of course, was Trigger.) I sat bolt upright in my chair when I saw it, that poor mistreated apostrophe. For a program that deals with words and phrases, there is simply no excuse for that kind of sloppiness. Right, Pat Sajak?

That, nevertheless, was a one-time bobble. The all-time champion, by odd coincidence, bears the same name, and his long-running PBS program, uncontestably one of the best ever for kids, flouts the rules of punctuation, spelling, and pronunciation. *Mr.* **Rogers'** *Neighborhood*, as the title appears on the screen is consistently pronounced as if it had no possessive ending – "Mr. Rogers neighborhood" – and the possessive *s* is unspoken as well. If the punctuation is even close to acceptability, the pronunciation should be "Mr. Rogers's," and in all the years my kids watched, and even today, nothing has changed. It's as if some little kid said it that way in the beginning and no one wanted to contradict him for fear of hurting his little feelings. Awww.

Head-scratcher?

Even when spelling, punctuation, and grammar are all OK, sometimes the logic goes bad, as evidence this offering from R.R. of Camarillo, Calif.:

> In a write-up of a new business venture, the Camarillo *Daily News* included the following: "The shop will sell hand-carved Welsh loving spoons, made by the nephew of the only Welsh craftsman left who makes the spoons ..."

Well now, it didn't say that the nephew was Welsh, now did it? But what are the odds? Could a Norwegian make Welsh stuff? Remember, those Vikings really got around.

Display ads are always suspect. Big ones, such as those for department stores, cars, etc., are prepared by ad agencies, which we could always hold accountable if we could ever identify them. However, the small ads, like the one G.D. of Las Vegas, Nev., found, may not always be done by professionals:

> An ad in a local newspaper [I include this reluctantly] for licensed business consultant David Guardino explains that he "formerly operated as 'JAMIL,' one of the world's foremost **physics**."

There are several ways that could have happened – perhaps an ad agency or newspaper staffer prepared it – but if Mr. Guardino himself put it together and presented it as "camera ready," as we used to do in the old days, then I owe him an apology, but only insofar as he was not a "professional" in the sense that it applies here. It was, however, too good to pass up. Then there's the possibility that the mention here might be good for his business, that is, if he is still in the consulting business.

One willing audience

Here's another excerpt from my early columns, this one in June 1980:

> Whoever devises a way to correct the speech or writing of
> another, without discomfort to either person, shall be enshrined
> in history forever, or, at the very least, be guaranteed a place of
> highest honor in the SOTS Hall of Fame. The secret, unfortu-
> nately, has thus far eluded all of humanity, including yours truly.
> SOTS, therefore, has little or no alternative but to continue
> to point one forefinger at the transgressors and slide the other
> forefinger across the first.

Less than a year after I wrote that brilliant (?) piece of logic, I joined an
organization about which I had been curious for several years – Toastmasters International – and discovered the secret to which I had alluded.
Believe it or not, there are people who willingly submit themselves to
judgment of their written and, more particularly, spoken words, and they
do it happily as well, week after week, year after year.

Members of Toastmasters not only learn to conquer that greatest of all
human fears – that of speaking in public (according to the *Book of Lists*) –
but they share their knowledge of the English language with their fellow
members. At each meeting, a grammarian is designated – a different one
at each meeting – to listen for language usage, good and bad, and report
to the group at the end of the meeting. Some grammarians, obviously, are
better than others, but since the Toastmasters program extends over periods of months and years, all members can correct their errors and improve
their overall performance. And when new people join, they gain the
benefit of the experience of the veteran members. Not all observations are
valid, of course, because there are many misconceptions, but the end result
is totally positive.

Whenever there is a dispute about the use or pronunciation of a particular
word, someone will look it up in a dictionary and carry the finding back
to the club at the next meeting. Frequently, there is a good deal of humor
involved, and everyone takes the end result in the spirit of helpfulness and
camaraderie that is intended, along with the accompanying educational
benefit.

As is carefully pointed out to new members, correcting each other's speech is intended only to be helpful, and advising a member of the overuse of a word or phrase, such as "y'know" or "like," or "I mean," can make the member aware of a speech problem he or she did not know existed. Most speakers actually do not hear themselves saying certain things that fall uncomfortably on the ears of others, and they are glad to know what they can do to improve their speaking, whether in groups or to individuals. In a job interview, for example, the applicant never knows how well educated the interviewer might be, or how sensitive the interviewer is to the use of good English. In that way alone, Toastmasters has helped thousands of people to have a better chance of success in the business world. Just ask author, public speaker, and businessman Harvey Mackay.

Unfortunately, Toastmasters fell unwitting victim to the well-intentioned provider of a very prominent and very large billboard in 1991. An out-fit called Marketing by Design accepted the commission to prepare a message for thousands to see on a major thoroughfare that read: "Ahhh … Ummm! For Better Listening, Thinking, Speaking – **Toastmaster's** [phone number]." Any member of the organization could have caught the apostrophic gaffe, but apparently no member was asked to proofread it. I never did get an explanation. (Toastmasters is the full and correct name, and an apostrophe is used only as a possessive as it relates to an individual member, as in "Each Toastmaster's responsibility is to add to the knowledge and skills of other members.")

It's a crime

I have occasionally been accused of including typos, and I swear I have never reported on a single one, unless it was clearly identified as such. Carelessness, ignorance, and bad hearing are most often the causes of journalistic errors, such as this one delivered to us by R.E. of New York, N.Y.:

> The story concerned the Mafia, and, according to the *New York Post*, "… the mob has **metered** out its own version of justice."

Painfully too, no doubt. Make it "meted." Wondering whether justice was served is the ever-alert J.S. of Coon Rapids, Minn.:

Actor James Garner was hospitalized for a week after a road-side altercation following a minor traffic accident. According to the *St. Paul Pioneer Press*, "Los Angeles Superior Court Judge Charles Woodmansee found free-lance photographer Aubrey Lee Williams guilty of assault ... **Woodmansee** faces up to two years in state prison, or probation." A photocopy is enclosed.

Go ahead, I'll wait. Got it? The item was bordered and included Garner's picture. As usual, of course, it was unattributed, but I'll bet that the newsroom denizens got a big laugh out of it. Then there's this one that hit close to home (for me) from B.R. of Tulsa, Okla.:

KMRG Radio offers: "Remember, don't miss our beauty tip of the day. You'll be glad you **did**."

("Don't fail to miss it, if you can.") This reminds me that in all of the thousands of TV and radio commercials I wrote during my years in advertising and broadcasting, not one ever ended with that goofy phrase, "You'll be glad you did." What's funny is that every ad agency hack who ever used that sentence thought that he or she had invented it, and even today we hear it, often breathlessly and earnestly delivered. Am I right or am I not? Yes, I am.

Words, words, words

It was always rare to find an error in the Ann Landers column, but that's precisely what F.L. of Somerville, N.J., did:

Responding to a question about telephone etiquette, Ann replied, "Anyone who doesn't have the **patients** to wait one minute for someone to answer the phone must not want to talk to him very much." ["patience"]

Here's one numismatists (coin collectors) will love, dropped in the SOTS slot by D.M. of San Rafael, Calif.:

Stephen Hall, writing in the *San Francisco Chronicle*, includes the following: "Under the theory that even worthless money is worth collecting, mini-checks have been a big hit on the

pneumismatic market, too." Talk about inflationary monetary systems! ["numismatic"]

Eschewing research was whoever wrote this one found by M.M. of Ann Arbor, Mich.:

> Headline in the Ann Arbor *News*: "Minnesota Governor **Trods** Shaky Ground."

Keeping in step is L.H. of Chicago, Ill.:

> A book review [the title is irrelevant] in the *Chicago Tribune* was headlined: "**Trodding** through some truths."

The words needed are "treads" and "treading" – there are no such words as those M.M. and L.H. found in those otherwise respected newspapers. The word "trod" is the past tense of "tread" and is preceded by the proper auxiliary verb – "has," "had," or "have" – and the writers are again anonymous, as is whoever came up with the next bit of nonsense forwarded to us by J.G. of Martinsville, Va.:

> A White Cloud toilet tissue commercial begins, "Most bathroom tissues **talk** about softness, but ..."

Yes, I know, they speak in whispers, and I hate it when I can't understand them. Mine just hangs there and rustles quietly, sort of like the newspaper being read by S.W. of Framingham, Mass.:

> A rather macabre item in the Boston *Globe* states that "Eight of the 89 persons killed in a 1973 plane crash at Logan Airport are suing ... in U.S. District Court ..."

Does anyone need help with that? I thought not.

Huge pet peeve

Education is good, no matter when it comes or where it comes from. Some came to me a few years ago from H.P. of Seattle, Wash.:

> Royal Brougham, associate editor of the *Seattle Post Intelligencer*, began his column with: "Another **kudo** for the Seahawks'

Norm Evans." And the following headline appeared in the Encinitas, Calif., *Coast Dispatch*: "Animal center chief wins **kudo**." Look it up.

I did, in 1980, and I learned. For whatever reason, I had not had any reason either to use the word or to question it on the part of others, because it was not in popular usage at the time. Since then I have cringed on hearing the word used, almost always incorrectly. There is no such thing as a kudo, and there are no such things as multiple kudos. The word is *kudos*, it is Greek, and it means "praise, glory, grateful recognition." It is pronounced KOO-doss or KYOO-doss; it is not pronounced KOO-doze. Similar words of Greek derivation include *chaos, cosmos, bathos, pathos, ethos*, etc., and they are neither singular nor plural, nor is *kudos*. Also, since the Kudos candy bar came out, I have refused to try it. I might like it, and that would create a *chao* in my stomach and a *patho* in my heart, going totally counter to my life-long *etho*. Note also that some of the newer dictionaries disagree with me, as does the Associated Press, but that's their unfortunate choice, isn't it?

Most embarrassing was one of Isaac Asimov's Super Quizzes, published in newspapers nationwide, that dealt with "CURRENT WORDS: All answers are a single word. The first letter of the answer is provided." The 7th question – on the Ph.D. level, no less – was "An award of honor (K) _____." Down at the bottom of the page the answer given was "7 / kudo." If former International Mensa vice-president Isaac Asimov were alive today, he would roll over in his grave. (Yes, yes, I know, I know.)

The singular use of "kudo" to mean an award, honor, or compliment comes from the desire of certain individuals to flaunt their so-called erudition, supposedly making them appear more "worldly wise." What seems not to bother them is that there are many who choke at hearing the nonword used, and that the ignorant could just as easily speak more plainly and assure universal understanding and accord. To repeat: say it wrong, irritate only a few; say it right, irritate no one. And never mind those permissive dictionaries. If we accept *kudo* as a word, what happens to the original meaning of *kudos*? You tell me.

And if you think that's bad, wait 'til we get to *déjà vu*!

10

Speak now or ...

C.J. of Rapid City, S.Dak., says she had difficulty dealing with this one:

> It's from an article in *McCall's* magazine on the subject of undertaking: "At present, American undertakers embalm routinely without consulting **corpse** or kin ..."

No comment. Make up your own.

Does anyone care?

During 1980 and 1981 I took a hiatus from contributing a SOTS column to the *Mensa Bulletin*. It lasted 15 months, and the only reasons I resumed were: (1) At the 1981 annual Mensa convention – called Annual Gathering by Mensans – in Louisville, Kentucky, more than a few members asked me what had happened to the SOTS column, and (2) several others had no idea what it was – mostly new members, of course. Also, the editor had been catching flak for not running a column that had not even been written. So I explained my own laziness and the multitude of distractions that had kept me from giving the column the attention it sorely needed. Further, the mail had been accumulating, so I had a huge backlog of submissions. So, yes, it appears that there are indeed those who care.

C.M. of Mobile, Ala., threw this log on the fire:

> From an article (no byline) in the *Mobile Press-Register*: "There never **was** very many American billionaires ..."

It's unlikely that that writer will ever be one – billionaire, that is. Fortunately, more and more newspapers are providing bylines than were provided in the past, but there are still some that don't. "Was" should be "were," and never mind why – something to do with plural past tense indicative. I told you before, this is where I get lost. No matter, we'll continue to cast our aspersions regardless.

V.F. of Escondido, Calif., has offered to help:

> On the *Match Game* evening show July 5, 1979, "I wish I **was**
> ___" was used as an audience match phrase.

In spite of that once very popular song "I Wish I **Was** Single Again," the word, as before, is "were," as in "If I Were a Rich Man" from *Fiddler on the Roof*. In this case, the use is in the subjunctive, which I eventually learned means that something is "contrary to fact."

Beg pardon?

Hey, who turned on the TV and woke me up? Oh, well, since it's already on ... Oh, no, did I hear what I thought I heard? "(Authoritative voice) What do hospitals use for constipation?" That one threw me for a loop, it did – so badly that I totally missed the name of the product. I haven't heard it since, so someone must have said something to someone. When I included the item in my column I answered the question with: "Well, in my area the best bet would be Roto-Rooter Sewer Service, what with so many indigestible meals being dumped into the drain (just kidding, my dietitian friends, if I have any left)." Oddly, no one complained. Not even dietitians.

On the edge

Here's one that is borderline – public to a limited extent, but doubtless prepared by a hotshot advertising professional. P.D. of Crystal Lake, Ill., found it for us:

> A subscription-renewal letter from *American Art Review* begins:
> "Dear Recently-Expired Subscriber: YOU'VE MISSED AN
> ISSUE ..."

There are a lot of bad things about it, but the key element is the reference to the supposed "dearly departed." Deal with it as best you can. And you're right if you noted that the hyphen after the adverb "recently" is out of order, which is the case after almost every adverb ending in -ly. Also, if the subscriber were indeed "expired," it's doubtful that he or she would have missed anything at all.

For more on that subject, we turn to W.S. of Willows, Calif.:

> A glaring example of the misuse of adverbs [is] in the TV com-
> mercial for Ex-Lax. Originally, the statement was "Contains a
> medically-proven-effective ingredient." Because the actors and
> directors could not follow the intended meaning, the statement
> has evolved into "Contains a **medically-proven**, effective ingre-
> dient," which is contrary to the original intent.

Unquestionably, there is a difference, since "a medically-proven ... ingredient," with or without the unnecessary hyphen, is a nonsense phrase.
Medically proven how? It is the *effectiveness* that one hopes is medically
proven, not the ingredient itself. Are you still with me?

Have a cold one

Don't throw that hyphen away, though. Dad's Root Beer, for one, can use
it in its advertising, inserting it in **Caffeine Free**. Without the hyphen,
"caffeine free" means that there is "no charge" for the caffeine. Put in the
hyphen and the meaning changes significantly, that being "without caffeine." OK, so it's not a big deal, but so long as people are getting paid for
this sort of thing (and people like me are on their case), let's have them do
it right.

A newspaper ad for Walgreens (note the missing apostrophe, gone now
for many years) advertised the laxative Swiss Kriss with this bold heading:
"WHY TOLERATE JOY KILLING CONSTIPATION!" Two things bother
me: It appears to be a question, so where is the question mark? Also,
who or what is "JOY," and why is "JOY" killing constipation? Shouldn't
constipation be killing JOY? And why are we making fun of all this while
knowing all along that what we're talking about is constipation that is
JOY-KILLING? See that little hyphen there? That's all it takes.

H.W. of Des Moines, Wash. (yes, that is correct), was one of many who
squawked about the decline of perfectly good adverbs. In the *Seattle Post-
Intelligencer*, he found this:

> B. Jay Decker edits a column on contract bridge. This morning
> his column was headlined: "Make Haste **Slow**." Of course our

traffic signs have advised us to "Drive **Slow**," but must we lose the adverb "slowly"? (Or slowly lose the adverb?) Bring on the SOTS book, please!

Check this

Spellcheckers can't handle inappropriate but otherwise correctly spelled words used in place of those actually intended, but somebody is responsible for typing (keyboarding?) the wrong one in the first place. A perfect example of this comes from W.F. of Clearlake Park, Calif.:

> A 20-point headline in the *Press Democrat*, Santa Rosa, Calif.: "High winds **reek** havoc in Empire."

Depends on what direction they come from. Downwind from a turkey or pig farm … well, that would be another story. The "Empire" is the Redwood Empire area of California.

Autumnal caption under a *Star Tribune* photo depicting pumpkins, squash, and a cat: "A black cat and squash from the fall harvest **conger** up the spirit of Halloween goblins and goodies." ("conjure")

Further proof that caption writers need copyediting comes from J.M. of Colon, Mich.:

> Under a picture in the *Sturgis Journal* that shows damage from a recent storm was the following: "WINDBLOWN – Eric Borgman and his wife, Linda, clear a fallen tree from in front of their house Sunday on Shimmel Road, just north of U.S. 12. A brief windstorm **blew over the tree and blocked the road**. …" If the wind blew over the tree, then what made the tree fall down?

Well, now, that's getting on toward picky, but I have to allow that the criticism is justified. If the writer had been a bit more careful, she or he would have written "… blew the tree over, blocking the road. Better yet would have been "blew *down* the tree, blocking the road." The windstorm did not block the road, the tree did, although a case could be made … never mind.

What's on the tube?

Don't you just love *TV Guide*? In trying to condense their program list-ings, as Red Buttons used to say, "Strange things are happening." Here's one from L.K. of Brown Deer, Wis.:

> Description of the *David Susskind Program* in *TV Guide*: "A discussion of television programming includes comments on the amount of sex and violence from network executives. (90 min.)"

It's called truncating; another word or two would have helped a lot. Another airing of the same program was listed in a local paper, and M.G. of N.Y.C. spotted errors in it:

> The *New York Daily News* listed: "DAVID SUSSKIND SHOW: 'We Can't Read or Write: Why 23 million American's Are Illiterate?'"

Can you identify the two errors? They are (1) the apostrophe in "Ameri-cans" does not belong, and (2) no question is being asked, so there is no need for the question mark. That item appeared sometime during the 1980s, but in 1979 an Associated Press story headlined: "Ford study claims 64 million illiterate." The article used the example of illiterate citizens being unable to address an envelope. It also said that "there are more illiterates in the South than in the North, more in the East than the West."

The AP story qualified its statements by admitting that defining illiteracy was difficult: "Using the number of adults who haven't completed high school, there are between 57 million and 64 million adult illiterates. Or, the number might be as low as four million adults, counting only those who are totally unable to read or write." I wonder what those figures would be today (in 2011), or if any such figures really mean anything.

Tickets, please

And how about this eye-popper of a movie listing in *TV Guide*?

> "*Commando*/Human killing machine John Matrix goes off heavily armed with an airline hostess to stop a Latin dictator ... Arnold Schwarzenegger ..."

Now, that's what I call a *weapon*! Thanks, *TV Guide*.

A.M. of Bronx, N.Y., returns, having checked the TV lineup in the *New York Daily News* and having seen listed "A MAN CALLED HORSE Richard Harris plays an English aristocrat captured by **Sue** (Ch. 5, 11-1.20 a.m.). *Powerful.* – Hank Winnicki." A girl Sue, or a boy named Sue? Oh, I see, a whole tribe named Sue – or Sioux, maybe?

I have a hunch that some of you are graduating from simple eye-ball-rolling to the primal scream once used as therapy. Or maybe it still is. Go ahead, let it all out. That is, unless you're laughing instead.

Still not convinced?

"Why doesn't someone do something?" That's what I keep hearing when I give speeches about our language, and I have to confess that it's a hard question to answer. There are those who "do" do something when their hackles are raised enough, but most of us do not have a low-enough boiling point. Mine is pretty low, but it could be lower yet, and I'm working on it. Poking into the world of TV, newspapers, etc., is not something most people feel comfortable doing, which is not totally surprising.

So, not much action is what it comes down to. There is, of course, the occasional situation when a SOTS member will write to an offender, or use the telephone or e-mail, but relatively speaking, it is rare. Why? Probably because the feeling among most of us is that it "wouldn't do any good," which is rather sad but probably true.

Then there are those who will chance upon SOTS in one form or another, and will take it as a personal attack on their own use of English. Perhaps they will feel threatened, but they really should not. This is still a free country, and citizens may speak and write as they wish, so long as they avoid libel, slander, or defamation of character (along with shouting "Fire" in a crowded room).

Stepping outside the public communications arena for a moment, let us consider the effect our efforts might have on the population at large. No one, not even SOTS, has the right to dictate how any member of society should speak or write. Conversely, neither is anyone to be prevented, prohibited, or discouraged from using good English, and no one should ever be criticized for being correct. But it happens, and we need to be aware of the ramifications.

Peer groups differ. Social conditions differ. Any school kid can tell you that he or she had better not pretend to be above the norm in language usage, for example. If peers are using *like, y'know, I mean*, and *he goes* or *she goes* as they interact, each will be wise to do likewise, even if it means lowering one's standards for the time being. An erudite college professor does not flaunt his erudition in a bowling alley full of construction workers (no offense, guys). Adapting to societal norms is no crime, and most often it is recommended as a way to "fit in."

Nevertheless, the use of *y'know*, for example, most often carries the connotation that "if you do not understand what I am saying, you are the dumb one, not I." This is why hardly anyone responds to the term by saying, "Yes, I know, I know." It might result in bodily harm.

Nor do the wise among the educated offer to correct their companions' speech. Such is done only by invitation, and even then it is best to be discreet. This also applies to errors in organizational newsletters, church bulletins, and other forms of communication prepared by unpaid volunteers. Criticizing them is "looking a gift horse in the mouth," and no, you don't want to do it anonymously either; you could lose the services of a perfectly good volunteer. (However, if the job is being done so badly that you just can't stand it, offer to do it yourself – gracefully, of course.)

Children, in their formative years, are the ones hardest hit by sloppy English coming at them from all directions – parents, teachers, peers, and especially the media, which have what is probably the strongest influence on their language development. Some are able to relearn as they mature, but many will not. Teachers themselves, sadly, are very often not learning English well enough to give students the indoctrination they need in order to become successful practitioners of English communication. This will undoubtedly raise the hackles of some of my good friends, but I cannot in good conscience withhold it. The grammar I hear and the pronunciations of some of the simplest words that come my way would never have been tolerated by those teachers who indoctrinated me in the language, and who taught me to use a dictionary, for pity's sake. Where, I ask you, is the credibility when there is no consensus?

So, are teaching requirements becoming more relaxed and permissive? The answer is yes, and it is not entirely the fault of the teachers. Surprised to hear that? Well, it's true: It is not teachers themselves who are determining curricula for either teachers or students; it is other administrative types, many of whom are so-called social engineers with a variety of philosophies, including the levelers. There's that word: levelers. These are people who are so terribly concerned with "equality" that they succeed only in lowering levels of achievement among the capable, with little or no attention being given to encouraging the slower students to upgrade their performance. The result, as has been widely publicized, has been to lower test scores nationwide, and some of the newer programs, such as the No Child Left Behind, have been so badly designed and managed that failure has been inevitable.

Perhaps you saw the *60 Minutes* TV program on which the subject was education. An interviewer asked one woman, "And what is your job?" She answered, "I teaches English." Why the producers allowed that interview to air is beyond me, but perhaps they too were trying to make my point. If so, I congratulate them.

Then who or what is *more* to blame for the decline of proper English (to use the concise term), the media or the educational system? With no hesitation whatever, I say that it is the media that must be held accountable for the greatest damage.

There is no question but that education has fallen far, but the public communications media have an audience that goes beyond the schools. Almost every adult, as well as every child, watches television; many listen to radio (loaded with music containing rotten grammar, along with otherwise questionable lyrics); some read newspapers, and many read magazines of one genre or another. It is in these areas where the public is most vulnerable, and adults do not have the opportunity to be corrected or have questions answered by teachers – assuming that teachers would actually have answers.

It is here, then, that the worst of the problem lies, and it is here that thus far no good solution has suggested itself. What is even more saddening is that the media have the educators at a serious disadvantage. The media are able to take shots at will at the educational system, blaming it for declining test scores and the reduced abilities of children to read and write. Educators, however, have no such similar access to the public at large. This may someday change as new communication methods are developed, but by then it may be too late.

It is now, today, that appropriate shots must be taken at those in control of the public communication channels, and this is the reason for the existence of SOTS, which may be a small voice in a vast wilderness, but it is at least something. The questions remaining are: Where do we go from here? and What are we to do next? Let's hope that we can come up with something. While we all think about it, allow me to put a few more linguistic logs on the fire.

Whatization?

Having a reader report on a successful upbraiding of an offender is always gratifying, and special recognition went to D.P. of Atlanta, Ga., for writing to the Chevrolet Division of General Motors to protest the absurdity of an advertisement that claimed "good gas **mileization**" for a Chevrolet product. Carl Uren, Chevrolet's director of national advertising at the time, responded, in part, with Shakespeare's "What's in a name? etc." Uren also had the nerve to say that "It is my sincere hope that this unfortunate incident will not deter you from paying a visit to your nearest Chevrolet dealer first, when you are in the market for a new car." The upshot was that the made-up word quickly disappeared from Chevy advertising, replaced by the much simpler *mileage*. Score one for our side.

Some newspapers have deservedly earned the title of "bird-cage liner," and the following from O.Y. of Norwalk, Ohio, does little to disabuse us of the notion:

> Headline (very large type) in the *Cleveland Plain Dealer*: "Rita Hayworth's daughter is different from you and **I**." You can't hear me, but I am screaming!

OK, but try to scream silently. At least it wasn't "different *than* …" Make it "different from you and me." Let's be happy that it wasn't worse.

Not so fast, says G.N. of Beechhurst, N.Y.:

> Another expensive slick-magazine ad in *Town & Country*, no less, was for Lufthansa, the airline whose slogan was "People expect the world of us," and was headlined: "Why flying to Munich is considerably different **than** flying to Muncie." ["from"]

In 1992, after three years of talking, Northwest Airlines and KLM Royal Dutch Airlines were still trying to get together on sharing transatlantic passengers. The *Star Tribune* headlined: "KLM-Northwest partnership may still be a long **ways** off." ("way" is sufficient)

Oops!

Remember Greg LeMond, who won the Tour de France bicycle race several times? His picture appeared in the *Star Tribune* with the caption: "Greg **Lemond** of Medina [Minnesota] **beared** down during Monday's Tour de France time trial. …" Note that I spelled his name right, but the caption writer didn't. As for "beared," there is no such word. What's wanted is "bore."

Same paper, same year, another unknown headline writer produces: "**Deciples** and detractors tangle over [controversial diet guru and author Jeremy] Rifkin's conclusions." ("disciples")

Things got no better in 1996 for the lovable local rag: An item about TV sports producer Tim Scanlan was headlined: "**Scallen** joins ESPN." Once again, no copyeditor for headlines.

In 1967 the *Strib*'s Carolyn Petrie reviewed an appearance at a local theater by comedian Jackie Mason. She wrote, "Jews and Gentiles, Italians and Puerto Ricans, husbands and wives all get run through the **ringer** in Mason's act, but the only person Mason really kvetches about is himself." Well, now, he has one more person to kvetch about – his reviewer. ("wringer")

Another copyeditor's day off resulted in this from D.Y. of Brookfield, Conn.:

> An item in the *New York Post* led off with: "Ernie Holmes defensive tackle for the Pittsburgh Steelers was arrested Saturday for **investigation** of drunk driving."

Obviously, the officers were just protecting their jobs. "We'll do the investigating here, Ernie! We won't be needing your help." No doubt they were also on the lookout for a comma thief. Two are missing. Surely you can tell where.

Strike!

Here's a category that I don't think I've touched on yet. Advertising comes in many forms, and F.B. of Washington, D.C., found this one in his travels:

> In a matchcover made for Piedmont Airlines is the following line: "Piedmont flies where America **happens**."

It was a copywriter's way of saying, "Piedmont flies where things are happening in America," but it turned sour in the making.

Total lunacy I cannot cope with, but ordinary nonsense I can. Case in point: these from N.S. of Bamberg, S.C.:

> [These are from TV ads.] Dynamints: "They look so little, but they refresh so **big**." Burger King: "Two hundred million people, **each** doin' things **their** own way." Close-up Toothpaste: "Whiter teeth and fresher breath **turns** girls on."

How's that for a trifecta? It's not called the "boob tube" for nothing, you know, and these are perfect demonstrations. The first two need to be sent back to the drawing board, and the last is pretty obvious ("turn").

Inhuman?

Anthropomorphizing never ceases. C.G. of Miami, Fla., picked up the paper and found this:

Headline in the *Miami Herald*: "Colonial group fights crimi-
nally insane hospital."

I decided not to boldface that one so that I'm not accused of overkill. Yes,
I suppose Jay Leno would have used it if he had had it, but I suspect not.
Besides, I have the item in my files and he doesn't.

Another headline that I can't reasonably highlight is this from Q.H. of
Los Angeles, Calif.:

> I enclose a banner headline – "Illegal Alien Raids Resume" –
> clipped from the *Los Angeles Times*. I believe it has four [possi-
> ble] interpretations: (a) The raids were illegal. (b) Illegal aliens
> did the raiding. (c) Raids were conducted against illegal aliens.
> (d) Raids were conducted *in search* of illegal aliens. The huge
> [84-point type, more than an inch] headline could just as easily
> read: "Raiding Resumed in Searches for Illegal Aliens."

I would reduce it even further to: "Searches for Illegal Aliens Resume."
The word "raids" was hyperbole, implying that weapons and perhaps air
support were called for. The type size, too, was overkill, and my suggested
headline, or even Q.H.'s, would have fit without difficulty and still been
readable at some distance.

Also in my files is part of a bill-payment envelope with a tear-off coupon
from the Cooper Rand Corporation that offers "The $29.95 Floor Lamp
that thinks it's $50! The Most Versatile Lamp We Have Ever Seen." I
suppose that if some people can believe that computers can actually think,
maybe a versatile floor lamp can, too. This one, however, is having an
identity crisis.

Crunch!

I don't have the actual item in my files, but it would have had to have been
stolen, so we'll take the word of B.Y. of Virginia Beach, Va.:

> On every table in a Shoney's restaurant in Chattanooga was a
> slickly produced special-feature card offering the "**Desert** of the
> month – cheesecake – topped with blueberries." What makes it

worse is that only about 3 out of 10 people to whom I show it are able to find the mistake, and only 1 of the 3 did so within 5 seconds.

That reminds me that I once saw "Sahara *dessert*" in print somewhere, but I cannot recall where. If I run across it, I'll put it in my next book.

I'd also like to take the opportunity to thank the many who sent items that referred to "just deserts." All maintained that the term should be "just desserts," as in proper rewards, symbolically after a meal. Sorry, folks, but you are misinformed. "Just deserts" [and not the Sahara kind] means those things that are "deserved," and the terms are somewhat similar in spelling but different in meaning. But thanks, anyway.

11

Trippingly off the tongue, if you will

They say – there *they* are again – that our language is flexible and constantly changing. So how much of this flexibility and change is good, and when does it become a problem? It depends, I guess, on how high our tolerance is, and how it affects our eyes and ears. Television and radio people, in particular, should pronounce English words without grating on our ears, especially the ears of the reasonably well educated.

It's really quite easy: All that's needed, usually, is almost any dictionary, even one of the smaller ones that contain the smaller words, at the very least. (Was that a bit arch? Sorry.)

Take, for example, the word (or article) *a*, as in "*a* peach" or "*a* donny-brook." The word is spelled with the letter *a*, but the two are not the same, nor are they interchangeable. The word is pronounced "uh," while the letter is pronounced ā, as in "bay" or "way." Before a vowel sound, another word, "an," is substituted. Examples: *a* banana, but *an* orange.

There's a cassette-tape program called the "Successful Living Series #7700" in most public libraries. Lesson #1 is "Improving English and Speech." The narrator begins:

> "During the next few minutes I hope to give you a few new
> words, their meanings and pronunciations – and to stimulate
> your interest in improving your vocabulary. Let's start with *a*
> few commonly used words …"

Yep. You guessed it – that ā was the long one. People who don't speak the language correctly should in no way be permitted to teach it. In Lesson #2 – "Building Word Power" – was an example of a rhetorical question: "What are you, some kind of nut?" That's not a rhetorical question, it calls for a punch in the nose. A rhetorical question is, by definition, one that requires no response. Boy, were those folks off the beam on that one. Also, whoever was doing the narrating was (as my doctor likes to say) "habituated" to the glottal stop (see following). The grunting was positively atrocious, if you can imagine.

Pay no attention, however, to the contestants on *Wheel of Fortune* who want to buy "uh *a*" or "uh *e*" or "uh *o*." They are not professionals and they are exempt from SOTS's criticism, no matter how much their uninformed speech detracts from our enjoyment of the program otherwise.

(I confess – yes, I watch the *Wheel* when I eat supper and I watch *Jeopardy!* when I have my lunch. So does that make me a substandard human? To some, perhaps, but I don't care. You probably watch those silly sitcoms or "reality" shows, and I don't. Your meat, my poison, and vice versa, OK?)

As long as we're on the subject, I might as well mention the glottal stop. What's a glottal stop? It's that peculiar grunting inflection heard in the regretful "uh oh," the most common (and correct) usage. Otherwise, depending on how severe it is, it can be truly bothersome. Many singers overuse it, but not all. Listen to Sinatra or Rosemary Clooney sometime. Doris Day is another who phrases really well without the grunt.

The problem with the glottal stop is that so few people have learned to use their diaphragm when they sing or speak. In years past, school children were taught to breathe with the diaphragm, but not any more, sad to say. A good example is the correct and official pronunciation of Hawai'i. Note the apostrophe; it indicates that the two letter *i*'s are to be broken apart so that both are enunciated. Also, the *w* has the sound of *v*. Oh, sure, it's not the end of the world, but those of us with ears attuned can hear the difference quite easily. If you, the reader, have now been infected with the sensitivity, I hope you will forgive me, if not thank me, but it had to be said. Besides, we can always blame it on the commercials, where the grunt is often used deliberately, for emphasis or effect.

Get a grip

Contributions to SOTS concerning packaged goods, which are certainly public enough for our involvement, have not been as plentiful as those in the newspaper and broadcast media, but here's one that hit close to home. It was sent in by A.L. of Pottsville, Pa.:

Printed on a card attached to a roll of Scotch brand freezer
tape: "Holds **tight** on papers, films, foils … Performs at -40°
below zero." Are there minus numbers *above* zero?

The 3M Company, manufacturer of the product, employs a few people I
know, since it is headquartered in Maplewood, Minn., a suburb just east
of St. Paul. None of them would own up to the goof, so I have to assume
that they all *know* that the word should have been the adverb *tightly*. And
yes, the temperature indicated is redundant. Choices are -40°, minus 40°,
or 40 below.

Taking charge of the remote control is J.B. of Dallas, Texas:

> The Dallas public TV station promoted National Public Radio's
> live coverage of a particular U.S. Senate debate by reminding us
> not to miss the "**emotionally** packed" forthcoming debate.

If you're packing a debate, you might as well do it with some fervor.
Ohhh yah! That should be "emotion-packed."

Now, here's one that almost qualifies for the SOTS Department of Lost
Causes, but let's not decide just yet, at least until we've heard from S.W. of
Livingston, N.J.:

> From an article in *The New York Times* by Pranay Gupte:
> "What was it that urban blight virtually stopped at the **param-
> eters** of the neighborhood?"

Parameter is listed in most dictionaries as a mathematical term, one that
would do no good to include here (you either know it or you don't). Over
the last few years, however, it has come to mean a whole assortment of
things, from *boundary* to *perimeter* to *specifications* to the contents of a list
of anything one can think of. I believe it deserves to be here, if only to
illustrate how common usage can actually subvert the true meaning of a
word. Math folks can still use it, I suppose, but it must give them pause
when they hear or read its many other permutations. Some things, sad to
say, are unstoppable.

Don't leave 'em dangling

When it comes to cockeyed syntax, it's hard to beat the dangling modifiers. Scooping one up for us is P.M. of Somerset, N.J.:

> Photo caption in the *Daily Home News* of New Brunswick, N.J.: "RESTORED – Built 200 years ago, Betty Sturkie and her former husband Victor Failmezgar purchased this Fern Road home … and began restoring it themselves."

"Highly waxed and gleaming in the sunshine, my neighbor proudly backed his new car out of his driveway and waved to everyone in sight." See? Anyone can do it, and I made that one up to prove it. You'd think, though, that hired hands in journalism would have at least *some* awareness of danglers. Far too many don't.

Another example of a dangling modifier is this from J.L. of Westchester, Ill.:

> On the mentioned Chicago television station: "Indestructible even in death, WGN-TV9 presents a one-hour special on Bogart …"

And this from J.B. of Charlottesville, Va.:

> Peter Kaufman, a free-lance writer from Hartford, Conn., appearing in the Richmond, Va., *Times-Dispatch*, began a column headed "Barbecue tips to help fire up your next date" with a paragraph that began: "As a single guy, women are always amazed when I cook for them."

Arriving in the same day's mail were reports from K.D. of St. Paul, Minn., and B.G. of Washington, D.C. Both pointed out that the *CBS Evening News* anchor (neither of the two provided a name), doing a story on marijuana smuggling, intoned: "While interviewing a customs official, the fuel tank exploded."

In case anyone doesn't know, the term "dangler" or "dangling modifier" refers to the introductory phrase in a sentence being inappropriately connected to the subject of the phrase that follows. For example, in the foregoing, it should read, "As a single guy, I always amaze women ..." If you can take "I" and put it in front of "as a single guy," you know you're OK. Otherwise, fix it, please. As for the other examples, all that's needed is rewording them so as to keep people like us from laughing at them. But what fun would that be?

More? B.W. of Bloomington, Ind., sent along a kiddies' place mat from Pizza Hut. In a fill-in-the-blank puzzle, the sentence was "While seated at your _ _ _ _ _, a waitress will take your order." The missing word, of course, was "table," and the waitresses should never sit down to take an order. Only when delivering an order, and only when the place is not too busy, is it ever permissible for a waitress to seat herself at the occupied table and chat a bit, and even then management does not allow in most restaurants. It does happen occasionally in small towns, however, but seldom in cities of any size. (The place mat was copyrighted 1984.)

Here's another from R.F. of Kenosha, Wis.: "Living Books (a Random House/Brøderbund company) comments in a magazine ad, 'As A Book, You Loved *Dr. Seuss's ABC*.'" Hey, watch it there! Who're you calling a book?

There's what?

Over there in a dark corner, we have the peculiar phenomenon that mixes *is* and *are*, especially when they are used following *there*. With what has seemed for several years to be an alarming increase in frequency, we are hearing professional communicators lose the distinction. I forgot to note the offender's name, but a local anchorperson not long ago clearly said, "**There's** quite a few crime **stories** in our report tonight ..." and a car dealer's ad proclaimed, "**There's** over 300 **cars** on our lot, and **there's** many **ways** we can arrange financing for you."

Remember Sam Patrino? I thought not. Speaking in TV ads for Kellogg's Raisin Bran, Sam was the fellow who told us that "**There's so many** raisins in there now, the package is purple." Not far behind was the Sears ad for a carpet sale: "**There's all kinds** of styles and colors."

A radio ad for King Oscar's Restaurant in Richfield, Minn., said: "**There's** people **that** come in ..." There's no telling what made the writer goof twice in so few words, but it should have said, "There **are** people **who** come in ..." People are not "things," so the customary usages in English are "people who ..." and "things that ..."

Where has the word "are" gone? My wife got sick of hearing me say, "There is?" so often, and I'll bet I'm not alone in that. For the record, one "is," and two or more "are." *There are* just too many professional communicators who get it wrong. Agreed? Good! No? Too bad!

Quite frankly, I think that the biggest problem is that the professionals don't even know when they are wrong. Who's going to tell them? If you were an employee of an organization and knew that one or more of your fellow workers were sending out flawed messages, would you point their errors out to them? Very unlikely, unless that was your job, such as that of copyeditor. Otherwise, you'd keep your mouth shut, for a whole variety of reasons, not the least of which would be a reluctance to hurt someone's feelings. But that's what I'm here for.

OK, so it's possible to hear it wrong. When someone says, "There're several of ... something," and the words are slurred or elided, it can sound as if it were "There's several," but my argument still stands. Let's watch it.

Approval

Before we get back to more screwball grammar, etc., I'd like to mention another boost that came SOTS's way. Mensa, as a society, has no opinions about anything, with the possible exception of its gifted-children's program. We were all "gifted kids" once and we members have agreed to do anything we can to help kids today from falling by the wayside because of "dumbing-down educational practices." The gifted and talented too often are held back by otherwise-well-meaning teachers who handle the class smarty pants with, "Sit down and shut up!" In my own case, more than once a teacher would see my hand go up, and say, "I know you know, Gordon, but let's let the others try to answer the question." So the gifted program is really the only one we all support. (After a while I stopped raising my hand, and lost interest.)

That is not to say, however, that Mensans have no opinions. Whoooey! You never saw such a conglomeration of opinions. Put three Mensans in a room and you will come up with 17 opinions. But we do not share those opinions "as an organization." To do so would create factions, and, very likely, warfare, within the society. Instead, we have created special-interest groups, which put members sharing their likes and dislikes in touch with each other, often locally in person, and nationally and internationally by mail and e-mail. At various times there have been more than 200 of these special-interest groups, which we have abbreviated to the acronym SIGs. Each SIG has a coordinator, and twice each year a complete listing of SIGs is published in the national *Mensa Bulletin*.

Upon joining Mensa, members are asked to fill out a questionnaire, which includes check-marking their hobbies and other passions on a list provided, and from time to time American Mensa has published a membership directory that tells members who others are who share their interests, so that they can contact each other directly. With hundreds of possibilities on the interest list, 152 readers indicated that SOTS, as a feature of the *Bulletin*, was among their favorites, which delighted me, as you might well imagine. I have, of course, been urged to develop a SOTS SIG, but my energies are required elsewhere, such as by this book, and the need to clean out the garage.

Keep out! (Unless ...)

If I can find the photograph, I'll include it here, but in case I can't, I will tell you what it shows, and credit D.N. of Baltimore, Md. The metal sign is attached to a large post next to the entrance to the town dump, and it reads, "NO TRESPASSING – EXCEPT AUTHORIZED PERSONS – CITY OF LAUREL, MD." The contributor adds that he plans to apply for a license authorizing him to trespass.

Picking up the theme is H.W. of Midland, Texas:

> BTA, a well-to-do independent oil company in Midland, has a large sign at the entrance to [its] parking lot: "PRIVATE PARKING – Violators will be Impounded." What do you suppose they'll do with their cars?

[Also], Henry J. Taylor, a Washington columnist writing in the *Lubbock* [Texas] *Avalanche-Journal,* wrote: "Scotland has found oil. Teeming Aberdeen faces the North Sea. Oil's first whisper came from beneath the dangerous northeast waves. Then oil seekers found immense oil **stratas** throughout the northern region's entire area ..." I wonder where he got the *datas* for the article.

Singularly, it's "stratum," so the plural is "strata." I found "stratas" in one dictionary, but it was noted as being *"considered nonstandard."* The words, referring to layers, are not used often enough for most of us to know the difference, but columnist Taylor and/or a copyeditor should have looked this one up.

Uncertainties

I asked myself, is a handbill public enough for SOTS, and was it likely to have been prepared by an advertising professional? If not, I apologize for inserting this item that came from M.V. of Los Angeles, Calif.:

> A handbill from the Party & I advises: "Must Liquidate Antiques – Old & New."

Need I bold-face the "New"? OK, I won't. Nor do I think it would do any good in this next lulu from R.W. of Philadelphia, Pa.:

> Headline from the *Philadelphia Bulletin*: "Court Bars Sex-Based Rape Laws." Are there any other kind?

Only if you're discussing a relative of the turnip (look it up).

Signs of the times

Here's one that could not be more public, seen from behind the wheel by J.L. of Ossining, N.Y.:

> The town of Mamaronek, N.Y., has an electric sign along a highway that reads, "You are speeding when flashing."

Best if we go by that one quickly. J.M. of Loveland, Ohio, has this:

All along the highways in Indiana [1976] are signs exhorting drivers to "WATCH YOUR SPEED – WE **ARE**."

Let's hope they've been changed by now. The short fix would be "Watch your speed – we *do*."

Even though we're pretty clear on what sorts of things are acceptable as targets, I'll slip another "borderline" one in from R.G. of Lonedell, Mo. (the SOTS borderline, that is, not the one across the bottom of Texas):

> A sign near the registration desk of a Holiday Inn in Galveston, Texas, says, "We are not responsible for lost articles of clothing being sent to the laundry." When I pointed out the error to the desk clerk, he didn't understand!

Gee whiz, do we have to do everything ourselves? That admonition, by the way, is almost exactly the same as one I saw in a Tokyo hotel.

Kid stuff

Here's something more from the wandering-attention department, again courtesy of L.H. of Chicago, Ill.:

> Heard on the [WBBM-TV] Channel 2 news: "Unvaccinated children will not be permitted to enter school next fall without proof of vaccination."

But ... but ... oh, forget it. Better to move on and see what's causing eye-rubbing by K.O. of Wappingers Falls, N.Y.:

> From an article in the Lancaster, Pa., *Intelligencer Journal*: "The .45-caliber handgun accidentally dropped out of Tientjen's hand ... hit a magazine rack beside the sofa where Eddie [Funke] was sitting, and went through his [Eddie's] lower left lip ..." The writer was Marybeth Wagner.

Made a hole bigger than a bullet would, no doubt, and wouldn't it be nice if we could be privy to the guffaws she most likely got from her fellow reporters?

Guns make news, but C.A. of Brawley, Calif., found a different angle on them in an Associated Press story in the *Imperial Valley News*: Datelined PUEBLO, Colo., it told of a shooting contest involving cowboys. Referring to contestant Peyson Peterson, it read, in part, "Gun **swinging** sometimes takes its toll on his fingers, as they weigh nearly 3 pounds when loaded." The two letters could hardly be farther apart on the keyboard, and the sentence structure could be a lot better – his fingers weigh how much? Loaded? The simple fixing changes it to read "... as *the guns* weigh nearly ..." Any good copyeditor could tell you that. Also, "swinging" should be "slinging," according to Western lore.

<u>12</u>

Save ink

Hereinafter, anytime you see AP, it is the abbreviation of the Associated Press, an organization that provides news services to subscribing newspapers. Also, it often happens that I get sent an error attributed to the AP, but it may indeed have been committed by the staff of the newspaper publishing the piece, and those folks should catch anything the AP misses. On other occasions I simply do not have the name of the paper, so if the AP is not at fault regarding any item published here, I apologize.

Case in point: K.M. of Fayetteville, Ark., sent me an actual piece of copy ripped right off a teletype machine in 1982, the kind I don't think are used anymore. How's this for tortured prose?

> IT STARTED OUT AS A ROUTINE TUESDAY FOR VICE-PRESIDENT BUSH. THERE HE WAS, RIDING IN HIS LIMOSINE [*sic*] TO THE WHITE HOUSE, WHEN THERE WAS A LOUD BANG. AT FIRST, SOME THOUGHT IT WAS A BULLET. BUT THE F-B-I LATER DETERMINED IT WAS JUST A CHUNK OF CONCRETE FROM A **CONSTRUCTION SITE** THAT **HIT THE CAR ROOF**.

Yes, as K.M. adds, falling construction sites do play hell on paint jobs. All scratchy-like. Once again, the only remedy is to recast the sentence, and I'll let you play with it this time.

Hot stuff

Back down to the Sunshine State we go for this rather dark bit of news from E.C. of Boynton Beach, Fla.:

> Headline in the *Miami Herald*: "Old Jersey Inn **Raised** by Flames."

Tried the old "Phoenix trick," I suppose? Try "razed."

S.M. of East Orleans, Mass., has another one for us:

> A magazine ad for Kero-Sun portable kerosene heat-
> ers says that "There's no smoke, no **order**, and you need no
> chimney-venting."

Believe it or not, I own one of those things, although it sits in my garage
unused since the warnings came out about their toxic characteristics, and
the 1979 claim of no "odor" was false at the time. It is not possible to
burn kerosene without creating a stink, unless there's something about the
newer models I don't know. I see vented models advertised on the Internet, so apparently they are still being used. With no word to the contrary,
I have to assume they are now safe, and useful too.

M.M. of Chicago, Ill., caught some unusual static in the air:

> From a radio announcement by the A&P Stores about green
> stamps: "Stamps will not be given for cigarettes and other
> items prohibited by law."

I believe A&P went out of business some time ago, but it will live forever
in this book. I would have reworded it to: "… for cigarettes or for any
other items as prohibited by law." Quite a difference.

The Rationale

While I always knew I was writing this stuff for a reason, it wasn't until
March of 1990 that I put my philosophy about English usage into the words
I had been searching for. As it appeared in my column, it went like this:

> SOTS has mellowed a bit [since the early columns]. Those who
> favor the sardonic, as well as the occasionally sarcastic, remarks
> we made may not be as happy as they once were. However,
> although SOTS is more positive in tone, I believe that we can
> still have some fun poking our targets in their linguistic ribs.
>
> Where we once razzed and jeered the errors, goofs, gaffes, and
> boo-boos we heard on the air and read in black and white, we
> are now less likely to differentiate between right and wrong.

Rather, SOTS prefers to encourage the use of language that is most acceptable to the largest segments of the reading and listening public; that is, usages that result in a smooth flow of information, uninterrupted by expressions that make us stop and wonder what is really meant.

Example: When we hear "nuclear" pronounced as it is intended to be, no one takes note or objects in any way. But when many of us hear it as "noo-kyu-lar," it puts a temporary block on the smooth flow of communication. Some people I know even scream when they hear it, and the information that follows, usually in a newscast, is lost to everyone within earshot of the screamer. Even for those who are only mildly distracted by the fault there is a loss of continuity, which turns those particular moments into a complete waste of time.

Some will say that so-called "errors" are usually not a serious matter because everyone knows what the writer or speaker means, and that is all that is important. What's more, most "errors" don't really hurt anything or cause anyone any real problems, so why make a big deal out of it? I disagree, and I am sure that many of you do, too. If we don't agree on a system of spelling, punctuation, and logical rules of grammar, a lot of time and money has been wasted on the printing of dictionaries and other language reference books.

To me, bad grammar is like having a hot dog for lunch and spending the rest of the afternoon with a gob of mustard on the end of your nose. It doesn't hurt anyone who sees it, but it certainly can have an influence on perceptions other people have of you. What is so odd is that most people won't tell you about it, any more than they would tell you about your panty hose being ripped or your fly being open, in order to avoid hurting your feelings or being thought of as critical. It's for those very same reasons that we almost never tell each other about language faults, and I think that that is terribly unfortunate. We really ought to be helping each other present ourselves as favorably as we possibly can. [I also mentioned Toastmasters here.]

Question: Has any sports writer or sports broadcaster ever looked in a dictionary for the definition of "destiny"? I would guess not. In every sport, throughout a season but mostly as a season nears an end, we hear and read repeatedly that this or that team is "controlling their ("its" would be more correct) own destiny." Singling out any individual writer or broadcaster would be unfair, because so many of them do it. What's wrong with it? Destiny is defined in every dictionary as something that is predetermined or foreordained; synonyms are "fate" (often similarly used) and "doom" (occasionally used, but not in the same context). It is no more possible to control destiny than it is to control the advance of time or the positions of the planets. Shape up, sports guys.

Remember when the early grades used to be called "Grammar School"? Today it appears to be an oxymoron, and for good reason: They don't teach it there no more.

A clothing store in a nearby town had a "Going-Out-of-Business Sale" a while back. Radio commercials for the sale emphasized that it was "just in time for Christmas." Planning is everything, I guess.

I don't know about you, but I have had it up to here with people who use apostrophes the same way they throw darts at a dartboard. On NBC's *The Today Show*, a feature on advancing technology was titled "Countdown to the **90's**." On ABC-TV's *Good Morning America*, the graphic on the screen introduced discussion of "The **90's** Environment." A special Fall 1989 issue of *Life* magazine had "the **80s**" (no apostrophe at all) in huge figures on its front cover. (Let's move that apostrophe out front, replacing the "19" in "1980s.") The worst offenders of all, however – and I do technically consider them to be professionals, but only because it's part of their paid employment – are those who write the display ads for used-car dealers. Pick up almost any newspaper and you'll see "**Chevy's, Buick's, Toyota's**, etc." for sale. Up to here, I say.

Philosophies aside, I find Paul Harvey (ABC Radio) interesting to listen to, but when he tells me that the economy is on the "DEE-cline," my eyeballs roll skyward. Also, I get the feeling that he is just waiting for someone to ask him if he is deliberately using the word *strange* as a noun (as in "Here is a strange": ...) to see if anyone is paying attention. The word is an adjective only, but maybe he is betting that his continuing use of it as a noun will eventually give it currency. If it ever winds up that way in a dictionary, he'll have something to brag about, won't he?

If all this hasn't depressed you enough, here's one that should do the trick: In an article by Patricia Corrigan of the *St. Louis Post Dispatch* (reprinted in the Minneapolis *Star Tribune*) regarding publication of the new Third College Edition of *Webster's New World Dictionary* by the Reference Division of Simon and Schuster, Inc., is a quote from editor-in-chief Victoria Neufeldt: "The **criteria** for a word to make it into the dictionary is not a quantum thing."

And so it went in the last century, if you can believe it. What was really hard for me to believe was the few pieces of mail asking me what was wrong with those apostrophes in that column. I explained all about the use of apostrophes in the next column and heard no more about it. (The correct shortened form of "the 1980s" is "the '80s." The apostrophe replaces the missing figures, in case anyone didn't know.)

Showtime

It was also the time when Disney released the movie *Honey, I **Shrunk** the Kids*. Shrink, shrank, have shrunk, is the way it goes, or is supposed to, anyway. Having no proof of the filmmaker's motives, I still think it may have been done that way deliberately, with the hope that it would generate free publicity. No, I doubt that anyone stayed away from the theater because of the gaffe, and I'd also bet that most of the general public had no clue. Still, it got my goat, and I know I'm not alone. When this sort of thing is done "for effect," the effect should be obvious to everyone, or at least to the literate. Otherwise, it's done on a subliminal level, which is a sneak attack on preferred usage.

For the record, my seven dictionaries agree, except that Merriam-Webster's *Third New International* once again lets us down, this time by equating shrank and shrunk. Yes, I know – language is formed through usage, and grows and changes. T.K. in Blue Jay, Calif., adds that changes usually come about by way of errors, and that while the French are trying to keep their language pure, perhaps we would be wise *not* to emulate them. You'll soon note, however, that T.K. appears in this book several times, each with a knock at what is clearly an error. T.K., or as you'll see, t.k., really does have an ox susceptible to goring. Read on.

One I swear I heard was on KLGT-TV. Promoting the showing of a movie, the announcer intoned, "Tyrone Power, starring in *Old Chicago*." But that, of course, was goofy. The name of the movie is *In Old Chicago*, but Mr. Voice couldn't bear to say "in" twice in a row, so he just left it out. Sorry, no name, following in the tradition of agency copywriters, headline and photo-caption writers, and those amazing creators of matchcovers, billboards, and swizzle sticks. Anonymity is the great protector from the ire of SOTS. Just watch them slink away, cackling gleefully at our distress.

Just to keep me honest, I'll tell a tale on myself so that I won't be thought of as holier-than-thou: On the cover of the December 1976 *Mensa Bulletin*, as editor I had "**Seasons** Greetings" without the apostrophe. It got by a lot of other people, too. Well, nobody's perfect.

Celibate?

How come so few people know the difference between "celibacy" and "chastity"? A *TV Guide* listing for that great old show *Cheers* used "celibate" to mean abstention from sex. On the program itself, however, "chastity" came through loudly, clearly, and correctly. For the record, "celibate" simply means unmarried; "chaste" and "chastity" are the ones that say "no sex." Have you ever heard of a "celibacy belt"? I thought not.

Lingering at the *Cheers* bar (which I actually did on a visit to the Hollywood museum that contains the actual bar used in the series), I can recall the episode in which barmaid Diane Chambers (played by Shelly Long), while failing to guess that the capital of South Dakota was Pierre, pronounced it PEE-air, like a Frenchman's first name. Those who live there say PEER. Hey, it's their town.

Those who remember *Cheers,* or those who still see it in reruns, may recall how poorly educated bartender Sam Malone was, and often how proud he was of his ignorance. M.R. of Apalachicola, Fla., wrote saying that Sam's "**I could care less**" really got under her skin. Meanwhile, overeducated waitress Diane Chambers always correctly said, "I *couldn't* care less." Oddly, none of the characters on the program ever took note of either usage.

Whether it's still around, I don't know, but a while ago a magazine ad for Drixoral Cold & Flu Tablets said, "They [the virus] **could care less** that **you've got** kids. They **could care less** that **you've got** to make a living ..." referring to the influenza virus magnified in the background. There's yet another ad agency cloaked in anonymity, although not totally at fault. The ad had to be approved by one or more company representatives. ... Sigh. ... Then there's the all-too-ubiquitous "**you've got**" instead of "you have," which is well on its way to the Department of Lost Causes. I once wrote, myself, in my column, that "We've got to face the music," and had it pointed out to me in no uncertain terms. "Gotcha!" wrote P.W. of Ipswich, Mass. Hey, I want it known that I am not untrainable. I've done a lot better since.

(Many years ago Jimmy Van Husen and Sammy Kahn wrote a song titled "I Couldn't Care Less," sung by Bing Crosby in the 1959 film *Say One for Me.*)

Speaking of state capitals (as I was a few paragraphs back), E.K. of North Miami, Fla., once again takes her local paper to task:

> The *Miami Herald* once featured after-hours entertainment, the article including: "... and Miami Beach was the nightclub **capitol** of America."

Once again, not everyone knows the difference, so here's the clear dope: "Capital" as it refers to a geographic location, means that a city or town is the governmental seat in a state or country. "Capitol" refers to the specific building in which governmental affairs are seen to. The *Herald* should have used the former, not the latter.

"Appropriate anywhere, so why not here?" is E.K.'s comment about my spelling the word "yuchh," rather than "yechh," which is the more common way. "Your spelling is much closer to how the word is generally pronounced, it seems to me." Can it really be called a word? I guess so.

E.K. also sent along a 32-point headline from that same paper: "Good Cheer **Aides A** Troubled Trip Going Down the Eastern Seaboard." Well, OK, so it was past deadline – no time to proof – hurry, the presses are rolling. That could explain what is most likely a typo for "aids," as well as the capitalized article *a*, with the other article *the* done properly. I was a newspaperman once myself, and yes, I did occasionally get blindsided by the pressures dictated by the clock. Time, tide, and newspaper pressmen wait for no one.

Not far off the subject, V.R. of Georgetown, S.C., was irked enough to send me this:

> A magazine ad for Gilbey's Gin contained the line "And it's still **drank** the same way ..."

V.R. wrote to the manufacturer to complain. Gilbey's director of communications, Nancy T. Albert, responded with the claim that *Webster's New Collegiate Dictionary* allows it, which, sad to say, it does, if we admit that inclusion equals permission. Personally, I consider it a flaw in the dictionary. On the bright side, however, Albert also said, "We will be rewriting the line for upcoming ads." SOTS accepts victory in any form.

Hierarchy?

In my relatively short time working for advertising agencies I learned that there is ordinarily a definite chain of command, but that the chain can vary from one agency to another. Small agencies have few employees with titles, but the bigger ones have many, and the work responsibilities can be shared by several people. In no particular order, there is the owner or partner, account executive (salesperson seeking clients and serving as liaison with clients), account supervisor, creative director, creative group head, associate creative director, art director, assistant art director, copywriter, print producer, and broadcast producer. (Note that I do not list a copyeditor.)

Before an ad ever gets to the public, it is supposed to go through just about every position in that organization, and it also requires approval by the advertising manager and associated individuals on the client's side. With all that involvement, you'd think that *someone* would catch the errors we are talking about here. My guess is that hardly anyone scans the material, relying on the old "Let George do it" syndrome, trusting that others will spot any goofs and fix them. When I was working as a copywriter, both in ad agencies and at TV stations, I was constantly amazed at how much sailed right on by the eyes of those who should have been paying better attention. Am I saying that I never committed errors? No, I can't say that, but early on I developed the habit of re-reading my own material, knowing that any mistakes I made were unlikely to get caught before it was too late. Even then, though, one occasionally got through. Do I have any such examples? Sorry, no, but that's only because I didn't keep track.

In contrast, I have to say that ad agencies are not deliberately opposed to the use of good English. Bill Reber, one-time vice-president of a large agency, was quoted some years ago by an interviewer:

> [Reber] listed as desirable qualities for ad-making: "An inventive and curious mentality ... the ability to write and to appreciate the language when it's used well ... an appreciation of music ... and a kind of competitive attitude that applies not only to our business, but to our clients' as well."

Oh, wouldn't it be wonderful if that philosophy held sway in today's world. As for business-to-business advertising, it's important to remember that we do not write to communicate with the people we know best, we write to communicate with people we don't know, or at least don't know very well. We must use language they are most likely to accept – or that they are least likely to find fault with. Colloquialisms and today's street jargon have no place in messages to those whom we are trying to influence, no matter how embedded "modern" words and phrases have become in our society. We had best play it safe, because we never know who is going to read what we write or hear what we say.

Peek-a-boo

Dan Rather is off the *CBS Evening News* now, but there are others who use his tag line "See you tomorrow night." OK, so it's colloquial and informal, but some of us twitch briefly at it. On the other hand, how would it sound to say, "So long, see me tomorrow night"? I have no answer to that, although I can think of several better ways to express the same thought – yes, grammatically, of course.

But in no way can I account for the off-camera voice heard by R.W. of Philadelphia, Pa.: "For news of the day ahead, watch the *CBS Evening News* tonight." So was that back when they were testing a crystal ball? I don't recall hearing a similar claim in recent days. Think about it – it'll come to you.

Incidentally, it was during the 1988-89 season that CBS Television used the slogan "Are You Ready!" They never said what we were supposed to be ready for. The new programs? How ready would we have to be? It was one of the few times I talked back to the TV set, remarking on more than one occasion, "No, dammit, I'm not ready!" Also, note that there was no question mark. How presumptive can you get? CBS not only assumed we were ready, they seemed to be saying, "Boy, are *you ever ready*!" I doubt that anyone was ever as ready as CBS might have thought. Mercifully, the campaign died at the season's end. I forget what replaced it.

Another once-thriving concern, the Montgomery Ward Co., similarly asked a question without using a question mark: "Why Shop Anywhere Else!" Again I found myself answering without being heard, "How many reasons would you like?" (All right, so I did shop there on occasion.)

Which is right?

Pronunciation is always difficult to discuss, particularly because there is so much regional variation in the U.S. For example, is it COO-pon or KYOO-pon? On radio and TV I hear it both ways. Most of my dictionaries give a first listing to the former – even though dictionary publishers maintain that the order of listings means nothing – while three of my Merriam-Webster books (the old 2nd *Unabridged*, the new 3rd *International*, and the condensed *New Ideal*) give us K(Y)OO-pon only, which I take as indicating no preference. My folks invariably said KYOO-pon, and it stuck.

Well, then, how about "culinary"? L.G. of Santa Ana, Calif., wrote that Judy Muller, substituting for Charles Osgood on CBS Radio's "The

Osgood File," in a report on the first George Bush's distaste for broccoli, pronounced the word "KULL-in-ary." My "battle of dictionaries" gives the edge, 4-3, to KYOO-lin-ary, with those same three Merriam Webster ones mentioned in the previous paragraph on the losing side, and a fairly recent (at the time) American Heritage among the winners. In all fairness, I have to concede that either is acceptable, even though I favor KYOO-lin-ary. As PBS's Red Green always says in The Man's Prayer, "I could change, if I have to, I guess."

There once was a time when everyone in broadcasting pronounced *finance* and *financial* with the short *i* and the accent on the second syllable – fi-NANCE and fi-NAN-shul. Not any more, and I have about given up the fight. It was partly the permissive dictionaries that caused it, and partly the British, who also gave us *mercantile*, *versatile*, etc., with the long *i* again. American radio and TV people, for whatever reason, have picked up these quirks and refuse to let loose of them. But, as I say, it's probably a lost cause. Sometimes the deck is so badly stacked against us that we might as well holler "Uncle!" However, that won't stop us from complimenting American Express Fi-NAN-cial Advisors for getting it right, the old-fashioned way. Most dictionaries, by the way, allow both. Dan Rather on the *CBS Evening News* was among the few who said it right, but, oddly enough, it stood out like a sore thumb. Was Dan just showing off? Not in my book, he wasn't, but it's such a shame that certain correct usages somehow now begin to sound either wrong or old-fashioned. I sincerely hope we are not headed in that direction.

Incidentally, I have a Discover card, and when I needed to speak to someone at Discover headquarters recently, I listened to a telephone "hold" message that is likely intended to make everyone happy by pronouncing "financial" both ways in the same message. Hmmm. Also incidentally, Jim Giebel, an announcer for radio station KNXR in Rochester, Minnesota, said fi-NANCE correctly, as did the voice on the commercial for Homes of Harmony, a real estate development. A tip of the SOTS hat to both.

Easy for me to say?

Speaking of dictionaries and pronunciations, which, as any fool can plainly see, I do often, I received an interesting letter from Rima McKinzey, pronunciation consultant for American Heritage Dictionaries, who also served on the pronunciation editorial staff for both Random House and American Heritage – powerful credentials indeed. In her writing she cautioned me about becoming too much of a "prescriptivist," as opposed to a "descriptivist." She also said that modern dictionaries had become more of the latter than the former, and that the "descriptivists" (describers) now must prevail, but she also noted that professionals should be more careful than they have been. She concluded:

> In ending, I must say that in general I like reading your column in the *Bulletin*, and that I agree that speech by those who have access to the media should be watched for accuracy. Standard speech should be upheld, but sometimes there is a fine line between that which is acceptable and that which is not.
>
> Keep the watch, but also guard against too heavy-handed prescriptivism. Sincerely, (sig)

I am indeed trying to walk that fine line, and I can only leave it to my readers to determine whether I am succeeding or not. I'm sure I'll find out, soon after this book is published.

Where credit is due

I haven't heard her on the air for a long time, but one of the best at pronunciation and the most wonderfully clear enunciation I have ever heard was Deborah Potter of CBS television and radio, later of CNN, and now with an organization called NewsLab, as of this writing. If SOTS had been presenting awards, she would have gotten one. There are others, of course, but not many. Jed Duvall scored very high in my estimation, and for a long time I wondered whatever became of Dale Schornack, an extremely literate news reporter and anchor who worked for a while in the Twin Cities before leaving for Phoenix. As I write, he is the lead anchor at KXTV in Sacramento. Dale was another of the few who measured up very well, in my estimation, and I have a remarkably good ear.

Carole Simpson of ABC-TV News is and/or was also very good.

W.H. of San Francisco, Calif., wanted to confer honors upon David

McElhatten, a news anchor for KCBS Radio, not only for "his impeccable syntax, but his enunciation is an outstanding example of the fast-disappearing perfection that was once, alas, standard in radio." Yes, there are a few left, but only a few, sad to say.

But not Phil

Apparently without affecting his popularity, Phil Donahue occasionally fumble-tongued his way through such dubious attempts as when he and a bunch of celebrity lawyers discussed "pre-nup-chew-al" agreements. E.B. of Pompano Beach, Fla., heard it and objected. Once again, according to *most* dictionaries, nuptial is pronounced NUP-shl, but even those famous folks at Merriam Webster have given us a good example of why their dictionaries have earned more than a little criticism: In the MW *Webster's Third New International*, NUP-shl and NUP-chl echo even the otherwise-suspect Random House *Dictionary of the English Language* (unabridged). But in MW's 1984 *Ninth New Collegiate* (now replaced, of course), which is based on Webster's 3rd, the addition of NUP-chew-ul and NUP-shew-ul (phonetics mine) are there for all to see. The *Collegiate*, however, qualifies that by adding that such pronunciations are regarded by many as unacceptable variants. That helps some. But as I have often said, there is nothing so common as common speech, and it becomes more common every day.

On a related note, L.H. of Chicago, Ill., heard WGN-TV's newscaster speak of Madonna's upcoming "**wedding** nuptials." Are there any other kind?

OK, now it's Larry King who gets it in the neck: M.S. of East Templeton, Mass., heard the well-known radio and TV interviewer ask a guest about a crime that King characterized as "HEE-nee-us," I too seem to recall once hearing him pronounce *heinous* that way. It's HAY-nus, of course, and it means "abominable"; on this all dictionaries agree. What's right and what's wrong? If it rings peculiarly on the reasonably well-educated ear, there is undoubtedly a better way to say it.

By the same token, if it looks funny in print, there is always a way to fix it. Case in point: M.E. of River Falls, Wis., sent a letter to the editor of the *River Falls Journal* that carried the headline, "Worried city trees may die." I can think of several possible improvements, as I am sure you can as well.

Reading his local newspaper was T.K. of Blue Jay, Calif.:

> In the weekly *Mountain News & Mountaineer* was an article
> concerning "bed and breakfast" establishments. Attributed only
> to the CPS news service, the report included: "And they turned
> right around and granted the permit without review or any
> further **adieu**."

T.K. signed off by bidding me a fond "ado." In my subsequent comment
I pointed out to T.K. that he had missed a second gaffe in the article.
In the opening paragraph was: "**Two** words describe the … hearing on
the Special Use Permit …; 'acrimonious and frustrating!'" But when I
pointed out that those were **three** words, D.R. of Los Angeles, Calif., took
issue with me, saying that I had ignored the fact that only two words were
descriptive, not including "and," and that the error was one of punctuation
rather than one of counting words. There should have been single quotation marks after 'acrimonious' and before 'frustrating.' Deduct two points
from SOTS, and give them to D.R.

_____

13

Our sympathies

The following is precisely as it appeared in my column:

> In Birmingham, Mich., as D.S. of that city proved with a photocopy, an ad in a publication called "Marketplace" for the Sunheiser Construction and Remodeling Company asked readers to "Call now for a free design **consolation**." There, there, now. It's not such a bad-looking gazebo, is it?

She's right

Renowned actress Lillian Gish once said in a radio interview, "In France, if they have a dispute about the pronunciation of a word, or anything to do with language or their culture, they go to the *Comédie Française* to settle it. Wouldn't it be wonderful if we, too, had a national theater where English would be spoken perfectly and beautifully?" (from *Out Of the Air* – Mary Margaret McBride – 1960)

Hey, look!

Billboards never got a lot of attention from SOTS, but this one spotted by J.A. of Chapel Hill, N.C., certainly did:

> The big board being rented by the Raleigh Federal Bank offers "Just Rewards. For those who deserve them." I really hate the thought that *other* banks let folks have Just Rewards when they don't deserve them.

Long ago I ceased to be amazed at the weird stuff sent to me. R.F. of Kenosha, Wis., did a double-take on this one:

> In the men's room of the Ground Round Restaurant in New Hope, Minn., was an ad above the urinal for Town & Country Dodge of Hopkins, Minn. It noted that "Our trucks don't know **their** not expensive." ("they're")

Well, then, don't tell them, OK? We wouldn't want the poor trucks to feel cheap, now would we? R.F. followed up a bit later with another off-the-wall entry:

> Berlitz, the language people, ran the enclosed magazine ad that had the line "Learn (foreign languages) progressively, just **like** you learned English."

Folks in the language business should know better. That should be "just as you learned English" or "just the way you learned English."

Dratted hyphen

Technology has provided us with many modern miracles in our daily lives, but it does not always work in our favor. Creating computer programs that simplify our writing and catch our mistakes is a noble profession; however, it can backfire, especially when any sort of general instruction is given to the machines. Case in point: Some programs are instructed to break double-letter words in the middle of those double letters. Usually this is OK, as in bob-bin, beg-gar, etc., but some word-breaks turn out to be just plain dumb, as in what D.P. of San Ramon, Calif., found:

> Computer typesetting in newspapers often has hyphens in very strange places, mostly at the end of lines. *The Valley Herald* had "sidew-heel steamer," for one, and there were others.

That had to be a pure glitch. The program obviously recognized "heel" as a word, but why it created "sidew" as a separate word may never be known.

Oh, yes, and that one reminded me of the goofy computer I had to work with at the weekly *Sun* newspapers in 1990. The editors typed (key-boarded?) their own copy into the computer and it was my job to catch any errors they might make, as well as errors the computer made. I encountered "Draf-thouse" (the name of a local pub), "cor-nbread," "four-in-ch-diameter," "han-dguns," and my favorite, "dol-lhouse," all end-of-line breaks. There was something about certain letter combinations that took those words apart for no earthly reason. Well, yes, there was a reason: Somebody programmed them that way.

Handed to me by J.M. of St. Paul, Minn., was a business reply envelope addressed to "U.S. English," about which I know nothing except that at the top of the envelope, in red lettering that was supposed to look as if it had been hand-written, was: "IF YOU WOULD KINDLY PLACE A 1ST CLASS STAMP HERE, YOU COULD HELP US SAVE **MUCH NEEDED** FUNDS. THANK YOU." I guess there was a large quantity of needed funds. ("much-needed")

Also competing in the hyphen-deprived world of punctuation is this from D.M. of Norfolk, Va.:

> The Sunday *Virginian-Pilot and Ledger Star* included a flyer about the 1978 Oldsmobiles. Enclosed please find the clipping containing the sentence: "Now you can enjoy all the advantages of a family-sized Delta 88 – with a smooth-running V6 engine, standard – or a remarkable new **available** V8 that runs on **money saving** diesel fuel." If you're going to have a V8 that runs on money, it's a good idea to have it available, especially if it helps in saving diesel fuel.

Once again, a strategically placed hyphen ("money-saving") would have kept this item out of this book, and we wouldn't have had it to laugh at. Dare we hope that the copywriter sees it here?

The aforementioned D.P. also told us about a radio ad on KKHI that urged listeners to "plan an outing to Stanford Shopping Center, where each shop is more interesting than the next." Apparently our first stop would be great, but it's all downhill from there. (Each shop is less interesting that the previous one.)

Don't leave home ...

Clever is as clever does, so they say. But too clever is not good, as R.M. of Miami Beach, Fla., can attest:

> American Express seems to have caught some flak for its TV ad line "That's why we're here, **aren't** we?" I wrote to them suggesting changing it to "That's why we're here, isn't it?" I never got a response, but instead of changing it, they dropped the line altogether.

That's still a score for our side. You'd have thought that *someone* in the
ad agency, or even the advertising manager of the company, would have
raised a question about it, but apparently cleverness prevailed, if not
for long. As a former ad-agency clever person, I am reminded that I
once suggested a slogan for the Fedders Company, manufacturers of
air conditioning systems. It was, "You'll be tickled with Fedders!" I
was crushed when they turned it down. It would have been one of the
world's greatest advertising slogans, IMHO (in my humble opinion, for
the computer deprived).

Verbing

When a noun is used as a verb, the result can be awful. But there are
many words that serve as both verb and noun. The trick is to know the
difference. Words such as *jump*, *skate*, *somersault*, etc., go both ways, but
not those like the one deplored by D.S. of Birmingham, Mich.:

> A slick magazine ad for a Radisson hotel west of the Detroit
> airport, among other things, invites guests to "unwind as you
> **cabaret** and dance the Lambada in Players Lounge."

Or would you rather "theater" tonight instead? On a similar note, there
was a TV ad that boasted, "No one **potpourries** like Glade (deodorizer)."
It disappeared after a short run, for which we can all be grateful. Also,
I believe Kinko's has stopped advertising itself as "a new way **to office.**"
(That was by way of J.M. of St. Louis Park, Minn.) And if you think
that's bad, try Taco Bell: "Introducing the NEW way **to Taco!**" It makes
me want to dance. Will you teach me to taco?

Blithely playing the same kind of music in a slick insert in my newspaper
is the Don Pablo's Mexican restaurant chain (central and eastern U.S.),
which asks, "How DO You **Carnita?**" Well, I would probably take a fajita
in one hand and a burrito in the other, and carnita rhythmically between
the tables to my seat. No? Oh, OK, looking more closely, I see that a
carnita is a traditional Mexican dish that is new to the menu. Shucks, and
just when I was in the mood to dazzle everyone with my footwork.

Maybe you'd like to join me in the back yard for a barbecue. An advertiser
whose name I missed – and haven't heard again since – was having a sale

on barbecue grills, especially those with built-in rotisseries. What got my attention was, "When you **rotiss**, you get better results." Umm, yeah.

Well now, they revived *Life* magazine, but most recently as a newspaper insert, and there's a different crowd running it, obviously. On the cover of the self-described *America's Weekend Magazine* was the question, "Are You Ready to **Roller Coaster**?" Sure, right after I "car" over to the amusement park and "entrance" myself. I'll also want to "popcorn" and maybe "hot-dog" myself before I "Ferris wheel" and maybe "carousel" some, too.

D.G. of Akron, Ohio, comments: "I don't understand your problem with the use of nouns as verbs. It seems to me that there are hardly any nouns that can't be verbed anymore." Jumping Jehosaphat, I surely hope there are. Let's not go completely to pieces!

Well, all right!

USA Weekend, another Sunday-paper magazine-type insert, included an article on teenagers and their lifestyles, but on the front page was "Believe us! The Kids Are **Alright**." My dictionaries, along with other books on language, are in almost total agreement that the term is "all right." Dictionaries in particular make special note of the usage with "nonstandard," "poor choice," and other descriptions. Further, the Associated Press style manual says that "alright" should *never* be used in place of "all right," and I suspect that once again no one bothered to check. Oddly, my Word program's spell-checker accepts both forms, but that's not saying a heck of a lot. Word is often wrong. Gasp! What have I said? Without Word, I wouldn't have been able to write this book. I'm biting my tongue (wink wink).

Ouch!

D.S., that same previous "cabaret" contributor, later sent along an ad created for Fran O'Brien's Maryland Crab House in nearby Auburn Hills, Mich. One specialty being offered was "**Dungeonous** Crabs." Very tender, no doubt, after being softened up in the torture chamber. Make it Dungeness, OK? (I had one once; it took two hours to eat, along with two bibs and several napkins, but it was absolutely delicious.)

Before we get past that verbing business, I have another: When IBM introduced its computer known as the PS-2, the creative geniuses at the company's advertising agency came up with this dandy rhyme as a radio-ad slogan: "How we gonna do it? We gonna PS-2 it!" There are people in the back room at IBM working on improving voice-recognition computer programs. That slogan must have given them bad dreams.

Not to be outdone, one of a pair of KSTP-AM radio announcers named Scott and Tony (I never could tell which was which), referring to a heavy schedule of sports viewing on TV, said that he was going to stock up on drinks and snacks and just "couch-potato it out." I heard it as I was KSTP'ing, and I never thought in a million years that I'd find myself saying *that*!

How ironic

Initially, I didn't use material found in mail-order catalogs, but they have become so ubiquitous that I now consider them to be in the public and professional realm, as evidenced by a couple of earlier entries. E.H. of Healdsburg, Calif., found an item I could not pass up:

> In a Paragon Gifts, Inc., catalog was a descriptive blurb for *The Handbook of Good English* that included: "Indispensable for **everyone** who wishes to speak and write properly but may not be sure of **their** choices."

Equally contorted was the radio ad for Rubbermaid: "**Everyone** needs **their** space." T.B. of Louisville, Ky., echoed that one:

> An ad in *PC World* for ForeFront Direct, a learn-by-mail company, headlined: "Would You Believe This **Person** Is Training To Advance **Their** Career?" Pictured is a person who is obviously female. Couldn't they have said "her"?

Yes, they certainly could have, and I know it has become "acceptable" in some instances to use *their* instead of the supposedly sexist *his* or *her*, but there are so many ways to rephrase and recast that the ugly usage should not be necessary. In the Paragon case, I would have rewritten it to read: "Indispensable for those who wish to speak and write properly but may not be sure of their choices." Surely no one can find fault with that. The ForeFront thing was too easy, I guess.

Pitch it

Let's knock off another catalog while we're at it. V.M. of South Paris, Maine, flipped through his copy of the Colonial Gardens Kitchen catalog and found this corker: "[photo] A new high in storage. Our eight-shelf tower maximizes space, **without** taking up **hardly any**." There are several ways to fix it, but my inclination would be to replace "without taking" with "and takes." It's another one of those nasty double negatives.

And one more: J.H. of Brooklyn Center, Minn., received a Taylor Gifts catalog and extracted a few items of interest. Rugs were advertised as "**Country look** orientals from Belgium ..." Mahogany picture frames let you "Display **momentos** ..." And a rack furnished with salt and pepper shakers in the form of 10 different animals was offered as "Noah's **Arc**." Cute? Yes. Sloppy? Also yes. Literate? No. ("Country-look," "mementos," and "ark")

L.G. of Anaheim, Calif., in the radio business himself in 1976, caught Bernard Shaw on his *CBS Radio News* report stating that, in the wake of Representative Wayne Hays's resignation from Congress (remember Elizabeth Ray?), his Washington staff was "packing up his **momentos**." L.G. adds, "Gad, I'm such a rat fink, but it's for a higher good."

K-K-K-Katie

Watching the NBC-TV *Today Show*, the longest-running TV program in history after *Meet the Press*, was V.T. of Wappingers Falls, N.Y.:

> Because of a school holiday, I was able to watch the program. Suddenly, my ears were assaulted as host Katie Couric referred to speaking of something fondly, something remembered as a "real **momento**." I wrote to Ms. Couric about it – alas, to no avail.

My own thought is that someone *considered* mentioning to the woman that the word is *memento*, but didn't for fear of hurting her feelings, and I'd be willing to bet that your letter never reached her. To be clear, "memento" comes from "memory," not "moment," although often something is a souvenir of a particular moment, which I suspect was Couric's meaning. Nevertheless, she shouldn't have used a word without being sure of its definition. Subtract ten points and fine her a dollar.

What, again?

Why is it that so many writers and broadcasters can't seem to grasp the meaning of *déjà vu*? And why do so many want *déjà vu* to happen "all over again," a double calamity that many attribute to either the famous baseball coach Casey Stengel or the New York Yankees catcher Yogi Berra? Even *Newsweek*'s Larry Reibstein wrote that "Last week it was *déjà vu* **all over again**," as did an unnamed sports-type in that same publication. J.A. of Arlington, Texas, was the *Newsweek* reader. Almost everywhere you turn, there it is in all its unglory. Contrary to "popular" belief, the term does not mean the remembering of a past experience or event; it is the eerie feeling that one has experienced something before, *but actually has not*, and knows it! It most certainly is not a here-we-go-again situation, or the repetition of anything. In *French* it has that connotation, but not in English. Look it up and you'll see.

Speaking of sports, the front page of the *Star Tribune* sports section in April 2004, reporting on the return of the University of Connecticut's women's basketball team to the final four, had just those two words, "*Déjà vu*," emblazoned in 116-point type – an inch and a half high. You could read it a block away. Has the term been consigned to the trash heap of ignorance? One can only hope not. Oh, I know that many will give me heat about common usage, etc., but I'll refuse to swallow it. If we accept the newer definition, then what will we call that eerie feeling of false remembering?

Then there was the uncertain use by Mark Armijo in *The Arizona Republic*, writing about auto racing at Phoenix International Raceway: "It was almost *déjà vu* for Englishman Nigel Mansell on Saturday," indicating that Mansell was still recovering from an earlier crash during a practice session. I guess it's just too tempting for sports writers to use such a ritzy-titzy term, whether they know what it means or not. But wait! There's more, and not just in the sports arena:

The disease has spread to others nationwide. Outdistancing everyone and putting on it the oddest spin of all was Jean Prescott, an entertainment writer for the Knight-Ridder/Tribune news service, published in *The Arizona Republic*. Discussing reruns of *Kung Fu*, she comments, "It starred David Carridine as the enigmatic Caine, and [cable channel] TNT is about to **do some *déjà vu*** with 62 episodes of that cult classic." Egad! What's next? Maybe we can all go **déjà vuing**? Even accepting the French definition, these usages are way out in left field.

To top it all off, now there's even a song called "***Déjà Vu* All Over Again**," as heard on *Austin City Limits*, a public TV program. Will it never end?

Getting away

Travel is broadening, even just reading about it. R.Z. of Kalamazoo, Mich., did just that:

> In the travel section of the Sunday *Kalamazoo Gazette* was the headline: "Mexico City: **Clamor** up a pyramid, see a sky-scraper." Aimed at noisily enthusiastic tourists, maybe?

Apparently "clamber" is not in that writer's vocabulary, nor is it in that of another: My daughter Judy picked up a copy of *MSP Airport News* and had to look twice at the main headline: "NEARLY 30 MILLION PAS-SENGERS **CLAMOR** ABOARD AT MSP IN '96." (MSP is Minneapolis/St. Paul International Airport.)

Watch your fingers

I'm hoping that you've been paying attention and have noted that almost nothing in this book has anything to do with typographical errors, except perhaps very marginally when there is some doubt. And no, I will not grant that substituting wrong words passed by the spellchecker qualifies as typographical. For example, we hear from P.D. of Dixon, Ill.:

> In the prestigious *Harvard Business Review*, an article writ-ten by Jeffrey A. Sonnenfeld, a business school professor, who may or may not have been paid for it, contained the following, which should have been caught by a copyeditor: "I hope that

his debate may **diffuse** a new form of potential discrimination
…" I'm sure that *defuse* would have been the word intended.

That is correct. K.U. of Menlo Park, Calif., adds:

> *Now Showing*, a local TV magazine, listed "JUGGERNAUT
> * * * *Action Adventure*. When a blackmailer plants several bombs
> aboard a luxury liner, a band of demolition experts must race
> against time to **diffuse** them." Wouldn't that just make things
> worse?

It most certainly would – spread them all over, it would. Now let us direct
our attention to D.M., a resident of the Big Apple:

> An ad in the New York City edition of *TV Guide* brought me
> to a sudden stop. *Earthscope*, a program on the Learning Chan-
> nel, was touted with the line "The rape of tropical rain-forests,
> international oil spills and acid rain **wreck** havoc on nature
> around the globe."

Not only is it not a typo, the gaffe rates a mention in the *Harper Dictionary of Contemporary Usage*. The word is *wreak* (pronounced REEK), and
besides, havoc refers to something that has already been wrecked.

L.H. of Chicago, Ill., whom we all now know as having an extremely
sharp eye, favors us with yet another nonstandard twist:

> Tom McPheron, writing in the *North Loop News*, began an
> article with: "This past week, the Windy City's winds battered
> street signs, sometimes knocking them off their poles, pushed
> around pedestrians, sending them staggering, but most impres-
> sively, Mother Nature **reaped** havoc on Chicago's lakeshore
> beaches and break walls."

Classified jazz

Much as I try to avoid them, once in a while a classified ad will not be
denied – like this one from J.K. of Nashua, N.H.:

The help-wanted ad in the *Nashua Telegraph* sought someone to sell tuxedoes. Benefits offered included "paid holidays, vacation, **prophet** sharing."

Some classified ads, usually larger display ads, often in boxes, are prepared by ad agencies or advertising departments of companies, and a perfect example of that is this one clipped by T.N. of North Wales, Pa.:

> The *Philadelphia Inquirer* carried an ad for JJH, a division of Xeno Technix, Inc., "an established **Navel** Engineering firm with extensive commercial and **navel** ship design experience [that] is accepting employment applications for ship design contracts. Immediate opportunities for experienced engineers & designers. Strong bkgd & exp in detailed design of US **Navel** ships, boats & commercial supply vessels required. ..." Is "navel engineering" a branch of plastic surgery?

And the classic classified of them all, noted by M.L. of Binghamton, N.Y.:

> The Binghamton *Press & Sun-Bulletin* carried the opening for a "PROOFREADER: AT-A-GLANCE, the largest manu-facturer of time management products [calendars, etc.] is expanding and has an immediate need for a proofreader in our Electronic Prepress Department. Our ideal candidate will be detail oriented and have strong **grammer** and spelling skills. ..."

OK, that's it. No more classified ads. Someday I may write another book, containing a lot about classifieds, and I have plenty of material, but not now and not here. I swear. Meanwhile, here come two for the price of one from P.S. of Santa Barbara, Calif.:

> Would someone please tell Geraldine Baum, a staff writer for the *Los Angeles Times*, that there is no such word as **reknowned**? Note that the enclosed clipping also has it hyphenated "rek-nowned." Don't they have copyeditors or proofreaders on that paper?

Well now, maybe they were all out to lunch at the same time.

I gave it a shot

In 1993 I tried something new – for me, at least: I signed up to teach a 3-hour class at a for-profit equivalent of a community education center that called itself Open U. It was listed in the program catalog as "Enhance Your Career with Better English," and it got off to a great start with 19 in attendance. Feedback from the students was fully positive and I was much encouraged. Unfortunately, that was it. Only three signed up for the second session and it was canceled for "lack of interest." I had put a lot of work into preparing the handout materials, and the small fee I received for that single class didn't even pay for the printing. Ah, well, it was worth doing and it taught me something: Few are willing to admit to any sort of weakness in their language skills. It was yet another good idea that had only one thing wrong with it – it didn't work.

In creating the course materials, which consisted mainly of a 180-question series of quizzes, I developed what became for me a new approach to improving the spoken and written word – specifically, "effective" English. It was based on the rather simple reasoning that we do not always know who is going to be reading what we write, or listening as we speak; and even if we do, we never know just how "sensitive" (picky?) our audience might be. In a nutshell, my new "statement" said that we are judged not by how we present ourselves, but how we are perceived by others. There is a considerable difference, and I believe that those few words speak volumes.

My second basic premise says that it doesn't matter so much whether a language usage is "right" or "wrong"; instead it involves making the better "choice." For instance, where one might say, "We are **anxious** to do a good job for you," the wiser writer would replace "anxious" with "eager." (The first comes from the word *anxiety*.) As I stated earlier, the word "anxious" may bother only a few, but "eager" would bother no one, so why bother anyone, if we can help it? The idea is to put our best foot forward whenever we can; it greatly increases the odds in our favor.

A good fit?

Kinney Shoes, I believe, is now out of business, and maybe one reason is that they were advertising with the slogan "We **only sell** the right shoe."

By "right," of course, they meant the correct or proper shoe(s), but it left me wondering how to get a left shoe – or maybe it came free when you bought the right one. It may not have been improved upon if they had said "We sell only the right shoe," but at least the modifier "only" would have been in the right place. "Shoes" would have made it even better.

Speaking of being "out of business," I am aware that many of the establishments named in this book are no longer in existence. That doesn't excuse what they did, and keep in mind that any of your favorite retailers could close the doors at any time. Also, names get changed as big businesses gobble up smaller businesses, so some of our offenders may simply be wearing different faces.

14

Glorious food

Those slick coupon sections in the Sunday papers demonstrate how "creative" ad agency folks have to be, and how often they miss the boat. One ad I saved, for Mrs. Smith's pies, offered "**Free a la Mode**." The idea was that we could buy a pie and get ice cream at no extra charge. What the ad types ignored, however, was that "a la mode" is a way of serving, not the ice cream itself.

Is Nestea's TV advertising still asking us to "**Taste the Plunge**"? It showed someone falling into a swimming pool, and I swear I could almost taste the chlorine. Almost as bad is another TV ad for banana nut bread made with Banana Nut Crunch breakfast cereal. The voice says, "We're going to show you what it tastes like." Which is sort of like hearing what purple sounds like.

Then there's the Green Mill restaurant billboard seen by my good friend P.A. of Minneapolis that invites us to "**Taste** Our New Menu." Sorry. No plasticized paper for me. Not even with ketchup. Oh sure, we know what it means, but that doesn't make it any less silly. And how about the TV ad for another local restaurant, Culver's? It implores us to "**Taste** how much we care." I guess this is what happens when the creative juices dry up completely.

More? Knollwood Mall, a nearby shopping center, placed a newspaper ad that read: "Lunchtime? We're a place you can really **sink your teeth** into." Yuck! When you think about it, though, concrete can be very filling – or ruin your fillings.

In the soup

On TV, the Campbell's Cream of Potato soup ad boasts that "Great Taste Never **Looked** Better." What does taste look like? Crystal Pepsi says, "You've Never **Seen** a Taste Like This," also on TV. Same question. In a Sunday coupon ad, Kellogg's Special K claims, "Great taste never **looked** so good." At least Kellogg's didn't go overboard with the capital letters. But will someone please tell me what *any* of the five senses *looks* like? I am baffled.

Also, if I'm not mistaken, Campbell's is still pushing its Chunky "soup that eats like a meal." In today's jargon, it could be "soup that eats, like, a meal." Make of that what you will.

I.I. of Youngstown, Ohio, found yet another from our favorite(?) brand:

> A Campbell's soup TV commercial boasts that its "old-world vegetable soup" contains "**real zucchini**." I wonder what the others contain – imitation zucchini? Then there's Sizzlean (a bacon substitute) that advertises "50 percent more **real genuine meat**." Twice as good, no doubt.

Yep, much better than that *ersatz* genuine kind. And who is it that says, "**Eat Fresh!**"? Subway, the sandwich people, that's who. I'd like to know what "fresh" tastes like. Next time I crave some "fresh," I'll go to Subway and order a "fresh sandwich," just to see what I'll get. Also, it's Applebee's who says, "Eatin' **Good** in the Neighborhood." Yes, I know that "well" doesn't rhyme, but can language like that be good for our kids to learn? And for anyone who wants to claim that "food" is *implied* after "fresh" or "good," I have an icy stare. Implied? Not a chance.

Among my pile of notes is one about a TV commercial for something called Gardenburger, but all I wrote was "Eating **good** just got great." That time "well" would have worked, but the whole sense of the thing has me shaking my head, and I really don't know why. Maybe if I stare at it a while.

D.S. of Hollywood, Fla., offered this in 1977, so the price may have risen:

> I find references on TV to "colored TV owners." I find this of interest, as I am green myself. Of amusement is a [TV] commercial for J.M. Fields. They tell me that I should run to their store and "enjoy a hot dog and coke for a **mouth-watering 29¢**." I'd like to, but my teeth aren't what they used to be.

Another variation on the theme was on a floor display in one of my local supermarkets, Cub Foods. Certainly professionally prepared, the sign for Ruffles Flavor-Rush Sour Cream & Onion Chips read: "**See** the Flavor – **Taste** the Rush!" OK, that's it! No more! I give up.

Except for this one on a somewhat related note: Let's hear again from S.K. of Yardley, Pa.:

> An item in the Bucks County *Courier Times* about Austin's Rib and Steak House in Bristol, Pa., tempted me to read how their "newly expanded menu will surely appeal to your spicy **pallet**."

Spelling aside, can a "palate" be spicy? The word has two meanings – the roof of the mouth and the sense of taste – but "spicy"? Umm, no. I hope that the unidentified writer went on to better things, maybe as a menu taster?

Whoops – spoke too soon. He or she may be working for KARE-TV, right here in the Twin Cities. Staff reporter Boyd Huppert was the name attached to an item on the station's Web site that discussed the differences between walleye (walleyed pike) and zander (a European fish), which some restaurants had been serving as a substitute for walleye without telling their patrons. A chef said he could tell the difference; Huppert then asked, "But what about the **amateur palates** that have been fooled at some other restaurants by the walleye/zander swap?" Web surfer B.C. of St. Paul, Minn., called my attention to it.

Egad! How many ways are there? Self-professed die-hard member of SOTS J.M. of Boca Raton, Fla., returns with the answer:

> Our *Boca Raton News* contained an ad for Pal's Captain's Table, a restaurant on the Intracoastal Waterway. Included was the sentence "So join us for lunch or for dinner, relax, and let us please your **palette**."

All what?

Is it possible to get too picky? Maybe in most places, but not on these pages, I think you'll agree. Jiffy Pop microwave popcorn is eminently edible, for example, but the reading material on the box contains a head-scratcher: "**All** popcorns **are not** created equal because not all popcorns are made the same." The first part of that is nonsense, of course, but the second part says it right. To speak for all popcorns is more than a bit presumptuous.

Mario olives were promoted the same way in a Sunday coupon ad: "**All** olives **are not** created equal." That, of course, would make every single olive *unique*, and that's pushing it. Or are olives like snowflakes?

My local *Star Tribune* booted an otherwise perfectly good obituary when the headline over it read: "[name not relevant], 59, **infamous** 'bakery lady' of Cannon Falls." The write-up, of course, praised her sweet rolls, Danish pastries, wedding cakes, etc. *Infamous* was a bad choice, however.

Sometimes just the arrangement of words can create communication speed-bumps. L.S. of Coon Rapids, Minn., saw this on the America Online welcome screen: "Palestinian Cabinet Minister Saeb Erekat and Tayeb Abdel Rahim, a top Arafat aide, confirmed that Arafat died in a conversation with reporters at Arafat's headquarters in the West Bank city of Ramallah." Actually, Arafat died in Paris while in a coma. The reporters were not involved.

Here's another paragraph exactly as it appeared in my column:

> Same newspaper, different day: An article described the appearance on a local TV talk show of a man who showed "how handy pawnshops are as he **hawked** an electric guitar that turned out to be stolen." Excuse me, I have to do this: Ptooie!

Sorry about that. (The writer was not identified.) Anyway, the word is *hocked*.

Fooled her

In 1993 Marjorie Mandelblatt, at the time editor of the *Mensa Bulletin*, dropped me a note after she received my latest column. Marjorie's day job in North Hollywood, Calif., was as the owner of a company that bore her name and included on her stationery the line "Professional Publishing

Services." She was also president of the Publication Production Association of Southern California and a member of the Society of Professional Journalists. Since we had not been formally introduced and did not know each other, her note read:

Dear Mr. Andersen,

Thank you for the SOTS column. It is very cute. I will put it in my immediate active pile. I can already tell you that the May issue is full-up, and I expect quite a bit of that to spill into June. July/August is looking open, though, and that will have been a reasonable amount of time since the "Ad-Annoyed" piece ran in March for yours to not ring the same note.

I can't believe how self-conscious I am in writing to a language expert. My degree and training in Linguistics/English seems to be fading fast.

Sincerely, [sig]

I was, of course, flattered to be called an "expert," but there are many definitions of the word. For some, an expert is "anyone from out of town." For me and others, an expert is someone who knows just a tiny bit more about something than you do. (If you said to yourself that "seems" on her last line should have been "seem," you are correct, but dashing off a note intended for only one set of eyes, without having the note copyedited, should never be criticized. That would be looking the gift horse in the mouth.) Sadly, Marjorie passed away a couple of years later.

Corroboration?

Occasionally, I have been asked about the written references I use in my columns and speeches. In the introduction to this book I mentioned some of the dictionaries in my possession, and I can add to that list several other works that aid my accuracy, such as the *Chicago Manual of Style* (I buy each new edition), the British *Fowler*, and Strunk and White's *Elements of Style*. None is totally infallible, however, so it pays for me to check them all, and even go to the library for additional research when I need to. Even then, though, I sometimes get caught with my syntax down, and my alert audience is ever poised to call me to account. But isn't that how we all learn, by making mistakes? I do, and I appreciate the help.

I hope you don't get the idea that I am a slave to the stylebooks and other sources, because I do not wish to be thought of that way. If something makes more sense than the way it is treated in the language literature, I advocate going with what our audience is most likely to accept. There is, however, a point beyond which I will not go in "dumbing down" my language. Besides, I seldom hang out in workingmen's bars anymore, and, trust me, one hears things there that one would rather not. I used to be able to hold my own in the dives, but people change, and so, I'm sure, have I.

What's in a name?

What do you call the people who live in Michigan? Without sufficient research, I referred to them as "Michiganders" and caught holy hell for it. The term sounded perfectly plausible to me, especially since I had once lived there myself and had adopted that usage. But several denizens of the state, including W.G. of Troy, took me to task. Whether it's engraved in law or otherwise, I have no idea, but the proper appellation is "Michiganians," according to W.G. However, D.G. of Akron, Ohio, disagrees and says that "Michigander" is proper for a guy from that state, and a gal from there (his words, not mine) is a "Michigoose." I think I'll stay out of the way from here on. If you need to know how "Michiganian" is pronounced, you'll have to ask one of them because I do not know, although I expect to, as soon, that is, as one of them reads about it here.

15

Great sport

Have punsters gotten too much of a hold on sports headlines? I think so, and I am not alone. J.H. of Minneapolis, Minn., agrees:

> On the front page of the sports section of the Minneapolis *Star Tribune*: "Cleveland **slews** Seattle" – referring to the former's winning the 1995 American League (baseball) pennant. Using the name of a famous racehorse, Seattle Slew, to "coin" a word is unsportspage-like conduct.

That it is. The correct, albeit somewhat colloquial, word would have been "slays," but then someone's fun would have been spoiled, I know. On a remotely related note, B.R. of Edina, Minn., got a mail invitation to plan group outings to Canterbury Downs, our local horse track. Across the top it said, "AND **THEIR** OFF!" I can assure you that *they're* business is going better than *there* spelling.

Same newspaper, but a few years back: Sportswriter Jon Roe once declared, "On a national average, about 9 percent of every 100 people play golf." You figure it out. I can't. Aah, wait! I just did!

Another *Music Stand* catalog made its way through the mails, carry-ing excitement and joy to thousands, no doubt, perhaps including J.B. of Charlottesville, Va. The catalog was intended to increase sales, among other no doubt highly desired items, of taped telephone-answering-machine messages by declaring, "**Their** wonderful!" I was tempted to order them, if only to hear Willie Nelson sing "On the Phone Again."

Eighty-eight-point (more than an inch high) type was way too big for such a major gaffe on the front page of that much-maligned *Star Tribune* sports section. Announcing that the L.A. Lakers had won the National Basketball Association championship in June 2000, the headline read: "**Their No. 1**." Just for the record, it wasn't their first championship, but the headline was intended as a play on words – "They're number one." Editors caught a lot of heat for it, and explained later in print that it was supposed to be a pun, but admitted that it caught the ire of more readers than they had anticipated. We can never know for sure if that was the case, having no way to prove it, but it could also have been a simple spelling error. Anyway, I've been having fun with it ever since, mostly in speaking to groups. I hold that page up without saying anything and invariably the audience reacts slowly at first, then bubbles into a roar of laughter. Thanks, guys, for the humor. It's made me a hit on the rubber-chicken circuit.

Before high school football started again in the fall of 2000 the *Star Tribune*, in its usual front-page hoopla, rendered the following observation in a subheadline: "The stretching, sweating and speculating **has** begun." They has? It's news to me. (The word is *have* and yes, I am aware of the missing serial comma.)

Credit where credit is due – except: The *Star Tribune* is pretty good about printing corrections, and even retractions when the errors are bad enough, but there is one thing puzzling me: The paper has a sports columnist, Sid Hartman, who has been on the job for many years. What baffles me is the following correction: "A Sid Hartman column on Page C3 Sunday incorrectly reported the terms of a free-agent contract …" Since when is the column to blame for the error? Ahh, I see! By putting the blame on the column there is no *person* to take the rap. Did Sid make the error? Or was it a copyeditor, or someone who sneaked in during the night and loused it up? Let's be clear here. A *column* cannot make an error of any kind. Only people make errors. In this case, however, I guess we'll never know who.

And how's this for a coincidence? On the very day right after I wrote the preceding paragraph, a correction appeared and actually named columnist Sid Hartman as the perpetrator of the error. Now, that's spooky. I think it's also a first.

Check the speller

A.S. of Federal Way, Wash., reads an out-of-town newspaper:

> In the Arapahoe, Neb., *Public Mirror* was a display ad for REALTORS® Dawson and Associates: "This home is **emaculate** – one that you can move **in to** with no work needed."

Those should be "immaculate" and "into." If they would spell better, they might sell better, no? The same correspondent found another odd one closer to home:

> Headline in the Kent, Wash., *Valley Daily News*: "Pilots may have **mistook** Iraqi radar ..."

I had to look that one up, but sure enough, it's wrong. *Mistake, mistook, (have) mistaken* are the present, past, and past participle tenses, so "may have mistaken" would have been the correct form, although "Pilots mistook Iraqi radar ..." would have worked also. What the pilots may have mistaken the radar for was not included in the report.

Phew!

The Associated Press, a very large news service that provides stories for local newspapers and broadcast media, sometimes leaves the names of their individual writers on the items they send out, and sometimes not. I have long wished that the AP would consistently give us those names so that we would know whom to blame for their goofy errors. E.H. of Jacksonville, Fla., found a big one in a North Carolina paper:

> An AP story in the *Winston-Salem Journal* was all about a 2,200-ton load of garbage on 30 flat-bed rail cars whose owners traveled 3,000 miles in search of a suitable landfill and wound up on Staten Island, about 30 miles from where they had started. The [unnamed] reporter pointed out that "it didn't smell, and there **weren't no** flies to be seen." ["were no" or "weren't any"]

Since it was an AP story, it had to have gone past several editors before showing up in print, or at least it should have, but, unfortunately, we'll never know. Also, it says that the owners traveled all that way, but it doesn't mention whether the rail cars went with them. (Note that errors can occur in translation from the AP wire to the local outlet, but more often a story is run without editing, except perhaps when it might be cut – sometimes skillfully and sometimes not – for space considerations.

I was once asked if both national and local magazines qualified for SOTS. Yes, they do. Local ones, naturally, have smaller audiences, but they are nevertheless for sale on newsstands, and that is the main criterion. K.W.-D. of Kenosha, Wis., found this qualifier:

> In an obviously expensive full-page, full-color ad in the *Milwaukee* magazine, for Warehouse Shoes, a store or stores dealing in Nikes: "So **your** lookin' to get off the **beatin'** path …" Someone is earning a good living at this, but with no one looking on, apparently.

So it would seem. That probably also goes for what I received from V.R. of Tucson, Ariz.:

> "All major credit cards **excepted**" at Mary's, a New York City Italian restaurant, according to an ad in the TWA in-flight magazine. Does that mean cash or checks only?

Podium?

It's time we had a little talk about standing and leaning and pounding. L.W. of South Gate, Calif., starts the conversation:

> I wrote to *TV Guide*'s Lisa Stein, chastising her for having General H. Norman Schwarzkopf leaning on a **podium**. A lectern may be leaned upon, but a podium is for standing upon.

Frequently heard at airports: "Will Mr. Homer Simpson please come to the podium? We have a seat available." Language lesson: Podium is Greek in origin and is derived from *pod*, meaning "foot." Think podiatry, the medical treatment of feet, or tripod, meaning 3-footed. Consider where the winners receive their medals at the Olympics: standing on a podium. Consider where a symphony conductor stands: on a podium. It's a raised platform on which a speaker may stand, too. A lectern, as members of Toastmasters and others know, is the item of furniture for holding a speaker's notes. One cannot "lean on the podium" any more than one can "mount the lectern," at least with any decorum. Nor is "pounding the podium" a practical means for speakers to emphasize their messages. We appear to need a Society to Preserve Distinctions.

Some time ago, the lecterns on quiz shows such as *Jeopardy!* were called podiums (podia?), but that has not been the case in recent years, so far as I know, there being few quiz or game shows left. It persists, however, on dramas and sitcoms. On an episode of NBC's *The West Wing*, Allison Janney's character chastised Richard Schiff's character for "leaning on the podium" during a White House press conference. And as is almost universal at airports, the clerks stand behind counters, which may also be called desks, but not podiums. But let me give you one small but important tip: If you want a lectern in a hotel meeting room, ask the staff people for a podium; it'll save you no end of discussion. There's a time to educate and a time to "go with the flow," as is often said.

Huh?

Not strictly within our purview, but I think good for a laugh, is this sent in by M.T. of Brooklyn, N.Y.:

> Throwaway shoppers and publications such as the *Flea Market News* are not known for great grammar. Case in point: In answer to a question, columnist Mrs. Fleabody replies, "To all of you who want to could yourself in clothes before you buy, but don't want to try on, we have a surprise for you."

Oddly enough, I think I know what she's talking about.

Are coupons among our selected targets? Sure, why not? Especially when one is as bad as this one found by C.F. of Chester, Pa.:

> On a Wisk detergent rebate coupon, "receive" is misspelled once ["recieve"], "receipt" three times ["reciept"]. A nonexistent four-digit ZIP code [5553] is created, and a totally improper abbreviation for "fluid ounce" [FZ.] is invoked."

C.F. also says he sent them a "rather tart letter pointing out their string of errors," but I think he should have waited until he got his rebate – if he ever did, that is.

Bordering on a typo, this item comes to us from F.W. of Palmdale, Calif.:

> In the *Los Angeles Times*, unsigned: "A debate has been raging about the **effects** versus the benefits of alcohol when **drinken**

moderately." I guess that when you don't know what word to use, make one up.

Drink, drank, drunk are the forms, but more and more publications are reluctant to say "drunk" in any form because they fear it may imply "being intoxicated." Whatever happened to journalistic courage? It could be a typo, since the *i* and the *u* are adjacent on the keyboard, but I doubt it. Also, the odd use of "effects" puzzles me. If "adverse effects" was what was intended, why not say so? Tight deadline? Boss on vacation? Copyeditor sick? Still ...

My friend L.W. of Newbury Park, Calif., caught this one:

> On the front page of the *News Chronicle* (with no author iden-
> tified), an article included: "Several times during his speech ...
> Barrett was left speaking to only a handful of people when the
> crowd rushed away to watch **squirmishes** between demonstra-
> tors and police."

When the skirmishers are squeamish, you have squirmishes. What the heck's so hard about that? L.W. also reads another paper:

> In the *Daily News* (same area), the article reported that "Every-
> body thought I was such a **shoe-in** for college, she said."
> ["shoo-in"]

Several things come to mind, but ... let's not dwell on any of them. Instead, let's turn our attention to another of those wonderful headline hi-jinks from S.K. of Yardley, Pa.:

> The *Courier Times* of Bucks County, Pa., ran a four-column
> headline reading: "Teens **tow** line when 'they're' watching"
> (referring to authority figures). A typo?

Hard to tell. The *w* is right next to the *e* on the keyboard, so it's possible. But one would hope that a sharp-eyed copyeditor would have fixed it. It's marginal, but I'm leaving it in because it conjures a really weird image.

Those darn commas

Read this next one carefully; it comes from P.B. of Cornell, Wis., and it's a bit confusing:

> Here's an ad clipped from the *St. Paul Pioneer Press*, placed by an organization called Women's Healthcare, in which volunteers are invited to participate in a "research study designed to address improvement in the quality of life and osteoporosis during menopause." Being female, I certainly hope they can improve the quality of osteoporosis.

Don't ever let anyone tell you a comma can't make a difference. Add one after "life" and the entire meaning becomes clear. In exactly the same vein is one from M.J. of Winter Park, Fla.:

> Reprinted from the Religious News Service was an article in the *Orlando Sentinel* that discussed lawsuits, including "cases involving Jews who object to autopsies, Muslim prisoners seeking to avoid being served pork and Amish buggy drivers."

Again, put the comma after "pork" and the sky is blue once more. Newspapers, and I've yet to see one that doesn't, are determined (or so it seems) to save ink and space by eliminating the serial comma, and with total consistency, which leads to the dumb things you just read. Books from the better publishing houses, along with several national magazines, use the comma before "and," so that there is never any question about separation of items in a series, or about continuity of thought. The general public, of course, never knows what to think; some have learned to omit the last comma, and others never write without it. My motto is, when in doubt, do it. Hey, newspaper types, would it kill you?

Along with the serial comma, another comma is fast disappearing – the one that is needed in figures greater than 999, such as 1,000. Many ads for automobiles, for example, lack that comma, while others include it, but most advertisers use it for $10,000 or more. Just for fun, take a look at the car section of your Sunday paper and see which way the wind blows. I'll bet that the comma loses more often than it wins.

Also watching the supply of commas dwindle was C.W. of Indianapolis, Ind.:

> I could not believe what I saw in the *Indianapolis Star*, and I'm enclosing a photocopy of the write-up about an auction, which included this paragraph: "All the belongings of Mrs. Clara O'Connell, Mrs. Jackson's mother, will also go on the block. Mrs. O'Connell's home ... has been boarded up since her death eight years ago on Mrs. Jackson's orders."

One little itty bitty comma after "ago" would have deprived me of this item in this book. I try to imagine how it would have affected me had I run across in myself. I'm pretty sure I would have grunted "Huh?" at the very least.

Bouquets after brickbats

SOTS has never pretended to be even-handed, but on occasion I am inclined toward parity. In all fairness, I have to say that many newspapers handle the English language, in specific instances, with common sense. For example, where so many publications refer to "email," the better ones use the hyphen in "e-mail." My own local paper, the Minneapolis *Star Tribune*, uses it, and that pleases me. There are others, of course, but I haven't seen them all yet, so perhaps later I'll add to the list. Some will say that either use is correct, but I'm not yet ready to concede. Maybe someday.

Oh, the *Post*

Despite any shortcomings it might have, *The Washington Post* really is one of the better ones, but it too is subject to an occasional faux pas. K.D. of Bethesda, Md., opened the following can of worms:

> Reading the golden words of no less a journalistic luminary than Robert D. Novak, I found him saying, "The unconventional wisdom is that the bell has tolled for the [Liberal Democratic Party] and that a **jury-built** coalition between the party's defectors and Socialists will take office, however temporarily." I used to wonder about "jerry-built" too, but now I am even more confused.

Could Novak have fallen victim to a creative copyeditor? There's no telling, but for the record, the two terms "jury-rigged" and "jerry-built" are both correct and are quite similar in meaning. The first has more of a temporary connotation than the second, but both imply haphazard or sloppy construction. "**Jury-built**," though, is not in any of my seven dictionaries, and I had never heard of it either.

In that same paper, A.C. of Rockville, Md., read a story about a shortage of sour mash whiskey that was causing great concern because distilleries were having a hard time keeping up with demand. As described by James Branscome – "Special to *The Washington Post*" – we're told that "It appears Jack Daniel's has fallen victim to the same successful advertising campaign that has made squeezing Charmin' and having Big Mac attacks national **past times**." Charmin (pronounced SHAR-min) is not a contraction, thus no apostrophe is needed, and the term or word is "pastimes."

The sacred book

"Look, it's right here in the dictionary!" Yes, well, that's fine, but dictionaries are not infallible, as R.S. of El Cerrito, Calif., discovered in this corker:

> In *The American Heritage Dictionary of the English Language*, Third Edition, 1992, the definition of "mayday" (the international distress signal) includes two variations of its French word origin, and offers the additional comment: "*Mayday*, in fact, has nothing to do with the first of May. Instead, it is a spelling that represents the pronunciation of French *m'aidez*, 'help me,' or the latter part of the phrase *venez m'aider*, 'come help me,' either of which **are** quite appropriate at such a critical juncture."
> I wonder how many bleary eyes passed over that one.

My, my. Caught with their tense down, as it were. "Either" is singular, so "are" should be "is."

The Random House dictionary I referred to earlier also booted a big one: Under "league" was this definition: "**3.** an association of individuals having a common goal: [for example] *The League of Women Voters held **their*** *meeting last week.*" In England that would be correct, but in the U.S. we use "its" because the subject, "League," is singular. The Brits, on the other hand, would say, "The jury **have** reached a verdict," or "The staff **have** all received pay increases." (My bold-facing here is not meant to indicate error, but only to highlight the difference.)

P.M. of Union City, N.J., adds that while ad-libs are generally off limits to SOTS, it won't hurt to point out the all-too-common blurts by sportscasters who like to say things such as "Yale has the ball on **their** 20-yard line." Oddly, however, here's a case where common usage has such a strong hold on our language that "Yale has the ball on its 20-yard line" would sound funny, at least to some. I'm afraid that we'll have to leave it up to the play-by-play people, willingly or not.

You and who else?

I really do like pinning the tail on specific individuals, but sometimes the error goes by so quickly that it's almost impossible to lay proper blame. Exemplifying this perfectly is this godawful disaster sent in by F.R. of Fountain Valley, Calif.:

> I listened dumbstruck as an evening TV newscaster blathered, "Me and Tom will be back with more news at eleven, so please join Tom and I then."

I cannot bring myself to boldface those that are so blatantly obvious, but not so with this one from J.L. of Rolla, Mo.:

> The TV program *Prime Time Live*, during an interview with Sarah Ferguson, displayed across the lower part of the screen: "The **Dutchess** of York." The duchess didn't appear to notice. Also, during the interview, the duchess said, "That's between Andrew and **I**," thus demonstrating that, despite her royal connections, she doesn't speak the queen's English.

It's unlikely she even saw the graphic, but by then the damage was done.

16

Go get 'em

Really serious SOTS-folk do more than write to me; they also admonish the offenders. Here's what E.C. of Cornwall, Pa., did:

> I notified *The Daily News* of Lebanon [Pa.], at some length, of my astonishment at the quoting by staff writer Gene Sholly of a Civil War reenactment participant, as follows: "The typical day for a Union soldier began with **revelry** at 5:00 A.M. The guys who couldn't make **revelry** would go on sick call." I should certainly think so! Even the guys who *could* still make revelry at that hour were probably well qualified for sick call.

Speculating about how that might have happened would be fruitless, because there are so many possibilities. But if the newspaper people knew it – "Well, that's what the guy said" – they could have done the quoted one a favor and changed it to "reveille." Or it could be that they were feeling frisky that day and left it on purpose. We'll never know.

Department of Redundancy

D.W. of Reseda, Calif., was just one of many to report those increasingly common goofs about abbreviations, such as HIV **virus**, SAT **test**, CDW **waiver**, ATM **machine**, and PIN **number**. In each case, the last letter of the abbreviation stands for the word that follows it, and sharp folks know it.

Kara McGuire, a finance columnist for the *Star Tribune*, pointedly advised readers not to "write their PIN **numbers** on the back of their ATM cards." She also said that "PIN **numbers** should never be kept in your wallet." Good advice, to be sure, but if she felt that most people understood what PIN stands for, she should have used only the acronym. ("Oh, but that's what everybody says!" Well, then, everybody is wrong, and boy, will I catch heat on this one!)

More walking fingers

Somewhere back there I mentioned the Yellow Pages. Before flying to San Francisco in 1998, I went to the public library and found the S.F. phone book and looked up car rentals so that I could call and reserve one. In addition to what I was looking for, I found that American Rent-A-Car made the claim that "We Make Renting Much **More** Easier!" Since they had an 800 number, I gave them a shot at it, and mentioned the ad to the reservation clerk. "Thank you for bringing that to our attention," was the stock phrase in the training manual, I guess. Whether it went any further up the line, let alone to company executives, I sincerely doubt. Besides, I can't be the only one to point it out.

Of similar stripe is this from W.W. of Dahlgren, Va.:

> A Time-Life Records ad for a Chopin [album] says, "He had already produced a body of masterworks that would assure his **immortality for all time**." This, of course, is not to be confused with immortality for only the next few years.

Eat, drink, and be married

Once more we hear from R.F. of Kenosha, Wis.:

> Dewars Scotch whiskey distillers runs ads everywhere, usually in magazines. One boo-boo is so common I'm surprised it hasn't appeared in your column before. It says, "There should be nothing artificial about what you drink or **who** you marry." "Whom" would be better, no?

Yes, and I just know I'll get letters about "whom" being the snooty version of "who," but what really bothers me is the idea of marrying someone artificial. How would one do that?

There's something else about that ad that isn't quite right, and I now know what it is, thanks to notes from T.C. of Philadelphia, Pa., and M.M. of Germantown, Md. By tradition, most distilled-grain potables known as whiskies are spelled *whiskey*, as in the foregoing, but Scotch and Canadian varieties are spelled without the *e*, giving us the word *whisky*. If indeed the Dewars ad had it spelled correctly, without the *e*, I apologize, but I cannot locate the item originally received from R.F. (There's no way in which to keep this stuff in any kind of order.) Anyway, now everyone reading this knows the difference. You're welcome.

And if you thought that the preceding *who/whom* thing was confusing, it's no more puzzling than this found by C.P. of Franklin, N.C.:

> In a magazine ad for the Chevy Venture minivan is the legend "It can open a door by itself. Sing two songs at once. Sit up and **lay** down. Imagine that. A minivan that can do more tricks than your dog." To make matters worse, most people I showed it to didn't see anything wrong with it. I wonder if proofreaders exist anymore. If so, many of them don't know good grammar, probably because their teachers didn't either.

The "lay" ("lie") is bad enough, but the string of incomplete sentences in such profusion is a bit too much. But that's advertising, I guess. Tacky advertising. (See? I can make short ones, too.)

A newspaper ad clipped by A.S. of Elmwood Park, N.J., for a condominium in New York City called the Courant began its pitch with: "You'll **languish** in our bathrooms." Are these bathrooms the kind that are "to die for"? At the very least, we can expect to weaken and lose the desire to live; we might as well be in prison rather than risking drowning in the tub. The only word I can think of that would have saved that ad is "luxuriate," but it's too late now. Famous last words: "I don't need any dictionary!"

Oh, shoot!

Headlines provide so much grist for the SOTS mill. E.B. of Pompano Beach, Fla., sent this:

> Big and bold, the headline reads: "Man shoots neighbor with machete."

"Editor stabs headline writer with gaff(e)" would be even more pleasing. In case you're wondering, yes, Jay Leno would have used this, but he doesn't have it and I do. Also, I would have preferred to have at least the name of the paper, but it was just too good to leave out. Incidentally, several books have been written about goofy headlines, but I have yet to steal any material from them. I get too much good stuff straight from the sources without hijacking someone else's work.

From R.P. of North Myrtle Beach, S.C.:

> The *Sun News* was decidedly duty-derelict when it failed to edit an AP story by Neelesh Misra. Datelined NEW DELHI, India, the story began with: "Police were ordered to shoot riot-ers on **site** ..." during a national election protest.

"Hold your fire, fellows, they're off-site. Wait'll they come back."

Similarly, L.J. of Dallas, Texas, caught *The Dallas Morning News* put-ting the blame on the blameless: "Census increases number of disabled youths." Yes, we know what was meant, but there were many better ways to say it. No need to blame the census.

Personal

It was always difficult, but once in a while I had to set contributions from others aside and dig into my own private file. Here is a small but meaty sampling:

In an article in *TV Guide* by Ilene Rudolph about the Miss America Pageant, co-host Kathie Lee Gifford was described as being "thrown out of a beauty contest in her youth for **flaunting** the rules ..." Maybe that's what happens when you are caught "flouting" your attributes, if that were possible. Look 'em up.

Crossword puzzles in *TV Guide* are usually pretty easy, but at least one clue-writer was not a fan of Chinese food. Whether it was across or down I don't recall, but the clue was: "Egg ___ **Young**." None of that *old* egg foo for me, thank you. Not to be outdone, Citibank in 2005 was run-ning a full-page ad nationwide that said, "I threw out my bill with the egg foo **young**." Although a bit cryptic, the idea there was that losing your credit card from Citibank was no big deal, and there were no late fees as long as you kept running up your balance. Anyway, in case there is anyone alive who doesn't know, the Chinese viand is "egg foo *yung*." At least the Chinese restaurants have it right.

Time magazine was really not at fault (its advertising people usually have to accept what's given them) for printing an ad for Iberia Airlines that included the invitation to "Relax in style and made-to-measure comfort **wiling** away the time watching films, sports ..." Frankly, I think it was those ad agency minions spending too much time at the water cooler and leaving the airline in the hands of a rookie. I've worked for three ad agencies myself and have "whiled" a while at the tap now and again. Note too that those full-page ads in the top publications do not come cheaply.

There's more?

As I discussed earlier, the distinction between singular and plural has been buried in the mud of common usage. "There's" those and "there's" these, and "there's" lots, etc. I usually give sports types a little breathing room, but a *Star Tribune* story about the National Football League was headlined "**Here's** 50 ways to learn about the league," and began its first paragraph with "Here are the 50 things we've learned in the first 50 days [of the season]." Staff writer Curt Brown did OK with "Here are," but the headline writer was more than a yard short of a touchdown.

On a paper place mat at Denny's restaurants: "If there are 7 deadly sins, then **here's** 8, 9 & 10. Denny's Truly Delectable Desserts." They spent some money on it, too, with beautiful color photos of "Chills 'n' Thrills," "Peanut Butter Binge," and "Chocolate Challenge." What's surprising is that the makers didn't say, "If there *is* (or "there's") 7 deadly sins ..." Let us be grateful for small favors.

Speaking of small favors, Denny's sent us a mailer with three discount coupons on it, along with letting us know that "**Kid's** eat Free – Every night through March 10th." "Kid's," of course, just love those "burger's" and "frie's," don't they? Shape up, Denny's. You, too, White Castle.

Not doing us any favor at all is another *Star Tribune* headline, this time on the front page of the Arts and Entertainment section. Over photos and articles concerning the introduction of a couple of new stage plays, it read: "**HERE'S TWO**, FOR OPENERS." There was plenty of room for "Here are two ..." and how one headline writer was able to bamboozle his or her editors and layout people into allowing such an atrocity instigates the shaking of my weary old head. Or maybe not. Let's be fair – dead-lines, you know. No time. Just get it done and out. Funny – I don't recall anything like that from my own newspapering days.

Oh, no, not again

I'll let H.H. of Palm Coast, Fla., slip in here with another angle on singu-lar vs. plural:

> A huge headline on the front of *USA Weekend*, a Sunday
> magazine section distributed to newspapers nationwide, read:
> "**WHO'S** HEALTHIER: Men or Women?" The same was
> repeated above the article inside, which left me in doubt whether
> MEN IS HEALTHIER or WOMEN IS. I certainly learned
> that some editors have no idea how to conjugate the verb "to be."

Well, as it turns out, neither men nor women "is" healthier. "Who are" or "Who're" would have been better, of course. The plural object requires a plural subject, at any rate.

One of … ?

Then there's that all-too-common "one of those …" messes. A TV ad for Ambien, a sleep aid, says, "If you're one of the millions of Americans **who's** searching for a way to get back into the rhythm of life …" Millions of Americans "is not" searching, etc. Make that "who are," or "who're," same as before. There are millions of Americans. You are only one of them. A self-defensive copywriter may argue that the subject is "one who is searching," but that would then exclude the "millions of Americans" from consideration in the sentence, so why mention them in the first place?

A variation on the theme comes by way of L.S. of Coon Rapids, Minn., one of those people who *are* always alert for grammar goofs:

> Rosalinda Wagner, a staff writer for the San Gabriel Valley
> [Calif.] Daily *Tribune*, writing about memory, led off with this
> absolutely dismaying sentence: "If you're **one** of those people
> who **ties** a string around your finger in an effort to remember
> something …"

There went an article that crashed and burned before it even got off the ground, and L.S. puts everyone on notice that "if anyone ties a string around *my* finger and forgets why, so help me, I'll clobber him!" I'll volunteer to hold the miscreant while you do. Once again, "of those people" becomes an irrelevant insertion if the meaning is singular.

Dayton's department store once asked on TV, "Are you one of those people who **is** always running late?" If the question had been "Are you one who is always running late?" there would have been no problem, but inserting "of those people" invites the question "What people?" The answer has to be "people who *are* always running late." Pretty simple, eh? Even simpler would be: "Are you always running late?" I have several more of this kind of infraction, but I think those two make my point.

As you might imagine, however, I received argumentation on this subject, including a letter from a reader who identified herself as a former high school English teacher. She even went so far as to diagram a "one of those people ..." sentence, except that she used a specific definition of people, such as "He was one of those boy scouts who practices the golden rule." In that regard, she is almost correct. However, in the case of the unspecific "people," and even in this particular specific instance, some sort of qualification is needed, and this is why I'm not even using her initials (former students might remember her). If she had said, "He was one Boy Scout, among several, who practices the golden rule," there would be no question, but take away the comma-less inserted phrase and my original argument stands.

And much to his credit, Alex Trebek said to his *Jeopardy!* audience, "If you are one of those quiz show fans who really love it when the contestants do well on the program, then you'll have had a ball this week ..." Turn on the applause sign, please. He could have said it either way, but this was by far the better one.

Over easy?

Those sometimes shaded columns (usually short) running down the side of a newspaper page (frequently the front page) are called sidebars, and informative though they may be, they usually bear no writer's name. As a result, someone at my local daily now escapes SOTS shame for writing about a $100 fine for serving over-easy eggs: "As of January 1, it became illegal for restaurants in New Jersey to serve eggs with runny **yokes**. The intent of the law, according to the state health department, was to crack down on salmonella bacteria in eggs. But runny-yoke lovers are convinced that the state has its priorities scrambled." Pun aside, notice that I bold-faced only the first incorrect use, but not the second. I am not totally without mercy.

For a screwball reverse twist, and still in the *Star Tribune*, there was the syndicated Personal Health column by Jane E. Brody (who has been ordinarily very knowledgeable and thorough), on the subject of Parkinson's disease, with the following: "But with the help of medication and counseling and the support of a loving family and friends, she has shed the crippling **yolk** of depression …" Trust me, I have the evidence securely in my files.

17

Sometimes the mind wanders

Once a week, if the carrier is in a good mood, my copy of our local community paper, the *St. Louis Park Sun Sailor*, lands on my doorstep – or at least somewhere on my property, occasionally the bushes. There was no name of the person who wrote it, but the story about the search for a bank robber included: "According to the police report, the man handed the teller a **clerk** which said: 'Do not push the alarm. This is a robbery. Give me all your money.'" Yes, I too had to read it twice, but with no boldface to help me.

I mentioned earlier that my local *St. Louis Park Sun Sailor* is just one of 26 [or perhaps more, now] weeklies being circulated in the suburban areas surrounding the Twin Cities metropolitan area. J.M. of West St. Paul receives his local weekly paper as the *So. St. Paul/Inver Grove Heights, West St. Paul/Mendota Heights Sun-Current*, a long name but one covering a lot of territory. It seems that the South St. Paul City Council was asking residents to help determine a name for a new park on the Mississippi River by sending their suggestions to the Park and Recreation Advisory Commission. In writing the story, Blair Reynolds quoted a member of the commission, who said, "We want something that is fitting for that area. The **skies** the limit." Well now, let's not be too hasty here. I would bet that the commissioner said, "The sky's the limit," but where the kink in the keyboard came is anyone's guess. If the quotation had been on a recording, the typist *could* have mistaken the word, but after it had been set in type, *where were the copyeditors?* Who knows?

The publishing powerhouses, of course, are the juiciest meat for SOTS, and taking them to task is also great fun. Here's a dandy from H.F. of Mequon, Wis.:

> In the *Wall Street Journal*, over an article of peculiar interest to [your column], appeared the following headline: "**Some Times** Ad Agencies Mangle English Deliberately."

Et tu, WSJ? Gotcha! The term is "sometimes." The bigger they are, the easier the target. It's unfortunate, though, that it's the little rags that catch the most heat. One of my most prolific contributors has been B.R. of Forest, Miss., and her locally produced *Clarion-Ledger* is a lush "forest" of errors, some of which truly boggle the mind:

> The feature article was titled "Preventing Dog Bites," and one
> step toward a solution to the problem, recommended by the
> Insurance Information Institute, is to "Have your dog **spade** or
> neutered." Spell-checker? [do I need to say "spayed"?]

Spell-checker most likely, but unacceptable as an excuse. Here's another from that same paper:

> Staff writer Sherri Williams tells about a 3-year-old girl who
> "used to try to play songs on the family piano she had heard."
> How's that again?

"Songs she had heard, on the family piano" would have been much clearer. B.R. also reads *The Scott County Times*, another paper with insufficient editing:

> The City Council of nearby Morton approved a budget that
> needed some explaining: "Mayor [Charles] Steadman **eluded**
> to several reasons for the overages …"

One can only shake one's head. The word is "alluded," naturally. Most newspaper errors are spelling errors, and between the two papers read by B.R. there is a plethora of them, including **"reef"** for "wreath," **"quite"** for "quiet," **"know"** for "no," **"seems"** for "seams," etc.

Here's another spelling trick, this time in a catalog ad provided by G.L. of Salem, Ore.

> Placed by House of Wesley, Greenhouse Division, Bloom-
> ington, Ill., a few weeks before Easter, the ad reads, "Passion
> Flower – $1.50 ea. ASTOUNDING BLOOMS RECALL THE
> **CRUCIFICTION**." Someone was not too sure? ["crucifixion"]

Apparently not. What surprises me even more, though, is that my spell-checker says that the word is an acceptable one when it is bold-faced in lower-case 10-point capital letters, but not in 11-point regular text. I'm not sure what to make of that. Well, yes, I am sure. It's not a word, that's what I make of that, and it's to be found in none of my dictionaries. I will never completely trust the spell-checker, although it does catch some things I might otherwise miss. It's both a friend and an enemy.

Watch those shenanigans

C.T. of Bangor, Mich., found this one:

> I was checking a real estate insert in the Benton Harbor *Herald-Palladium* and saw an ad for a commercial building that was "PERFECT FOR VIDEO RENTAL: Or **connivance** store! ... Creative financing available."

I'd stay away from that place if I were you. They're plotting to overcharge you.

Your call

Look out, here come two sides of the same coin. Heads, it's S.K. of Chapel Hill, N.C.:

> In a TV listing in the *Dallas Morning News* about a series called "Millennium," the episode dealt with the hero's half-sister being "involved with drug dealers **pedaling** contaminated heroin."

And tails, it's S.M. of Huachuca City, Ariz.:

> The *Sierra Vista Herald/Bisbee Daily Review* had a headline declaring: "Bicycles no mere **peddling** machines."

Take your pick, folks. The latter paper mentioned is typical of small-town weeklies with rarely a copyeditor to be seen (I've worked on two of them, so I know). Those that have tape-recording telephone-opinion lines have strange things happen when the messages are typed up. Spell-checkers, of course, are of no help, because the wrong words are readily accepted so long as they are spelled right. *Gaul* is changed to *gall*, *set* turns into *sit*, *indigent* becomes *indigenous*, *slight* transforms into *sleight* (of hand), and there are countless others. All that aside, I am weary of blaming the machines and will henceforth speak only of poor editing, which is the primary reason for this book.

Sometimes those switched words have little meanings all their own, as in this that came in over the transom from L.B. of Lebanon, Pa.:

> I've been saving one for you from the *Montgomery Journal*, a Maryland weekly named for a county. It read: "**Dear** carcass removed from Rockville alley." What do you make of that?

Quite a lot, as a matter of fact. It had to be a "deer" carcass, of course, but it may also have been somebody's pet deserving of affection, poor thing, and *dearly departed* carcass would have signified something else altogether. *Dead* carcass would have been redundant, as we all know.

Mystical cymbalism?

Another in the substitution game is one found by P.P. of Norwalk, Conn.:

> In my local news rag, *The Hour*, captioning a photo of old wind-up toys, appeared words describing "an antique monkey with **symbols** [that clashed when the toy was wound up]."

By golly, I think I saw that very thing on *Antiques Roadshow*. (Did the boldface take the fun out of it?)

First what?

Taking an advertiser to task in his hometown *Herald News* is P.S. of Wolf Point, Mont.:

> A display ad for Mike's Bar announced the date for the estab-lishment's "**First Annual** Golf Tournament." Not possible.

Indubitably. Oh, sure, lots of events, including golf tournaments, have to start somewhere, but to call the initial one the first of what is expected to become an annual affair is illogical. An event cannot be called "annual" until at least the second one has taken place, because even when the "inaugural" one has been completed and another is being planned, no one can be absolutely certain that that second one, as well as any more beyond it, will transpire, regardless of any expectations for the future. (That's redundant, I know. Expectations can't have anything to do with the past or present, but neither can any other synonym, such as plans or hopes or wishes, etc. There's really no good way to say what I said, but I think I got my point across.)

At any rate, I must now confess that I was unaware of the "first annual" problem back in the late '60s when I organized the "**First Annual** Minnesota Mensa Golf Tournament." Oddly, no one pointed out my error, so the oh-so-common terminology may be headed for the Department of Lost Causes. (There never was a "second annual" tournament, so the only one we had wasn't even an "inaugural" one, technically speaking, because it really didn't inaugurate anything.) "First ever" would have worked, too.

But here's a fellow who should not have gotten caught with his chronology down. Stephen Wilbers, Ph.D., writes a column in the *Star Tribune* called Effective Writing. He is much more knowledgeable in the use of the English language than I am – actually more than almost anyone, because he teaches classes on the subject. His column is one I dare not miss, and his writings are flawless – almost. At the end of 1995 he decided to present his own awards for creativity and wit by those who write for a living. Headlining the column was: "Welcome to the **first annual** Wilbers awards."

I wrote to Dr. Wilbers, presented my credentials, and pointed out his error. Very promptly, he responded on a postcard: "Thanks for your letter about my column – and your vigilance in identifying sloppy use of the English language. Actually, I intended "first annual" to be humorous, but if my joke didn't work for you, it probably didn't work for others as well. That's why I like hearing from my readers. Yours, Stephen Wilbers." Having noted my credential as a fellow columnist, he later sent a note requesting copies of recent issues, which I gladly provided.

Sports, etc.

Looking ahead and slowly shaking my head from side to side, I move on to J.F. of Sun Prairie, Wis.:

Supposedly cheering for a local football coach, an unknown *Sun Prairie Star* sports writer included: "Defensive coordinator Tim Bass presented [coach] Hahn with a **plague** commemorating his 200th victory. But when Bass tried to talk his emotions got the best of him and his words became unclear, much like the stadium's faulty sound [system]." Geez, it must have been really contagious.

Came on really fast, too, didn't it? But down at the other end of the field we find Greg Gumbel (and I know I said I wouldn't touch ad-libs, but this is too good) announcing the AFC Football Championship for CBS Sports. When the Denver Broncos won (January 1999), Gumbel declared the victory, with "John Elway gaining all the **platitudes** here at Mile High Stadium." ("plaudits") Sorry, Greg, I had to use it.

Another fumble on the field was picked up by D.K. of New York, N.Y.:

> The [1976] television commercial that drives me right up the wall is one shown during the summer Olympics. It is for Brut (men's toiletries) and is done by Joe Namath [New York Jets quarterback]: "Well, the world's become a closer place, and Brut is part of it."

Perhaps what Joe really meant was that the earth, rather than the world, became a closer place every time he got sacked – and Brut kept him from offending the defensive tackles. Don't blame Joe, though, because he was only doing what the ad agency hotshots told him to do – in this case, deliver a badly constructed message. I suspect that what was actually meant was that the world of today is putting people closer to each other, and we should all be careful about how we smell, or some such. That's the best I can think of. Let's move on.

More sports?

Getting off scot-free, however, is the announcer (whose name I failed to record) and the person in charge of screen graphics (who was not identified at all), both of whom introduced the CEO of "Freeport-**McDermott**, Inc.," sponsor of the Freeport-McDermott Classic golf tournament. Alas, there was no such company as "Freeport-McDermott." The tournament was actually co-sponsored by Freeport-McMorran, Inc., and McDermott, Inc. File that one under Not Paying Attention.

Uh-oh, here comes another hit on the AP, but once again we don't know for sure whether the error was from the AP or the participating newspaper. Still, we have to follow the lead of H.K. of Pebble Beach, Calif., and report properly:

> In an article in the *Monterey County Herald* about Frank Lloyd Wright, AP writer Amy Sancetta referred to Edgar J. Kaufman, owner of Wright's Fallingwater house, as a "Pittsburgh department store **magnet**."

That should be "magnate," of course, and I still say that headlines and photo captions are rarely copyedited or proofread, except in truly first-class newspapers, and even then not always, especially as deadlines approach. I leave it to you to figure out which newspapers are "truly first-class."

L.H. of Chicago, Ill., returns just in time for the flip side of the foregoing:

> According to the Inc. column in the Sunday *Chicago Tribune*, the Chicago Zoning Board of Appeals has put up notices announcing a public hearing on a plan to build a public "**Magnate** Academic School" to replace Jones Commercial High School.

Grooming tycoons, are they? As Alex Trebek would say, "Now's the time for 'magnet.'"

Before we let the AP off the hook for a while, here's one more yank on their chain from C.A. of Brawley, Calif.:

> This one I pulled out of the *Imperial Valley Press*: "LOS ANGELES (AP) – Six LAPD officers have been relieved of duty with pay stemming from a Laughlin, Nev., trip where a police civilian employee allegedly was paid to **bear** her breasts for officers, a newspaper reported today."

No doubt they would have been willing to help with the load. Forgive me
– I'm just the reporter.

Brrr

Right in my neighborhood, J.M. of St. Louis Park, Minn., has been
keeping a *Star Tribune* headline taped inside her cupboard door and has
finally let it out for all of us to share. It reads: "**Down** airplane passengers reportedly survive blizzard." J.M. thinks it would be an advantage
for them. Would down jackets qualify as passengers? Even if wrapped
around their human counterparts? Makes you feel all warm and cozy,
doesn't it? ("downed") I think I need some fresh air about now. ... OK,
I'm back.

How good?

Credit R.S. of Smyrna, S.C., with a refined palate and an even more
refined eye. He enjoys his favorite cereal for breakfast, but has the edge
taken off by the following questionable legend on the box: *"What makes
our 7 Reasons™ multigrain cereal 'Too Good To Be True!'™?"* Now, there's
a phrase that's bugged me for years. So does that mean that it's so good
that it's false? Aside from that, how can they trademark a common saying, ridiculous though it might be? Another common saying, and a better
one, I might add, is the one that says, "If It sounds too good to be true,
best to stay away from it."

What adds to the interest is that R.S. removed the front of the cereal
box, wrote a message on the reverse, addressed it to me, added his return-
address sticker, and applied proper postage. I have never before or since
gotten a piece of mail on part of a cereal box. I'll bet it's a collectible I can
sell on eBay.

Sam?

I suspect that Sam Donaldson, the veteran ABC-TV reporter, originally
came from some part of the country where certain regionalisms in speech
originate. Donaldson has consistently referred to an animal doctor as a
vet-in-arian. Bob Brown on ABC's *20-20* has done much better, pronouncing every one of the six syllables in veteranarian.

In that regard, I always feel embarrassed for TV and radio news types who interview people who speak English better than do the interviewers. Reporter: "**Has** the media been unfair to you lately?" Subject: "Yes, they have, and I resent it." Sadly, it goes on day after day. "Media" is plural, "medium" is the singular form.

Hah! The estimable *Star Tribune* wavered. In an editorial, the phrase "the media have focused …" was expressed correctly, but a headline writer lost the ball entirely with "Media not only **reports** racial attitudes, **it aggravates** them." One point for, two points against. ("report" – "they aggravate")

And to top it all off, America Online, my Internet service provider at the moment, recently displayed on its Welcome page the opportunity for me to get the definitive answer to the question: "**Is** the Media Too Negative?" My own answer was, "Surely you jest," which then brought to mind the old journalism axiom about bad news, "If it bleeds, it leads." But now I'm off my own subject, and I apologize.

Need a word? Make one up!

Adding (?) to our language was an unknown radio reporter discussing a nominee for a Supreme Court appointment. The question asked was to the effect of: "Is this particular candidate **filibusterable**?" Ah, there's nothing like creativity, is there?

Time for *TIME*?

Then there's *TIME* magazine's "Special Edition: 2000 – the Year In Pictures." In the introductory article, writer Joel Stein asks and answers, "The Microsoft breakup? Not yet. Middle East peace? **Not hardly**." First-class journalism? Not by a long shot. "Not hardly" is a double negative.

Also reading *TIME* was R.D. of San Diego, Calif., who sent along a copy of the People page, edited by Lev Grossman. The headline over a story about Michael Jackson read: "Didn't He **Use** to Be A Musician?" Who wrote the headline is unknown, but whoever it was should have lower-cased the capital *A* and put a *d* where it belongs as the end of "used."

Castigating another of those anonymous photo-caption and headline writers is G.P. of Muscatine, Iowa:

> A caption writer for the *Muscatine Journal* wrote about dinosaurs in an exhibit getting a new paint job "to more accurately reflect what some scientists believe to be brighter coloration like their modern **ancestors**, birds. *AP Laserphoto*" This made me wonder how many people in the U.S. have ancient descendants who came to America on the *Mayflower*.

Which brings us once more to our old friend B.R. of Forest, Miss., and an even bigger load of nonsense from the *Clarion-Ledger*:

> Staff writer Jack Bertram did a nice article about the collecting of "… 'oral histories' from **ancestors** of slaves … and has already interviewed two such **ancestors** … [and that] **ancestors** of slaves buried at Mount Locust are still living in the vicinity." Bertram also had a different article about **ancestors** of a Civil War veteran who were about to have a family reunion.

The previously mentioned *Star Tribune* Backfence columnist, James Lileks, did a piece on preserving family histories and offered several suggestions as to how it could be done. His last one caught my attention: "Hire someone to follow you around and observe everything you and your family do. Have this person cryogenically frozen so he or she can be defrosted in a century and describe events to your **ancestors**." So help me, that's what he wrote. I suppose I could have called him – we've talked before – but I just never got around to it. Anyway, he might have tried to talk me out of exposing his foible, and there was no way I could let it go by. (My sources tell me that he is, however, a kind and gentle person. Besides, he's a fellow match-cover collector, so this is probably the last poke I'll take at him. Fair and square, James?)

Of passing interest is that "descendant" was at one time the only preferred spelling, but so many writers misspelled it "descendent" (and now the spell-checker goes both ways) that the latter eventually became an acceptable alternative. *Webster's Second International* appends the note: "now rare." With the publication of *Webster's Third*, the note fell off and has not been seen since.

That much, eh?

It can be hard to pin blame on many of our linguistic miscreants, none more so than whoever is designing the packaging of various consumer products. Often it is a specialized design studio, sometimes called an industrial design company. Also, there is sometimes a separate department in an ad agency devoted to package design, depending on how big the agency is. We have no one to grab by the neck, but coupon-clipper M.L. of Na'alehu, Hawai'i, sent me some hard evidence:

Land O' Frost luncheon meats offers ".55¢ OFF" on any variety.

Fifty-five one-hundredths of a cent? That's not a heckuva lot – hardly worth the bother. Nor can we be sure about the wonderful offer from Zale's Jewelers in their TV spot that both E.W. of Boca Raton, Fla., and I saw. The hype was for a sale where we could get "Up to 50 percent off, **or more!**" I am occasionally compelled to yell back at the screen, "How much more?" It does no good. As a former advertising copywriter, I am proud to say that never once did I use such a phrase. If a client should want it, I was always able to talk that client out of it simply by asking that same question: "How much more?" Worked every time.

Franklin Hobbs was an extremely popular radio personality for many years here in the Twin Cities. He was very picky about delivering commercials, especially those he did "live," but one got by him when he was on KLBB-AM. In 1991 the copy for a company called Financial Independence of Minnesota had him saying, "Earn **up to and even more** than 9 percent." I seriously doubt that he ad-libbed it.

The *National Reporter* of Bixby, Okla., ran some contests back in 1979 and came up with a plan to save entrants some postage costs, apparently by combining entries to different contests in the same envelope. S.M. of East Orleans, Mass., sent in the clipping:

Under the headline "Contest Entry Service cuts postage bill **by almost half**," the text included: "This means your entries will arrive at the contest sponsor's office exactly the same way as if you would have mailed each one at 15¢. However, instead of paying **15¢** each, you pay just **.08¢** for each entry." Isn't that eight hundredths of a cent? [Yes, it is.]

18

Arf!

This is not pleasant for me, but I have to keep myself honest. The following paragraph is extracted in toto from my column in the February 2001 issue of the *Mensa Bulletin*:

> The *Suislaw News* is read by A.G. of Florence, Ore., who sent along an article by writer John Fiedler. Checking conditions in the Suislaw River, he noted a "die-off of algae called **fido-plankton** in the water." Unless it has changed, it's phytoplankton, the plant element of plankton. Some people just hate to look things up.

Before you folks in Oregon get all lathered up, I heard from plenty of you when that item was published. Flying in the face of what I had said about looking things up, I failed to check the spelling of that river, which is correctly "Siuslaw," and is pronounced sigh-YOU-slaw. I own one of the largest geographical dictionaries, the Merriam-Webster one, and I absolutely dropped the ball. But I still think that "fido-plankton" is funny. Sit. Stay. Fetch.

Typographical errors, also known as finger-fumbles, are not a significant SOTS concern, as we all know. On occasion, however, some errors come awfully close to being typos, but are usually caused by temporary short-circuits in someone's brain. Case in point: another goodie from J.B. of Charlottesville, Va.:

> An Associated Press write-up in the *Richmond Times-Dispatch* reported on Al Gore claiming that his health-care proposals were "the best way to **reign** in HMOs ..." ["rein"]

Headline in the Business Section of the *Star Tribune*: "More calling for **reigning** in credit bureaus." (same)

Hee-yah!

B.S. of State College, Pa., gives our imagination a strenuous workout:

> Our city's *Centre Daily Times* includes Paula Dill's Good Morning column. She recently mentioned a fellow named "Michael Kaye, who is now a master and instructor of the Penn State **Marshal Arts** Group at The Athletic Club North." ["martial"]

Comma to me, my melancholy baby …

A comma missing, a comma in the wrong place, or a comma used instead of a correct punctuation mark (usually a semicolon) is called a comma fault. B.R. of Roseville, Minn., tests our comma skills:

> The neighborhood weekly *Focus News* announced a Sunday morning program at a local church "discussing the differences between men and women and why we often have a difficult time understanding one another at 9:45 A.M."

The comma goes after "another," of course. One more like that is my own discovery in the otherwise estimable *Star Tribune*: On the front page of the feature section – once named Variety, later called Source – was (and currently is as I write) a weekly column edited by John Ewoldt called Dollars & Cents, in which he tells readers how to save money in various ways, this time on a weekend at the Marriott Hotel. He says, "The executive king romance package ($189 per night) includes champagne, chocolate, breakfast and valet parking in a large room with a whirlpool tub." Can't you see it? I can. He did say it was a large room, didn't he?

And here's one so goofy I almost laughed out loud (in fact, I'm sure I *did* laugh out loud): In that same paper, television programs are listed in a section all by themselves, and it can't be an easy job to put them together, what with so much going on on the tube. The source of my hilarity was the title of a self-improvement program on public television: "There's a Spiritual Solution to Every Problem With Dr. Wayne Dyer." Now, I have no idea what kind of problem(s) there might be with the good Dr., but I certainly do wish him well. Oh, and if you put a comma after "Problem" in the blurb, it changes the whole picture and takes the fun out of it. Your choice.

A.D. of Milwaukee, Wis., found another just like the previous one:

> Dermatone Laboratories in Cleveland, Ohio, ran a slick maga-
> zine ad for Zsa Zsa Gabor's Beauty Cream Z-11 that contained
> this line: "A message to every woman who dreads lines and
> wrinkles from Zsa Zsa Gabor." Somebody should stop Zsa Zsa
> from going around giving people wrinkles.

Once again, the comma makes the difference. If it had appeared after
"wrinkles," there would have been no problem. Copywriters just have to
learn that readers do pay attention, quite often more than copywriters do.
Personally, I would have recast the sentence to read: "A message from Zsa
Zsa Gabor to every woman who dreads lines and wrinkles."

Big or awful?

Here's one that a lot of pros have trouble with, furnished for our enlightenment by T.M. of North Wales, Pa.:

> Regarding a televised Barbra Steisand concert, *TV Guide*'s
> article was accompanied by a sidebar that included: "Execu-
> tive producer Martin Erlichman explains the **enormity** of the
> production."

Although some dictionaries waffle on this, the majority agree that the
definition of the word, which is actually a noun, is "horror, ghastliness,"
"wickedness." Not a very nice thing to say, even about his own show. But
there's more:

Staff writer Catherine Watson created a true oxymoron in her *Star Tribune* article – her swan song, actually – about her impressions of a special
event on the Mississippi River: "When the big white paddlewheelers of
the Grand Excursion rounded the final curve into St. Paul last month, the
heartwarming **enormity** of that celebration brought tears to my eyes."

And again: Judy Foreman of the *Boston Globe* is usually very knowledgeable in her writings about health and medicine, but joined the preceding
offenders with this in an article about colds: "You would think that with
61 million cases of the common cold each year in this country alone, the

sheer **enormity** of the market would goad drug companies into an all-out attack on cold viruses."

All right, just one more and I promise not to bring it up any more. Surely everyone knows by now of the huge Mall of America in Bloomington, Minn., a southern suburb of the Twin Cities. The giant shopping center, largest in the U.S., really is something to see, but it's much too big as far as I'm concerned. OK, yes, I have gone there on specific errands, but only once did I take the whole thing in and walk down every corridor. As of today, in August 2005 – and I say that in view of the current proposals to make it even larger – there are four levels and the lower three are each approximately one mile around. On my initial tour I had to stop and rest part-way. So in that context, the *Star Tribune* early on published a good-sized article bearing the headline "Mall / Developers concerned that **enormity** might be intimidating." In all instances, the word needed was "enormousness." Yes, I know that some dictionaries allow both. I don't. Let us not lose valuable distinctions.

Hyphen or not?

V.T. and C.T. of McAllen, Texas, tsked at this one:

> Our local paper, *The Monitor*, headlined – in very large lettering – over an article on the front page of its feature section about dining out in Japan, "Tokyo – **take out**." Shouldn't that be takeout, or take-out?

Either will work, but a hyphen would be necessary for take-out. Both are much preferred over the bold-faced one.

To your health?

There's a cure for almost everything except bad spelling. Proving it is E.F. of Buena Vista, Colo.:

> In the *Denver Post*, Dr. Mollen mentioned that shark **cartridge** is being used for arthritis.

What caliber, pray tell? I believe that should be shark "cartilage." In fact, I'm sure of it.

Sears and sawbucks?

As a fairly handy type around the house and in the basement workshop, I have collected a rather nice assortment of tools over the years, many of which are the Sears Craftsman brand, considered by most to be of the highest quality. However, I had to blink twice when I saw what J.D. of Oregon, Ohio, sent me:

> The Sears ad had me asking serious questions about saving $20.00 on a two-piece socket set that has "8-in. and 10-in. adjustable box end wrenches [that] contact all **4** sides of **hex** nuts and bolts."

One question J.D. didn't mention was, how can a socket set come in only two pieces? I have to assume what was meant was that the set came with two *handles*, a large one and a small one, like the two sets I have. Another question is, since when are box-end wrenches part of a socket set? They are two completely different kinds of wrenches. Some ad agency's ace staff really fell asleep on that one.

"Where's that **number 9 socket wrench?**" That was the clarion call of a beleaguered handyman on a radio commercial for Rubbermaid products that featured a tool organizer for workshops. Anyone ever hear of a #9 socket wrench? A 9-millimeter wrench, yes, but not a "number 9." (Sockets are identified by the size of the bolt or nut they can accommodate.)

Scream therapy is good

The Associated Press takes yet another hit, maybe or maybe not unfairly, this time from H.M. of Fullerton, Calif.:

> In the *Whittier Daily News*, AP writer Don Thompson reports that "Energy **conservation** is dropping across California even as the state begins an aggressive campaign urging businesses and residents to turn off the lights and turn down the heat. ... **Conservation** during peak periods has dropped ... The drop in **conservation** – despite a new $20 million ad campaign by the state – comes as Northern California braces for a cold snap expected to stretch well into next week." The headline writer,

not to be outdone, composed "**Conservation** drops as voluntary lights-out urged." Can you say *consumption*?

My suspicion is that there was another article in the same edition being copyedited at the same time, one which had "conservation" mentioned several times, and that the copyeditor did what is called a "global" correction, which for whatever reason carried over into this article. A global correction will affect every use of a word or phrase in an entire document with a single keystroke. Then again, someone should have checked.

So who do you think is the better-paid, the headline writer for your local suburban weekly or the headline writer for the *Wall Street Journal*? Aside from frequency of publication, can there be any doubt? Our reader and reporter this time is J.E. of Eugene, Ore.:

> Headlining the Potomac Watch column was "Fat-Cat Calvary Rides In to Rescue High Taxes." Paul Gigot writes the column, but I'm sure he had nothing to do with the headline.

That is correct. I deliberately didn't bold-face it, so if you missed it the first time, read it again. Maybe someday newspapers will bite the bullet and assign copyeditors to headlines and photo captions. In the meantime, C.T. of Bangor, Mich., returns with this doozy:

> I gasped at the photo caption in the *Kalamazoo Gazette*: "Andre Agassi leaves the court in **disjection** after losing to Spain's Alex Calatrava."

On examining the photo, I decided that he did indeed look "disjected" and maybe needed to get into another racket. *Hold your fire!* Actually, there is such a word as "disjection," with "disject" meaning to disperse or scatter. Agassi, you'll be happy to hear, remained in one piece.

Electrifying!

B.H. of Linn, Mo., definitely got my attention with this shocker:

> During Dr. Emily Senay's report on the CBS News *Early Show*, she said, "At first glance it's hard to tell that electrical engineer

Kenny Whitten is a double amputee. He lost both arms when he was **electrocuted** fifteen years ago."

It wasn't easy, but we had to tell her that she had inadvertently killed him with her words. Electrocution is terribly fatal, every time.

Town cryer?

I'm going to let you guess where these came from; they are otherwise perfectly good words that were substituted for others and easily passed the spell-check test:

Articulate for matriculate – **weather** for whether – **steal** for steel – **fare** for fair – **flue** for flu – **beat** for beet – **road** for rode – **morality** for mortality – bichon **fries** for bichon frise – **aloud** for allowed – **wedge hills** for wedge heels – and on and on. Yes, it was a small-town weekly, and in the interest of mercy, I am not naming it. I'm sure its staff suffers enough from their readers' e-mail, cards, letters, and phone calls, so out of pure pity, its identity will remain between the contributor and me. Thus far, none of the words or their incorrect counterparts have appeared in this book. Oddly, there are many more where those came from. See my next book.

Just having fun?

Here's a quickie from regular reporter E.F. of Buena Vista, Colo.:

> Once more the *Denver Post* conjures images with its headlines: "Slay suspects **tousle** in cell." That should be tussle.

No, no, they were playing noogies in the pokey. Shucks, they have plenty of time for it. OK, tussle would be correct, tousle meaning to dishevel or rumple, such as someone's hair

S.N. of Whitefish, Mont., didn't hit the mute button fast enough and got an earful:

> A TV commercial for the law offices of James Sokolove referred to a class-action suit about "a rare, **malignant** type of cancer."

Pass ol' Jim the dictionary, will you? There is no other type of cancer. All cancer is malignant, by definition. The phrase is redundant.

Also redundant was the review snippet by Jeff Strickler in the *Star Tribune*: "Pinocchio – Not screened for review – A live-action adaptation, starring Roberto Benigni (who also directed). This is Italy's **most costliest** film ever."

Another? Remember the poisoned-Tylenol and -Anacin situation back in the eighties? W.R. of Piedmont, Calif., clipped a short AP item from the *San Francisco Chronicle*. The report stated that "The tainted capsules were in a 20-capsule, non-tamper-resistant bottle that was **not tamper-resistant**." Okey dokey.

And the Redundancy Sweepstakes winner is K.R. of Canton, Ohio, with this entry:

> A wedding announcement in the *Canton Repository* informed us that the bride "is a dental hygienist in her husband's dental practice here who is a dentist." There was no writer's name.

Bad shot

T.W. of Plano, Texas, got yanked up short when he opened his morning paper:

> A headline in *The Dallas Morning News* read, "Man's death ruled self-**afflicted** gunshot." I wish they hadn't inflicted that on me.

In Dallas itself, J.R. of that city picked up that same paper and got an eyeful:

> From the Associated Press: "WASHINGTON – Organ donations from the living reached a record high last year, outnumbering donors who are **dead for the first time**."

Are we talking about zombies here? Maybe a second time disqualifies you. As before, a simple little comma – after "dead" – would have kept it out of this book. I would have recast it entirely.

Bless you

Cruise-line magazines are not technically public, since their distribution is limited, but H.P. of Libertyville, Ill., gave me one that I just had to include:

> A travel writer who is (safely) unidentified, while walking the streets of Sorrento, Italy, reports that he saw "a trio of young acolytes, scrubbed Sunday-clean in white **hassocks** with teal sleeves ... a city transit bus pulls up and stops; the monsignor hops out, tugging on his **hassock** ..."

Make of it what you will; need I say "cassock"? Keeping an eye on another kind of toggery was D.L. of Dunedin, Fla.:

> The *St. Petersburg Times* had a Fall Fashion Preview, description of which included: "John Baldwin – Can any woman deny herself the exhilaration of slipping into a Halston? Sarah Baldwin models this creation in studded crepe with a **surplus** top and dolman sle[e]ves ..."

Can't blame the spellchecker on that one. The word is "surplice." My wife said so. She also said that dolman sleeves are large at the armhole and small at the wrist. I looked it up, and darned if she wasn't right.

Sign in the lobby of a Holiday Inn: "Please excuse our dust! We apologize for any areas that are inappropriate." They were remodeling, which was, of course, perfectly appropriate, except in a few areas.

Ten-hut!

From W.B. of Woodland Hills, Calif.:

> I've given up all hope of creative writers and the American press ever agreeing to the need for syntactical usage of common English. This was the front page introduction to the second lead article of the Woodland *Daily Democrat*: "Jack Delmage, a World War II veteran, is scheduled to receive medals for serving in the 551st Parachute Infantry Battalion he never got because he was thought to be killed in action during a special ceremony today."

Hey, you! Journalist! Yeah, you. Go back and start over, OK?

From T.M. of Maplewood, Minn.:

> In a four-page, full-color newspaper ad insert, Audio King [an
> electronics store later known as Ultimate Electronics] offers
> "FREE **Instulation**" of a dish antenna.

Where that went wrong is anyone's guess. Spell-checker rejects it, but the
line of type may have been set using some other kind of typography. No
excuse, though.

Incidentally, A.H. of Brooklyn Center, Minn., points out rather pointedly
that no one should rely on the spell-checking feature of a word-processing
program, by pointing to three words in most dictionaries that can be
confused with each other – minim, minimum, and minium. That last one
was rejected by my Word spell-checker, but so are lots of legitimate words.
Two words of advice to anyone who writes for others to read: Look up
every even slightly questionable word; and let at least one other person
read your stuff before you send it off for publication. Those two things
will give you your best chance of staying out of books like this.

19

With what?

Although I really enjoy my SOTS mail each day, I especially love it when I see things myself that I can share with others. Here's one I found as I pushed my cart through my favorite grocery store. There on a shelf was Johnny's French Dip Au Jus Sauce, a product of Johnny's Fine Foods in Tacoma, Wash. It might be good stuff, but someone should have told them that *au jus* means "served with the natural juice the meat was cooked in." OK, so I know this isn't the usual SOTS target, but it couldn't be more public, and someone got paid, I'm sure, to create the product label. In any event, the name is nonsensical.

Among other dopey things I've seen was the sign on a newspaper rack for the weekly *St. Louis Park Sun* that read, "FREE, TAKE ONE." When the rack was empty, another sign at the bottom said, "SORRY, SOLD OUT." The paper has since changed its name and those signs are now gone, but the malady lingers on right here in my heart.

The vacuum cleaner department of a Sears store had a sign reading: "Less than a **nickle** per square yard to clean carpets ..." The salesperson said that I was only the third person in two years to point out the error. I elicited no promise to change it, however.

Along the same line, a former Minneapolis City Council member, Van White, once told the *Star Tribune* that he liked to do public speaking. Staff writer James Walsh then quoted White in print as saying, "If they want to give me a few **sheckles** for it, that's fine, too." Close, but no cigar: The word is "shekels," once a Hebrew coin, but now a slang term for money.

Apropos of nothing else in particular, I have always found it quite odd that the three-volume Merriam Webster's *Third New International Dictionary* contains no listings for any of the planets in the solar system. Earth is defined only as dirt, etc. Further, there are no proper names in the book. Fortunately, I now have several sources available to me on the

Internet, so I should have no excuse to screw up anything in this book. I hope. Come to think of it, though, that dictionary would have to be a lot bigger in order to contain proper names – even though my Random House seems to have plenty of them. I wonder what the Random House one is missing.

To be fair, the offshoots of Webster's Third, the *Ninth* and later *New Collegiate Dictionarie*s, all contain geographical and biographical names in back.

Boy or girl?

P.D. of Houston, Texas, chimes in with this one:

> The ABC Baby Furniture & Infants [*sic*] Wear store advertised its "FAMOUS BABY SALE." I think I'd like one.

Girl or boy? Prices vary with degree of celebrity, I suppose. Down the road a piece lives G.W. of Austin, same state, who is a previous contributor:

> An article in the *Austin American Statesman* contained the following: "His prison term saw Krueger develop into … a **vociferous** reader and a social worker in alcohol and drug abuse programs." Disturbing, no?

"Voracious" is the word, and while I don't ordinarily deal with books, which is not to say there isn't a fertile field there, someone sent me a photocopy of a page from an A.E. Van Vogt science fiction short story, "Project Spaceship" (1949), that included: "He was an **avaricious** reader." Looking for ways to make money, maybe?

Stick 'em up

From K.U. of Santa Clara, Calif.:

> The *Vallejo Independent Press* reported that "A man **simulating** a gun robbed Payless Drug Center …" Another story was headlined "Gun Toting Man Arrested."

Well, so much for gun control. E.L. of Canon City, Colo., is eager to share this one with us:

> In a *Rocky Mountain News* article about singer Debby Boone, Walter Saunders wrote: "Boone is accompanied by a four-member trio ..."

Izzat so? On a more somber note is this from B.W. of Bloomington, Ind.:

> In a *Family Weekly* [magazine] article about George Burns, Isobel Silden writes, "Their 38-year marriage, which ended with Gracie's death in 1964, was the most tragic thing that happened in his life."

That syntax is tragic as well. Shortly after the item was published in my column, I received a letter from M.Z. of Park Forest, Ill. In part, it read:

> This kind of muddle-headed prose makes the whole SOTS effort worthwhile. This execrable sloppiness is inexcusable, even if it comes from the typewriter of a busy person calling himself a journalist. Off with his head! If he does it again, he should be instantly fired, except if he has a dependent family of six, but then he must be demoted to copy-boy.
>
> GOOD FOR SOTS! But let's not forget that journalists, or as you call them, communicators, whether they be scribes or heralds, are under enormous pressure of time and the requirements of accuracy, and that occasional slips are unavoidable. It's easy for you and me, writing at leisure at the comfort of our desk, to avoid such errors, and even we don't go blameless. But sloppiness and flabbiness of style, born of laziness of mind, set a bad example to a younger generation of aspiring authors, and cannot be forgiven. This is where SOTS can shine.

Despite my having to agree with my readers that "Isobel" is a female name, I have to tell you that M.Z. is one of those who are no longer with us. Nevertheless, he was one of the few who could have figuratively torn this book to shreds, as he did with several of my columns. He was unquestionably in favor of what I was doing, but didn't miss a chance to remind me to pay attention to what I was writing as I reported on the writings of others. A self-confessed nit-picker, he reveled in pointing out such things as going over something with a "fine-toothed comb," rather than with a "fine-tooth" one. Of course, there have been others who caught me in my own quicksand, but M.Z. was the champion.

And just to show that I am not without the guts to take the heat, I will add right here that more than one reader joined S.G. (of a city not shown on the submission) in saying, "I hope that some day you choke on one of the nits you seem so fond of picking in your column." Perhaps that day may come, but not too soon, I hope. Thanks anyway, critics; at least I know you're paying attention.

Lastly, for now, I repeat my earlier caution to those who take personal offense at what I write about professionals, even though the offended themselves are not among them. To those I say, I in no way attempt to deny you your right to speak as finely or as sloppily as you like. Speak in the parlance of your milieu, as we all should do, but allow us to hold higher standards for those whom we *pay* to communicate with us. It is not too much to ask.

Jeopardy!?

Earlier I confessed to watching what is one of the two most popular game shows on the air at the time of this writing, *Jeopardy!* (Note that the exclamation point is part of the title, which is why both it and the question mark after the subtitle are appropriate, since a question is asked.) The other is *Wheel of Fortune*. Sharp-eared viewers of *Jeopardy!* have heard announcer Johnny Gilbert (a former game show host himself) change his description of contestants' winnings: What was once "Twelve thousand, four hundred and one dollar" is now correctly "Twelve thousand, four hundred one *dollars*."

Sometimes the *Jeopardy!* quiz-makers create a laugher like this one: In the category of "'50s Movie House," the answer was "In 1956 she starred in 'High Society' & also appeared on a postage stamp." The question, of course, was "Who was Grace Kelly?" But her appearance on the stamp was not until 1993. Besides, no one except a president of the U.S. can appear on a stamp until the person has been dead for 10 years [now changed to five], so being in a movie and on a stamp in the same year is impossible. Substituting the word "later" for "also" would have cleared it right up.

Chomp!

Are the makers of Trident Gum still telling us that "millions of teeth can't be wrong"? By golly, I wouldn't want to see all those teeth make a mistake and chew on something else, for heaven's sake. Sorry, but I was not aware that teeth had a choice. Fifty million Frenchmen, maybe – teeth, nooo.

Tongue-tied?

Earlier I mentioned "nuclear" as being a difficult word for many to pronounce. Interestingly, while so many people have trouble with it, it is also the number one pet peeve among lovers of the language, and is the most often mentioned word during question and answer sessions following speeches I've given. Once when our local electric power company (formerly known as Northern States Power but now called Xcel Energy) made a series of TV commercials, their ad agency hired a narrator who found it impossible to say "nuclear" correctly. Because of time commitments and a lack of available substitute spots, they had no choice but to run them on the air, knowing viewers were certain to notice. The company's advertising manager told me later that it was one of their most embarrassing times, and the spots were deep-sixed as quickly as possible.

Beg pardon

Very briefly, I'm going to break my own vow not to include ad-libs, but I will just this one time (I think): I won't name the perpetrators, purely out of mercy, but the radio station was KSTP-AM here in the Twin Cities. One announcer, who is now long gone from there, opined that "We're going to see the sunshine wind down this afternoon." Just like an old watch, I thought to myself.

Then, turning to sports, as they say, another former stalwart once declared, "The NFL draft is barely under way and there have already been some

surprises. I wouldn't be surprised if there are more surprises coming."
Nor would I, nor would I.

Pretty scary

Speaking of radio, from the Associated Press and running in several newspapers was the story of the commemoration of the 1938 "Martian inva-
sion" of Grovers Mill, N.J. It included: "Howard Koch, 86, who wrote
the radio adaptation of H.G. Well's novel *The War of the Worlds* for the
Mercury Theatre, was given a key to the town …"

And a TV spot for phone company US West said that it was "The Allen's
Choice." Which Allen?

Did you miss them without the boldface? Look at them again. I've seen
some pretty cute tricks with apostrophes, but these are gems. Not only did
author Wells get his apostrophe misplaced, it took his name apart in the
process, which is unforgivable. It should have read "H.G. Wells's novel
…," or for those who insist on using the more permissive newspaper style,
"H.G. Wells' novel …" It's a good thing that Orson Welles, producer of
that radio classic, wasn't mentioned, because it would just as likely have
come out as Welle's. As for the Allen family, it should have been "Allens',"
with the apostrophe serving as the possessive of the plural name. It's the
kind of thing we often see on those plaques on posts in front of people's
houses – "The Sullivan's," etc. I never do it, but I always have the urge to
knock on their door and point out that they should have asked for their
money back.

Most newspapers and some magazines, unfortunately (as a way to save to
save ink, maybe?), leave the possessive *'s* off plurals and other words ending in *s*. For example, if Gus left his hat after asking his supervisor for a
raise, in newspaper typography you can expect the question to be, "What
happened to **Gus'** hat?" And the answer would be: "Oh, he left it in the
boss' office." Usually the missing *s* is pronounced anyway – Gus's hat,
boss's office – but the silly custom prevails. Better publications, as well as
most books from top-drawer publishing houses, properly have that final *s*.

"If you thought the car was **James'**, you were mistaken." You can't put the
comma inside that apostrophe, so it sort of hangs out there in the middle

of nowhere. The possessive *s* would help a lot, so that it would read "If you thought the car was James's, you were mistaken." Much better. And along that same line, "I thought those were **Thomas'** English muffins, but they weren't." At least the radio and TV commercials have the announcer delivering the final *s*. Consider also: "Where did that gas smell come from? What is the source of the **gas'** odor?" Or "Someone sent a distress signal at sea, but we could not determine the **SOS'** purpose." If more of us do it right, there's hope.

"So you want to critique your boss' writing?" That was the headline over one of the Effective Writing columns by the previously mentioned Stephen Wilbers, who we know was not involved in the headline. Exactly one week later, Wilbers's column carried this headline: "Suffering from apostrophobia? Here's some help." Wilbers bemoaned the "apostrophobes" who create "apostrophomission," a perfectly good (if newly coined) word, I suppose, one that squarely hits the mark. However, he didn't come up with a word for those who liberally salt their writings with the little jot unnecessarily, so how about "apostrophiles" or even better, "apostrophiliacs," meaning those having an uncontrollable urge to insert apostrophes where they don't belong?

What is most remarkable about Wilbers's column is his advocacy of the possessive *'s*, despite the *Star Tribune*'s style dictating otherwise. Yes, he did it and they let him get away with it. Huzzah! To end that column on a really great note, he suggested that "If you or someone you know suffers from apostrophobia, seek counseling from a trained apostrophologist. Please. Act now. Before it's too late." Don't you just love it? (At one time, the *Star Tribune* used a combination of the New York Times and the Associated Press style books. Now, however, I believe they have formulated one for themselves.)

If I were convinced of the existence of hell, I have to think that whoever was first to drop the final *s* on a possessive ending in *s* is there right now, probably laughing his head off.

Comical strips?

What are sometimes called "the funny pages" (or "funnies" or "comics" or "jokes") often give us a poke in the eye. On one particular Sunday,

Blondie was trying to wake Dagwood for breakfast, but was having no luck. After dousing his father with a pitcher-full, son Alexander was seen to say, "Even the ice water didn't **phase** him." No, to phase him you'd need a phaser from the starship Enterprise. The word is *faze*, despite the fourth definition of "phase" in *Webster's Third* that says it is a "variation of faze." I never have completely trusted *Webster's Third*, and here's a reason I had previously missed.

Not particularly comical at all was the failure of the *Star Tribune* staff to catch this one about a man known so well in this area because he was a native of St. Paul. The identity of the feature's creator is unknown to me, but the little corner of the Kids' Page, which was assembled each week by cartoonists Craig MacIntosh and Steve Sack, was about "**CHARLES SCHULTZ (1922-2000)**" and the text continued with: "When cartoonist Charles **Schultz** died earlier this year, the world mourned the passing of an institution. For more than a half-century, **Schultz**'s 'Peanuts' characters had entertained generations of kids and adults with their playground antics. **Schultz** acknowledged that he had based the character Charlie Brown largely on himself. Like Charlie Brown, **Schultz** had done poorly in sports and was afraid of girls. He was even a failure as a cartoonist. When he submitted some of this cartoons for his high school yearbook, they were rejected. **Schultz** persevered, however, and later created one of the most popular comic strips ever." The man's name was Charles Schulz. No *t*.

While I'm at it, the "Schultz's" in the third use of the name in the preceding paragraph, which properly carried the *'s*, opens the door for another swipe at *Jeopardy!* On May 16, 2006, the category was World Authors and the answer was, "This literary **whiz'** name is sometimes transliterated from Bengali as Ravidranatha Thakura." The question, of course, was, "Who was Tagore?" In reading the answer aloud, host Alex Trebek correctly pronounced "whiz's" despite the lack of the final *s* on the screen. Altogether too many writers, especially on newspapers where it is often a matter of "style," are leaving off that last *s*, thus leaving viewers and readers uncertain as to whether it should be pronounced or not. Considering that I already covered the possessive *s's* infractions, I suppose the dead horse has been beaten more than is prudent, but I had to add this little item because it was different enough.

In that same position on that same kids' page on a different Sunday, the spotlight was on Candice Bergen of *Murphy Brown* television fame. It said: "Candice Bergen grew up as the **son** of the famous ventriloquist Edgar Bergen." In his act, Bergen often introduced Candice as the little **sister** of his dummy, Charlie McCarthy. Neither was correct, of course, and it couldn't have been pleasant for her.

The aforementioned Steve Sack has also been the main editorial-page political cartoonist for the *Star Tribune* for several years. In a cartoon he drew in 1988 he had George H.W. Bush being coached for a debate, and having the Pledge of "**Allegience**" printed all over the front of his body. Obviously, no one checked. ("allegiance")

Fry me

Delta Airlines a few years ago declared itself "The Official Airline for Kids," and ran a newspaper ad headlined: "How To Get Small **Fries** To Go." Aside from all those unnecessary capital letters, the "Fantastic Flyer Program" was undoubtedly great for traveling youngsters, but the plural of (small) "fry" is still "fry." The last line of the body copy was, quite properly, "The airline that serves your small fry some extra fun on the side." Obviously, there was a lack of communication within the ad agency. ("Fry" can refer both to small fish or to small kids, by the way.) Fries are what you get with hamburgers, etc. The agency probably claimed "creative license," but that license has long since expired.

There was also the time that Sears, Roebuck & Co. teamed with McDonald's for a special cross-promotion called "McKIDS," offering "Fun clothes for small **fries**." Tsk, tsk. Same agency?

In a word?

Alka Seltzer Plus Cold Medicine: "**In a word**, it works." Huh? How many words? Advertising types will tell you that this is an example of "literary license." I say, revoke that license, too. A.M. of Edmonton, Alta., Canada, concurs:

> Some sort of award should go to the creator of the Ivory Soap commercial in which the man says, "If there is **one word** I can use to describe my wife, it's 'healthy looking.'"

When you stop to think about it, though, how often has someone said, "I'd like a word with you"? I defy anyone to follow that statement with but a single word, unless you include the fellow in the movie *The Graduate* who said, "Plastics." But he also had quite a few other words, so, no, even though I can think of several responses of one word, there is none that could follow that original question. OK, so "Halt!" and "Freeze!" might qualify in some circumstances, but not following "I'd like a word with you." Whether a hyphen in "healthy-looking" was implied or intended we do not know, but even that would not make it a single word; it's still a two-word compound.

Achoo!

N.H. of Rochester, N.Y., heard an ad for Contac: "In this remarkable scientific capsule are enough medicines to cure most cold symptoms caused by every known virus." Now, that was a pretty wild claim, considering that symptoms cannot be cured, they can be alleviated, and it is the condition or disease that is subject to curing. Unfortunately, no one has yet found a cure for the common cold, at least not as of my writing this. One hopes, however. Worse yet, pity the poor person who has "every known virus."

Also from N.H.:

> On the radio: "Goodman Plaza Discount Furniture [in Rochester] will meet or beat the price of any comparable-priced furniture."

Yes, I had to look at that more than once myself.

What there was was a bunch of 'em

My favorite TV show, *Jeopardy!* (for which I passed the qualifying test in 1990 but never got called to appear on the program), provides an occasional tidbit for SOTS to chew on. Not too terribly long ago the answer on the screen was, "The second of Egypt's plagues was **hoards** of this amphibian." I suppose that if they had been accumulated as a collection for a while, "hoards" would be just as good a word as "hordes." But to be safe, go with "hordes." The correct question, of course, was "What are frogs?"

TV Guide writer David Chagall, commenting in 1981 on the popular *Hill Street Blues*, said, "There may not be **hoards** watching, but they are avid fans." I was one of them. (again, "hordes")

I was also among those who spotted *TV Guide*'s 1981 program note in which writer Jeff Hyde described one of the characters in the program as a "high school vice **principle** ..." ("principal")

Says who?

The annual *Jeopardy!* Teen Tournament should be free of inaccuracies, but no, sadly, it is not. In the 2004 edition, a category was Fix the Proverb and the answer was "That gold glitters is not all." The saying appears in Shakespeare's *Merchant of Venice* as "All that glisters is not gold," but Willie got his grammar wrong. *Some* things that "glister" can easily be gold, so his rendition should have read "Not all that glisters is gold." Shakespeare actually paraphrased earlier writers such as Chaucer – "Hyt is not al gold that glareth" (*The House of Fame*) – and a fellow named Alain de Lille (d. 1202) – "Do not hold as gold all that shines as gold" (*Parabolae*).

On the same day and in the same category, the answer was "All root is the evil of money." Contrary to popular belief, the saying is not "Money is the root of all evil." Straight from the King James Bible, Second Timothy, chapter 6, verse 10, it reads: "The love of money is the root of all evil." Even so, that's an awfully broad statement to make, seeing as how so many other human failings can foster evil, financial considerations aside. I always wonder who copyedited the Bible.

Educational TV?

Yes, we once called it Educational TV, but now it's called Public TV, and what children are learning from it is often quite disturbing. On a program called the *Electric Company*, one of its sketches that dealt with the word "if" had a character saying, "There **wasn't no 'if'** in there," and no one corrected it. Is this the kind of thing kids should watch? No wonder we are awash in ignorance. The program was similar to *Sesame Street*, and there was a time when I suggested an adult version of that show. Now I'm not so sure it would be such a good idea

Not on the air, but in *Woman's Day* magazine, was an ad for a videotape created for kids to "Learn Time The Blue's Clues Way – With Blue's New Video!" So far, only the writer's penchant for capital letters gets our attention, but in a little box that simulates a spiral notebook are the words "Contains 2 **Educational**-Filled Episodes!" Overkill is what it is.

Educational radio?

In my car one day I had a fine program of music interrupted by "Star Bowling and Golf **have** all the items you need." I wonder if that means that if Star Bowling doesn't have it, Golf does. (OK, "have" should be "has," of course; Star Bowling and Golf was the name of the store.) This is similar to the TV ad that boasts, "The law firm of Kalina and Wills **help** people …" It do? They does? Oh, forget it! (OK, "helps")

TV Guide has gotten several hits here, but there's another publication called *TV Week* that once noted: "**Kelsy Grammar**" [of NBC-TV's *Cheers*] was to be a guest on *The Magical World of Disney*. The poor fellow's name is Kelsey Grammer, for Pete's sake (Pete's my cousin, you know. Hi, Pete).

Back to radio, I caught Haskell's Liquor Store proclaiming that its "spectacular **annual** wine and spirits sale happens only **once a year**." Oh, is that so?

20

Identity theft?

Sometimes I think I am wandering alone in a vast wilderness, looking for sweet reason wherever I can find it. It's not easy, I can tell you. The media have stolen our states' identities, and I'd like them back. In all fairness, it's more the electronic – well, OK, TV – that is the biggest culprit, but print advertising is not helping one bit. Let me elucidate:

Several years ago the United States Postal Service created a means of simplifying mail delivery. Called the Zoning Improvement Plan, and abbreviated to the acronym ZIP, it later added two-letter postal designations for each state. Massachusetts became MA, North Carolina became NC, and so on. My own state, Minnesota, took on MN as its postal moniker, and is naturally the one that now bugs me the most.

Here in my area, TV newscasts are rife with variations: "Mn," "Mn.," (with the period), and "MN." (also with the period) are all shown regularly, but never "Minn.," the only legitimate abbreviation, according to most style manuals, and, believe it or not, that includes the Associated Press style manual. (The *Chicago Manual of Style*, 15th edition, waffles, but leans toward the earlier versions.) I'll give my local *Star Tribune* credit for using the proper "Ark." instead of "AR," and "Ariz." in place of "AZ," but too many others fall into the "TX" and "FL" habit. And at the risk of insulting some of my good friends who live there, the "CA" for California is all-too-often pronounced "Kah!" (I wonder whether people in Pennsylvania say "Pah.") I'll grant that the two-letter short versions are useful in charts, graphs, and lists, but when writing about a state, for heaven's sake, why not use the traditional tried and true?

Although not exactly in the public media, our governmental departments have been pulled under by the same tide. The Minnesota Department of Transportation is now called "MnDOT" (note the lower-case *n*) and is pronounced "Mindot." The Minnesota State Colleges and Universities comes out as "MnSCU," and is pronounced "Minskew." Ye gods and little fishes! What is happening to our most important means of communication?

Awakening?

I got pulled up short myself a while back when I first saw Duck Tape advertised. For years I had been using "duct" tape, and immediately thought "Duck" was a misspelling. I was astonished to find that it was no misspelling, that Duck Tape is one of the brand names of duct tape, and that it was available at my local hardware store. It just goes to show that anyone can be mistaken. The other time for me was back in 1937, but that's another story.

By the way, I too found out the hard way what many home handy-persons should know: Despite its name, duct tape, no matter the brand, should never be used on furnace ducts, especially not on the plenum (that sheet-metal above and around the burners that gets very hot). In small print on each package is the warning "Suitable for use at no more than 176° F." Get it hot enough and it melts into a sticky goo. (No extra charge for the handy hint.)

This is unnatural

It's been a while since I heard it, so it may not even be around any more, but Eucalyptamint pain reliever used to be advertised as "**100 percent all-natural**." Competing products, naturally, were only partly all-natural, or maybe 100 percent sort-of-natural. I never found out. Interestingly, when Tom Snyder had his own radio show, he had the product as a sponsor, but refused to repeat that slogan. I wonder how long it took for the sponsor to drop off the show. I also saw that same claim by Jolly Time Pop Corn – "Try Our **100% All-Natural** Pop Corn And Save 30¢!" Also puzzling is "Pop Corn" as two words, something I'd not seen before, and I've been eating *popcorn* since I was a very small child.

Incidentally, when Tom Snyder was still on late-night radio, he once gave a caller a succinct lecture on the use of "unique" and why it should not have modifiers. Tom was one of a kind. Had good jokes, too.

A local car dealer – Key Nissan in Wayzata, Minn. – ran a newspaper ad headlined: "Help! or I'll Lose My Job!" The copy began, "I must sell 35 cars ... etc." At the bottom it was signed "Mike and Jim." Did either or both lose his or their job(s)? I never found out that either.

I've bought shoes at Foot Locker, and may again if they're still in business, but not without recalling their TV ad that asked, "Where else **you gonna go?**" I don't know, but I gonna think about it.

Whack!

Sears once sold an item called the Weed-wacker, and maybe still does. My dictionary search reveals no such word as "wacker," although "wack" and "wacky" are there. There is a Wacker Drive in Chicago, and I used to work in the Civic Opera Building, which was located on that street, but that's a story I've told only in my autobiography. Anyway, whoever named the lawn trimmer Weed-wacker deserves a whack wherever it'll do the most good.

Speaking of "whacking," I know full well that sometimes there is no cure for a linguistic malady, and sometimes we have to consign certain usages to the Department of Lost Causes. Such it must be for *impact*, a perfectly good word gone totally astray. No longer do things or circumstances "affect" us or "influence" us. They "impact" us. According to every dictionary I own and some that I don't, "impact," as a verb, originally meant "to strike suddenly with great force." As a noun, it meant the "forceful collision of one body against another," as in an auto accident.

Nowadays, it can mean anything from "barely touching" to "creating change." Soon we will hear of school children studying the laws of "cause and impact (effect)," or the consequences of "outside impacts (influences)," or whatever creative minds can derive. No doubt legislative lobbyists will soon be described as "impact-peddlers." And the term "environmental impact statement" as it applies to governmental decision-making has long ago taken root, but I for one fail to see its logic, universally accepted or not. There! I said it.

That paper again

Yes, once more we pore over the pages of the *Star Tribune* in search of food for our kind of thought. J.M. of St. Paul is chewing on some now:

Staff writer Peg Meier, in an article about the census, told about "(1880 census study) project head Steven Ruggles, who is on sabbatical for a year at Cambridge University and is therefore **illegible** to be counted." Make that "ineligible," please.

Same paper, second verse. It's one from the Right-hand/Left-hand Department: A headline read, "Norwest [bank] plans to **loan** students $750 million over 3 years." Then, the first paragraph began, "Norwest Corporation ... plans to **lend** up to $750 million ..." Despite the bold-face, the second word is not an error. "Loan" is a noun; "lend" is a verb (and the past tense is "lent," not "loaned"). In this case, the (anonymous) headline writer blew it, and writers Lucy Hood and Michael Phillips of the States News Service had it right. Furthermore, old Will Shakespeare never penned, "Friends, Romans, countrymen, **loan** me your ears," now did he?

A test

1. Creative Lighting had a "SEMI ANNUAL SALE." ("Semi-annual" appeared farther down in the ad.)

2. Dayton's (department store, once Marshall Field's, later Macy's) had a "SEMI-ANNUAL CLEARANCE."

3. Talbot's (women's clothing) had a "SEMIANNUAL SALE."

4. And the Lenox China Store had a "Semi-Annual Sale."

Only one of the five ways (there are two ways in #1) is correct. If you guessed, or knew for certain, that the Talbot's way was the right way, pat yourself on the back. "Semi" is a prefix, and is not a word that can stand alone, unless you're talking about an 18-wheeler. The prefix rhymes with "hemi," as in the Dodge commercials, and a hyphen is inappropriate. (I found the five of those examples in newspaper display ads.)

Front-page main headline, *Star Tribune*: "Gorbachev warns Estonia to back off." Right below it was the second-deck head or subheadline: "He criticizes bid for **succession**." It wasn't until one read the second paragraph that the concerns being expressed about Estonia's moves toward "secession" became evident, an altogether different kettle of fish. It's too bad that copyeditors don't have time to read headlines and photo captions. Or maybe they're simply told not to. Good guess?

Headline in the same paper: "OPTIMA: Design concept takes some **queues** from minivans." Now, the word "queue" has several meanings, including "Chinese pigtail" and a line people stand in, but it is not a synonym for "cue," in this case meaning "suggestion." I'm still betting on there being no copyeditor for headlines. (Thanks to J.M. for that last one also.)

Look eastward

Over there, just on the other side of the Mississippi River from Minneapolis and points west, lies the mighty city of St. Paul, but I seldom see its fine newspaper, the *Pioneer Press*. I have friends who do, however, and they keep a lookout on my behalf. Once, right on the front page, was the headline: "Arizona **trys** to retain Super Bowl." Did I hear someone say *typo*? Not a chance. Try "tries," which is not even close.

Copy that

Three cheers for the Xerox Corporation for bringing back the word "guarantee" in their advertising. The usual dodge nowadays is to use "warranty," a weaker word that allows merchants to weasel on backing up their products and services, and one that is often preceded by the word "limited" in the bargain. (Small print sizes may vary.) Worse yet, some have said that they "**warrantee**" whatever it is they're selling. There is no such word. A "warrantee" is a person, the recipient of a warrant; nothing more. However, if someone wants to "warrant" that their stuff is what they say it is, fine with me. Paul Harvey slipped up on this one occasionally.

Speaking of Paul Harvey, A.H. of Brooklyn Center, Minn., had the radio on at work one day:

> Paul's famous pauses worked against him ... during one of his advertisements, which began: "You own a dog? (pause) You want to feed him the very best dog food, don't you? (pause) Well, so do I (pause) ..." at which point I yelled at the radio, "Good! Bring some over and feed my pooch, Paul!" at which

point I lost all interest in the rest of the pitch (for Purina). For a person who crafts his words as carefully as Mr. Harvey, this seemed like an awful gaffe.

A.H. also caught ABC Radio News with: "There have been two aftershocks (to the Seattle/Tacoma quake). The **strongest** measured 3.4 ..." ("stronger" – there's a difference)

Boo!

The TV screen showed Viking Chevrolet's big sale for "**Holloween**," which reminded me of how so many newscasters and others pronounce it that same way. It's "Halloween" as in ballot, shallow, or marshmallow, if you must be told. Kids grew up saying "Holloween," and never got over it. As for Dave Campo, the spokesman, it should probably be called "Hollerween," he's that loud. Please, folks, get over it. We're listening.

Say that again?

Reader D.I., somewhere in Arizona, got my head shaking with this one:

> Why do [newspaper] people use expressions they don't understand? Hardy Price, writing his On Stage column in *The Arizona Republic*, told us that "There's little doubt that **anyone** gets sleep while (singer Ronnie) Sessions is performing. Sessions' brand of country is a hard driving, honky tonk version."

"There's little doubt" means "I'm sure," and **anyone** should be "no one." There appears to be little doubt that Price dozed off for a moment while compiling his review.

It's time

I've been having fun jabbing at headline writers, but criticism should be constructive, and I think mine is. That same kind of criticism follows this from D.R. of San Mateo, Calif.:

> A headline from the no-less-than-venerable *San Francisco Chronicle*: "**Suspicious** Engines Slow Amtrak." Were they suspicious of their engineers or of their passengers?

Faced with limited space, headline writers have to come up with short, pithy condensations of the subject matter in the accompanying article or column. It is not an easy task; I know, because I had the same difficulty when I was editor of a small-town weekly. The trick headline writers often forget is that shrinking the type size can often solve a problem like the one just mentioned. Instead of the 36-point type used, dropping to 18-point and rewriting the head to read something like "Possibly Defective Engines Slow Amtrak" should work. I might have even considered "Defective(?) Engines Slow Amtrak." But to describe engines as "suspicious" is well off the track.

Wanted!

If there is anything more public than a post office, I'd like to know what it might be. J.S. of San Francisco takes us to visit one she used to patronize:

> From an FBI Wanted poster in the post office in Tecumseh, Okla., which I found before I moved from there: "… This **deposit slip** will bear a fictitious account number and if questioned, **will depart** the bank immediately leaving the documents behind."

This is the kind of thing I always have to read twice, because I can't believe my eyes the first time through. J.S. also enclosed an ad clipped from a drug store circular that was for "**AEREATED** Brand Hygienic Cotton Crotch Panty Hose." Shown in the ad is an actual package, with that same spelling, as it appeared for sale in the store, so it definitely qualifies as fair game for SOTS.

There has also been a recorded radio commercial running on KNXR-FM in Rochester, Minn., that has "aerated" pronounced AIR-ee-ate-ed. In both cases, the extra *e* after the *r* on the package, and the extra *ee* syllable in the radio ad are uncalled for. The word is "aerated" and it is pronounced AIR-ate-ed.

That same station, KNXR, is 90 miles from my house, but is nevertheless tuned in on my car radio and on my bedside radio (others in the house pick it up poorly, if at all). I regret that I did not get the name of the product, but the commercial had two glaring errors. In celebration

of *Syttende Mai*, the seventeenth of May (1814), the announcer called it
Norwegian "**Independence** Day." It's not; it's Norwegian Constitution
Day, which also coincides with Norway's independence from Denmark,
but not from Sweden, and there is a big difference. Complete independence from Sweden was gained on June 7, 1905, long after the constitution was accepted for use. When broadcasting historical information over
the public airwaves, it's best to research it first. So how did I know it was
wrong? All of my grandparents were Norwegian.

And as if that weren't enough, that same announcer went on to say that
the product gets something clean, "as white as the **snow-capped fjords**
of Norway." Sorry, but when snow lands on the open water of the fjords,
it melts instantly. I'm sure that what was meant was the snow-capped
mountains *on either side of the fjords*. Several of my friends of Norwegian descent got a huge laugh out of it, and made me promise to put it
here. Done.

Where?

It pays to know the territory, proof of which is provided by M.M. of Los
Angeles, Calif.:

> The following comes from the pen of *Los Angeles Times* journal-
> ist Nicholas C. Chriss: "Lufkin is in east Texas, which is more
> like the old Deep South than **any** part of Texas." If east Texas
> is not in any part of Texas, where is it?

One word would have saved the day: "more … than any 'other' part of
Texas." What's so hard about that? Must have been a really tight deadline.

Count 'em

From J.L. of Forestville, Md.:

> An article in the Lewiston (Maine) *Daily Sun* about applicants
> to U.S. service academies reported on a seminar attended by
> "**nearly** 18 persons." The same "nearly" appeared in a photo
> caption as well. There was no mention of the actual number, or
> fraction thereof.

Recruiter to candidate: "If you were half the man I think you are, you'd apply in an instant." Ah, that explains it. More than 17, but fewer than 18, hence "nearly 18."

A different way of counting was employed by the Savin Business Machines Corp., according to the newspaper display ad found by I.L. of Michigan City, Ind. In 64-point (quite large) type, we are told that "Now, 1 out of every 2 copiers we place – **replace** a Xerox." Make it "replaces."

Big sale!

Captured on film by D.B. of Akron, Ohio, was a billboard reading, in huge type: "We're Selling Houston." It was paid for by a company called Homes For **Living** REALTORS®, and the company's name was in a smaller block type. I wasn't aware that Houston was for sale, and I didn't know that REALTORS® built homes just for themselves, living or not. I suspect that the name of the company was really Homes For Living, but someone tacked "REALTORS®" on, not knowing anywhere else to put it.

Incidentally, I and others keep hearing "REALTOR®" pronounced REEL-a-ter, and "realty" as REEL-a-tee. J.M. of Fairfax, Va., was first to report it many years ago, and the situation has gotten only worse. The word "REALTOR®" is fully capitalized, of course, since it is a name trademarked by an association of REALTORS®. Say it with me now: REE-ul-ter and REE-ul-tee. Good. You all get an A. Unfortunately, Abigail Van Buren, aka Dear Abby, in pointing out the same error, in print, pronounced it REEL-tor. It would have been better had she had it as REAL-tor, because REAL actually has two syllables, run together though they may be.

<u>21</u>

Kind words

Changing direction for a bit, I'd like to note some of the comments that came from readers of those early SOTS columns in the *Mensa Bulletin:*

"The SOTS section is one of my favorite parts of the *Bulletin.*"
–M.W., Lansing, Mich.

"[I] enjoy SOTS and wish you continued success on it."
–M.M., Chicago, Ill.

"Dear Gordon, A note of thanks for all the hard work and time you put in as editor of the *Bulletin.* You made it a much better publication, and I am sorry to see you leave the post. But won't you please continue to write the SOTS column?"
–S.W., Orlando, Fla.

"I strongly support the Save Our Tongue Society and wish you and others well in promoting lucidity, clarity, precision, and plainness of speech."   –R.M., Scottsdale, Ariz.

"Congratulations, best wishes, and may a thousand Birds of Paradise nest in the wig of he who is the progenitor of SOTS."
–J.D., Chicago, Ill.

"Count me as another enthusiastic supporter of SOTS. It's an idea whose time has most assuredly come, and I'm delighted that a Mensan was the one to do it, especially since it gets so much exposure through the *Bulletin.*"
–H.K., Chicago, Ill.

"Yours is the only feature of the *Mensa Bulletin* that I truly enjoy. Unfortunately, although fascinated by words and their use, I am no grammarian and many of the horrible examples you expose appear perfectly in order to me. May I suggest footnotes explaining the errors? [But] do continue the column; it's very well done ..."

–B.S., Los Angeles, Calif.

Then there were those who sent excerpts from my columns to various newspapers and other media outlets. D.S. of Denton, Texas, for example, wrote a lengthy and laudatory article (published in the Fort Worth *Star Telegram*), which I can't reprint here, but for which I am grateful.

I will mercifully spare embarrassment to another reader who also wrote an article that included excerpts and had it published in the monthly magazine of another membership organization. Aside from identifying me as **George** K. **Anderson,** the write-up was fully positive. All I will say about the organization is that it is one that requires excellent command of the language, particularly spelling and punctuation. The reader/writer later apologized for misspelling my name. All is forgiven.

Old home week?

A.L. of Pottsville, Pa., was first to send me this one:

> An Associated Press article in the *Pottsville Republican* date-lined LOS ANGELES began with an incomplete sentence: "Together **again** for the first time: Glenda Jackson and Carol Burnett."

I guess I've seen worse sentence construction, but that "Together again for the first time" bothered a whole passel of readers, and yours truly as well. If they had been together before, wouldn't they be together again for the "second" time? No, not really, because if they had been together once before, the next time would indeed be the first time they were together "again." But if it's for the first time, doesn't it also presuppose that they may be expected to be together "again" one or more times in the future (note: not in the past). This is one of those take-your-choice-and-move-on things that I prefer not to dwell on too much, and have already done so – dwelt on, that is. No wonder the rest of the world has so much trouble learning English.

Head SOT?

I never thought I'd see the day, but here it came with this from J.T. of Enid, Okla.:

> Dear Head SOT: I felt I had to pass along to you this gem of purest ray which appeared in the *Enid Morning News*: "Since spring and lamb are **synonymous**, another way to serve lamb is a boned shoulder." Ah, well ...

Head SOT, indeed! OK, I guess I can take it, so long as J.T. buys my book. Unfortunately, I'll never know, I suppose. And yes, I know it should be "... is *as* a boned shoulder." And no, lamb is not a synonym for spring, even though it is often eaten then. The two, however, can be said to "go together."

Mispelled?

B.A. of Philadelphia, Pa., has this classic:

> Strung full-width across the front page of the Sports section of the *Philadelphia Inquirer* was the astonishing "Carlton Letter Is Forgery – Even Name **Mispelled**." It referred to a letter supposedly signed by former Phillies pitcher Steve Carlton, who died in 1973.

More newspaper stuff comes to us from E.C. of Towson, Md.:

> Once upon a time the *Baltimore Sunpapers* were admired for excellent grammatical structure and fine proofreading, but those qualities have been deteriorating. As evidence of this I found misspellings in three headlines on one day: "Red **Turbin** Leads Police To Suspect" (and the same word appeared *twice* in the accompanying article); "Rank Does Have Its **Priviledges** – At Least in Texas"; and "2 Who **Hung** Selves Had Suicidal History." Unbelievable!

"Turban," of course, would be correct; take the *d* out of "Privileges"; and remember that pictures are "hung," while people are "hanged." As William Safire once said, *You Could Look It Up* (the title of one of his many books). Egad! How much bungling can there be? To paraphrase Al Jolson in *The Jazz Singer*, you ain't seen nothin' yet! Try this one, from M.J. of Larchmont, N.Y.:

> Have you seen the Chunky Candy TV commercial in which it is proclaimed to be the "**thickerer** one"?

Just wait. Sooner or later will come the "thickererest," mark my words. Ad agency types are hard at work daily, trying to find new ways to bastardize the English language, and they seem to be succeeding. They, of course, will call it "creativity." I was once among them, but I call it a "travesty," especially since it is so often squarely aimed at kids.

Anybody?

I found this one to be particularly interesting because the blooper fits the headline so well. It comes to us from D.Q. of Boulder, Colo.:

> In our local *Daily Camera* was reprinted an article from the *Chicago Tribune* written by one Michael Kilian, who, upon seeing an ad that offended him, stated, "I was instantly **nauseous**." Over the article was the headline: "It Seems Anybody Can Get Into Journalism."

Indeed. In the event that enlightenment is needed, *nauseous* means "causing nausea," while *nauseated* means "having nausea," a major difference, although some dictionaries waffle on this. Being nauseated in the presence of others, however, can also make one nauseous, so please head for the loo when you become so. Thank you.

J.K. of St. Petersburg, Fla., clipped and sent a cartoon, drawn by someone named only Stinger and probably printed in quite a few papers. It was from a syndicated feature service called Country Life Features. In the single panel a male viewer is looking at a TV screen, on which is seen the following graphic (printed lettering only): "The **Alledged** Weather Report – sponsored by Smith, Smith & Jones – Attorneys." The intended gag, of course, is that attorneys reputedly hesitate to state anything as irrefutable fact. However, someone at the syndicate should have caught the extra *d* in the middle of "alleged."

Rejected

I may be sorry for doing this, but between what I still think was a good job of writing and the utter goofiness of it lies the middle ground of deciding whether to include it here. I'm talking about the only column I *ever* had rejected by an editor, on the grounds that "it simply went too far." The piece may not accurately reflect my philosophy today, but I think you'll find it at least entertaining:

> OK, folks, this is it! We've been fooling around and putting things off long enough! It's time for SOTS to get off the dime! We've been criticized and castigated for our efforts, in varying degrees, by a few readers whose motives (at least to me) are unclear, but whose effect, remarkably enough, has been exactly the opposite of that which was intended. Although their numbers can be counted on one hand, these dissidents have fanned the embers of SOTS into flame. They have uncorked the slumbering volcano. They have jabbed us right where it will do the most good. They have dug their spurs deep into our placid flanks and jolted us into full gallop. The pies they have flung in our face have coalesced into the fierceness of war paint. No more will we chatter among ourselves and indulge in wishful thinking. We have been challenged on our own ground and the gauntlet has been retrieved at full tilt to be held high on the pikestaff of inexorable and unshakeable purpose. Let the faint-hearted doubters stand aside. The time for resistance is past. The time to attack is upon us and the first arrow has already been notched. Read now, the
>
> ### SOTS Plan of Battle!
>
> **First Volley:** Casting all modesty aside, we begin by answering one question that has given us undue pause – "Who or what is the final authority and arbiter of correctness in the use of the English language in public communications?" Because of the great disagreement among dictionaries and the diversity of opinion among language scholars, none of which or whom has shown willingness to make the following forceful declaration, it falls by default to SOTS to pronounce itself as the **Syndic**

of Public English and guide to the use thereof. Others may influence, but no other may prevail. It is done.

C'mon, critics, get off your high horses. Before you start screaming about presumption, arrogance, and audacity, consider carefully. No one else has ever been willing to take such a stand with the boldness that it requires, although I have no doubt that many others will now make the same assertion, and there should be no question as to the need for a single authority. What Emily Post did for etiquette, SOTS will now do for the crumbling foundations of our language. And if not SOTS, who? Many are able, certainly, but not one has dared. SOTS dares. Even our critics should at least give us credit for daring.

Second volley: SOTS will publish! With luck, pluck, and a strong pull together, we will prepare and distribute one or more books, newspaper and magazine columns and articles, guidebooks for writers and broadcasters, and any other forms of communications in furtherance of our cause. This, of course, will take work and money. I have some ideas in this regard, and your suggestions will be most welcome. Federal and foundation funds may be available. Educational institutions should be willing to cooperate. I am convinced that all we really need to do is demonstrate our seriousness to the right people and their support will be forthcoming. In the meantime, though, it will be your help and encouragement that will keep us going, and we can all get the action started right now. We'll call it the **National SOTS Brainstorm**, and what follows will be an important part of it.

Third volley: SOTS will convince everyone that its work is needed and will be of benefit to all. This is a tall order, but I believe we can do it. I also believe it is a necessary first step toward eliminating all doubt, not only in the minds of our few outspoken critics, but in the minds of those who don't care, no matter the reason. When we can clearly demonstrate the importance of correct and fully understandable communication in the mass media, we will have surmounted our largest obstacle, that of apathy. To do this, I am asking [for] your help. I am looking for specific examples of situations where language errors, both written and spoken, have led to difficulty. These examples may be either real or imaginary, events that have happened or could happen, and they need not be confined to the media. The results of these language errors can range from the mildly irritating to the totally disastrous, and special recognition will be given to those who come up with the most horrifying. This collection of atrocities will make up the **SOTS Rationale** and will be the final proof that faulty communication diminishes our quality of life, even to the point of creating hardship and suffering. Remember, all types of examples are welcome, and you may even find some in literature. If you should remember an event that was your own fault, please don't hesitate to send it along. I'll honor all requests for anonymity, but please do include your name and address.

Well, there you have it. Making commitments is always a little scary, but it's the only way to get things done, and it helps a lot to know I'm not alone. Every day, my mail gives me a fresh charge and spurs my determination to keep this thing going. You people are great. Incidentally, I'm sure you understand why there was no room for your contributions this time, but we'll have a good load of them when next we meet. Adios. [sig]

As they say nowadays, Whoa! Remember that it was written in 1979 when I was much younger and wild-eyed. I was so caught up in what I considered to be a mission that I got completely carried away, and you can see now why the editor put the kibosh on it. She knew better than I that it was way beyond anything achievable, and that it would strike many of our readers as the ravings of a nutcase. Well, maybe not that bad, but I have no doubt that there would have been a serious outbreak of skepticism.

And if you think *that* was funny, what was going through my head was even more outrageous. My plan was to start a campaign to create a United States Department of English, overseen by a cabinet-level appointee to be known as the secretary of English. But was it really such an off-the-wall idea? I still think it would be a good thing, but I question whether there would be sufficient public support. We will probably never know. As for the unpublished column, I revised it considerably and resubmitted it. In it I included a request for material that would go toward making up The SOTS Rationale, and this was met with praise and encouragement from the readers.

My revised column included the following:

> All of us, I am sure, have seen or heard of instances where misspellings, mispronunciations, or improper syntax have created difficulties in one way or another. Such difficulties can range from mild aggravation [*sic*] to total disaster, and could have been prevented if the communicators had only been a bit more careful in the delivery of their messages. Misplaced commas in legal documents, for example, have denied rightful inheritances, deprived patent holders of proper royalties, and caused otherwise law-abiding citizens to unwittingly circumvent laws to their everlasting regret. There are cases on record in which travel directions were written that caused serious damage to life and property, subsequent apologies being of little help. The variety of such calamities is probably endless, and I think you now have a good idea of what I'm talking about.

So now you know what my state of mind was in 1979. Perhaps my wonderful dream will never come true, but you have to agree that the underlying thought was a good one, pure and noble, or you wouldn't be reading this book. The English language is integral to our society and deserves to be recognized as both a science and an art. It deserves the support of cultural organizations of all types, including foundations and other granting institutions.

Not everyone relates to art, nor to music, nor to literature, etc., but we all relate to the spoken and written word, particularly as it is used in our public communications media.

Down the hatch

Screwball language can be found almost everywhere, but I especially like to nail those big ad agencies who compose and place their clients' ads in expensive publications, such as big-city newspapers and nationally distributed magazines. Here's a perfect example, found by E.T. of Winston-Salem, N.C.:

> In a four-color ad for Samovar vodka: "Samovar is enjoyed in over 80 countries on every Continent, including France, England, Germany, Greece, and Australia."

One out of five is not good geography, and the ad types lucked out on Australia only because it is both a country and a continent. Also, the four other countries are all located on only one continent. There was a better way to say it. The ad was also shot through with incomplete sentences, such as:

> Just like the world's finest Scotch and Canadian whiskies, Samovar comes to you at 86.8 proof. The International Proof. 86.8, however, is more than just the International Proof. When it comes to vodka, it's the perfect proof.
>
> Perfect for drinking straight and ice cold – the ultimate test of a vodka. Just as perfect for adding a touch of perfection to your favorite mixed drinks. ...
>
> No other vodka is quite like Samovar because no other vodka is distilled like Samovar. Through a costly and pain-stakingly [sic] precise method.
>
> Resulting in a vodka that's Ultra Dry. And exceptionally smooth. Yet, with a lively quality that's unique and consistently rewarding.

"Perfect for adding a touch of perfection"? And how many ways are there to distill vodka? OK, that's enough of that. Let's have a look at what E.M. of Mansfield, Ohio, found in the paper:

AP Newsfeatures syndicates a helpful-hints column by Andy Lang. One question asked was, "When a screw works loose and is **too big** for the hole it was in, what is the standard procedure for plugging the hole?"

Yoo-hoo, is anybody home there? A screw too big for the hole? Copyeditor out to lunch, or just napping? Never mind, let's just move on …

E.M. also clipped an article from the Cleveland *Plain Dealer*, written by John P. Coyne. Regarding a new chief of police, Coyne wrote: "Hanton, with 29 years on the force, immediately vowed to **increase** police response time and get a handle on the police bureaucracy …" ("reduce" or "improve," I hope, or maybe "increase the speed of police response time …")

Smile and say cheese …

From R.C. of Concord, Calif.:

> In an article I clipped from the *San Francisco Chronicle*, staff writer Kathleen Pender tells of an attempt to trademark a particularly famous tree, the Lone Cypress near Carmel, Calif. She says, "Although it has not gone to court yet, Pebble Beach Co. recently warned at least two photographers not to use pictures of the tree without its permission."

Yes, we all know it's grammatically correct, but it was awkwardly written and conjures the image of two photographers standing on that rocky point pleading to the spreading branches. Replacing "its" with "the company's" would have removed that speed bump on the road to understanding. (I never did find out whether the tree was granted a trademark.)

Hit the road

Carmakers spend billions on advertising, so you'd think they would pay more attention to what their ad agencies are doing. Our old friend D.S. of Birmingham, Mich., sent along an ad for the Chevrolet Caprice that took up two full pages, face to face, in *Travel & Leisure* magazine. The ad boasted that the car "stops as **beautifully** as it looks." Stopping beautifully is a stretch, but looking beautifully goes way beyond the bounds of any sort of reasonable syntax. To top it all off, the ad ends with "So we invite you to see and drive the new Caprice. And come to your own **beautiful** conclusions." Aside from the incomplete sentence, what the heck is a "beautiful" conclusion?

What would a car be without a radio? And what would a radio in the car be without the advertising of related products? On my way to somewhere one day, I chanced to hear a golden-throated announcer intone, "If you want your car to go just a little bit **further** ..." The ad was for Gumout, a Pennzoil product. In this case, "further" implies making the car last longer, and it is "farther" that means "going a greater distance." Although "further" is not actually incorrect, it wasn't what was meant, which was "covering an additional distance." Quibble if you like, but that's my reading.

Restaurant chain Baker's Square's ad agency made the same mistake. Boasting, "Nobody goes **further** for fresh," the TV spot showed a man in a chef's hat driving a pickup truck to a farm and back. If the intention had been to illustrate exerting extra effort, "further" would have been OK, but the truck on the road requires "farther," because it relates to distance.

Baker's Square also provided a puzzler: In one of those Sunday newspaper coupon inserts was a full-page ad about some new menu items. Included was this imaginary restaurant review in the style of a movie review by Gene Siskel and Roger Ebert:

> "A MOUTHWATERING PERFORMANCE" – **Sitsill** & Eatum.
> LIMITED ENGAGEMENT – NEW FALL PREMIERES!

I have a hunch that it was supposed to be "Sitstill & Eatum," which makes a certain amount of sense. But I'm having difficulty picturing a performance as "mouthwatering." The food, maybe, but the performance? Sorry, but the weak "showbiz" tie-in misses the mark.

Group?

J.B. of Charlottesville, Va., returns with his hooks firmly embedded in *U.S.News & World Report*:

A section titled Washington Whispers, edited by Charles
Fenyvesi, led off with: "Take a memo. A group of seven leading
Republican conservatives **have** prepared an explosive memo to
the White House ..."

If the article had been in the *London Times* or some other British newspaper, or on the "telly," it would have been perfectly proper, because that's
the way the British speak and write, but as I mentioned earlier, Brits and
Yanks frequently do not speak the same language. (has)

22

Slick and shiny

Computer enthusiast B.B. of Raleigh, N.C., reads *PC Today* magazine and caught writer J.W. Huttig, Jr., in the middle of an article about online forums being "open 24 hours a day and the conversation is always as stimulating as a good cup of coffee." Unfortunately, that particular paragraph was preceded by a bolded subheading that read, "**WHERE TO KIBBUTZ**." Aside from turning an unlikely noun into a verb, one would never be able to do it in a chat room, even in Israel. "Kibitzing," of course, goes on everywhere, including online.

Speaking of coffee, A.E. of Madison, Wis., bought some Norelco filters and read the package: "Convenient: Filters are economical and easy to dispose of, **un-messy**. No **affect** on taste." "Affect" should be "effect," and I have no clue as to how anyone could come up with "un-messy." My suggestion would be to make it, simply, "not messy." "Unmessy" or "non-messy"? Or maybe "messless"? Maybe.

Multiple contributor K.W.-D. of Kenosha, Wis., cast a sharp eye – twice – at an article by Thomas Kostigen in a 1991 issue of *Financial Planning* magazine. It was all about financial planning, of course, and included: "The need for [financial] advisers to be **bluntfully** honest with clients over their future is important now more than ever." I must confess that I had never seen the word before and have not seen it since. Nor has any of the Webster dictionary folk, either.

Take the day off

P.S. out in Wolf Point, Mont., returns with nothing to celebrate:

> The Wolf Point *Herald-News* advised everyone to "Celebrate freedom – The Herald News will be closed on Monday, July 5, in observance of the Fourth of July." And a display ad for the First Community Bank read: "Hail to the Red, White & Blue! In observance of the Fourth of July, we will be closed Monday,

July 5." Whatever became of Independence Day as a holiday?
It just seems strange to me to celebrate the Fourth of July on
the fifth.

It would appear that a great many people now use "Fourth of July" inter-
changeably with the proper name of the day of observance, which is
indeed Independence Day. I am reminded of that old saying, "Live it up
on the fourth – buy a fifth on the third," even though I never did.

That same P.S. also reads the *Sioux Falls* [So. Dak.] *Argus Leader* and adds
a new one to the cause: It seems that a house caught fire on Minnesota
Avenue and Fire Captain Jerry Black was quoted as saying, "One of the
residents stated [that] he woke up and there was an entertainment **council** that was on fire." ("console")

Junk mail is a borderline area for SOTS, but the Book-of-the-Month
Club is so ubiquitous that it's public enough. The mailbox of P.S. of
Santa Barbara, Calif., yielded an offer for *Never Be Lied to Again*, a book
designed to teach us to "use certain words, phrases, and body language to
illicit the truth from others." By an odd coincidence, a companion book
on the same mailer was *Match Wits with Mensa*. Not that there's any
correlation, of course. No, really, there isn't. It was, to me, just an unusual
coincidence.

Also arriving by post at the home of E.R. of Hoboken, N.J., was a solici-
tation for *Book Digest*. It offered "**full excerpts** from volumes like *The
Armand Hammer Collection, American Folk Painters,* ..." I would certainly
not want to read only a partial excerpt, would you? E.R. also noted the
legend in the address area on a catalog from Inmac Corporation: "If the
above person is no longer **appropriate**, please pass this catalog on to the
right person in your organization." Hey, just because a person is no longer
working for the company is no reason to label him or her as "inappropriate." Sheesh!

I would hate to be picking on a nonprofessional, but I don't think I need
worry because it's the job of copyeditors to fix things before they go to
press. Or maybe not. L.C. of Pleasant Hill, Calif., read a book review
that contained a speed bump:

Written by a Harvard student who may or may not have been paid, the review in the *San Francisco Chronicle* was of *When Things of the Spirit Come First,* by Simone de Beauvior. Treating an individual story within the book, the reviewer writes: "In 'Marguerite,' the young protagonist takes up with her sister's husband; although this **elicit** liaison ends with the man's exposure as a self-absorbed chauvinist, it leads Marguerite to self-discovery."

Oh, copyeditor, wherefore art thou?

Correction?

If it seems as if I'm picking on the little weekly papers, I guess I have to confess that I am, but it's only because they give me such irresistible ammunition. This offering from the ever-present B.R. of Forest, Miss., takes the cake, as far as I am concerned:

> *The Scott County Times* wrote up a Lions Club event, including: "On Tuesday, January 16, Dr. John Smith, a local **denist** spoke to the Lions Club about his trip to the Holy Land. His talk was very interesting and informative as he explained about such places as the West Bank, Golan Heights, and the **Gay** Strip." In the next issue, the following appeared: "In last week's news, there was a **mispring** in one of the places Dr. Smith visited in the Holy Land. The place was the Gaza Strip, not the gay strip as printed."

One more from B.R., and then I'll ease off a bit.

> Ruth Ingram, assistant metro editor of the *Clarion-Ledger*, reviewed Jacque's restaurant in Vicksburg, favorably, I might add, but seemed a tad confused when adding, "Kelly had to **secede** his mashed potatoes to our oldest gal, who passed up the kids' menu for cheese-stuffed cannelloni ..." I cannot figure out what the writer had in mind.

Well, first he had to declare the potatoes an independent entity, separate from the rest of his plate. Then his daughter was required to grant them autonomy, but available to form alliances with other foods she had ordered. Secession, of course, was part of Vicksburg's history, so it all makes sense. Doesn't it?

Unrelated, but still "cheesy," came the coupon from S.C. of Sierra Vista, Ariz.:

> On the back of a package of Zesta soda crackers was the offer to "Save 10¢ on **any size** or flavor of **10 oz.** Cracker Barrel cheddar cheese."

Maybe I'll try a small-size 10-oz. first. If I like it, I'll buy the large-size 10-oz.

Really?

Those pamphlets that come in the mail from utilities companies certainly qualify for the SOTS treatment. They're public and they're prepared by professionals, although perhaps not in the same sense as ad agency types. Nevertheless, B.M. of Carrollton, Ga., was within his rights to present us with what came in his mail from the Georgia Natural Gas folks. The pamphlet began: "Colder Weather May Increase Your Home Heating Costs." Brilliant, no?

B.M. followed that a bit later with this one:

> This ad is so strange that I'm not even sure it qualifies for mention in my favorite section of the *Bulletin.* It pictures a man seated on the rim of a rubber boat, and the headline reads, "Wherever you go ... go fishing, too with Avon." In the ad's text is: "An Avon stows away compactly in its own bag, inflates faster with a powerful foot pump and launches in min-utes. **Avon's** are the safest, multi-compartments and positive stability."

A boat in a bag – now, that's not a bad idea. Too bad the ad writer fell overboard, starting with the misplaced comma that should have gone after "too," not before, and diving into murky waters with that unnecessary apostrophe in "Avon's" before drowning altogether in the last nonsentence (or nonsense sentence). The magazine, *Popular Science*, should have sent it back for rework.

Here's another TV news boo-boo, brought to us today by S.N. of White-fish, Mont.:

> Recently the pope visited Mexico. MSNBC's coverage was highlighted by the printing across the bottom of the screen of "Mexican saint **canonized**." A person is canonized to *become* a saint. This is either a redundancy or a *non sequitur*. In either case, you're welcome.

And consider yourself thanked.

Yes, books

I know I said that books were not one of SOTS's targets, but I'm going to make an exception, only because what follows is so closely related to broadcasting.

In *TV Book*, edited by Judy Foreman and published by Workman Publishing Co., N.Y., N.Y. (1977), across the bottom of almost all pages was "A Photo History of Television," compiled by Danny Peary. Three times, the name of **Durwood** Kirby appeared. What's wrong? The former sidekick of Garry Moore (a well-known TV personality) bore the name of Durward, not Durwood. But there were other goofs just like it.

In *Television: The First Fifty Years*, by Jeff Greenfield (Harry N. Abrams, Inc. 1976), a photo caption on page 69 reads: "One of the most successful variety shows of the late 1950s starred Garry Moore ... His announcer, sidekick, and commercial spokesman, Dur**wood** Kirby ... etc."

Richard Lamparski put together a series of books that were all called *Whatever Became of ...?* His tenth in the series, published by Crown Publishers, Inc., New York (1986), had on page 208 the same **Durwood** Kirby. It was beginning to look like a disease. I have since Googled Mr. Kirby's name on the Internet and found similar errors. However, there is at least one Web site that sets the record right, one called Seldom Asked Questions. Check it out.

Along that line, it must be noted that the error has been compounded. Readers may recall the TV cartoon series *Rocky and Bullwinkle*, in which there was a separate cartoon called "Mr. Peabody & Sherman." Mr. Peabody was a dog and Sherman was his pet boy. The two traveled through time in search of "The Kirward Derby," the wearing of which made the wearer the smartest person in the world. Unfortunately, most Internet Web sites have it spelled "Kirwood," and I have since discovered that on Google there are more sites with wrong spellings (672) than there are with right ones (54). It looks as if we have an "urban legend" on our hands. The man's name was Durward, for pity's sake.

Why is all this in my book? Because it needed to be said, that's why.

Is that a fact?

Another book, *The Golden Years of Broadcasting: A Celebration of the First 50 Years of Radio and TV on NBC*, by Robert Campbell (Charles Scribner's Sons, 1976), was not so much in need of a copyeditor as it was in need of a fact-checker. A photo caption on page 41 read: "'Hello, Duffy's Tavern,' Ed Gardner would say as he picked up the phone in his role as the genial **saloonkeeper**, Duffy." Just a cotton-pickin' minute, there, pardner. In actuality (and I was a regular listener), the phone would ring and actor Gardner would say, "Hello, Duffy's Tavern, where the elite meet to eat, Archie the manager speaking, Duffy ain't here ... oh, hello, Duffy." As Lily Tomlin's little Edith Ann would say, and that's the truth.

A bit further on in that same book, on page 56, the text read: "Little more than three weeks after FDR's unprecedented third-term election came Pearl Harbor." Author Campbell booted another one; Roosevelt was re-elected in November 1940, and it was indeed for a third term. However, the attack on Pearl Harbor came on December 7, 1941, "a date that will live in infamy," as Roosevelt said on the radio the next day. Campbell was close to a year off.

And then there was yet another goof, but this time only someone familiar with motion picture film would likely catch: On page 109 Campbell mentions the counting down of the beginning of a film by way of the "academy leader," and many have seen the numbers flash on the screen – 6 – 5 – 4 – 3 – and here Campbell goes astray. He adds, "2 – 1 – start," and calls them "optical markings," except that the "2 − 1 − start" are never seen because they are simply not there. The film is black for those last three seconds, enabling the projectionist to stop the projector, to have it ready, and on cue to show the opening of the film without showing the countdown. As Paul Harvey would say, "And now you know the rest of the story."

Stop the bleeding

All too common are common misconceptions about the English language. A word may be printed in dictionaries, but that's no guarantee it won't be misused *en masse*. A good example appeared on a *Jeopardy!* college tournament. The category was "Barber College," and the clue (answer) was "A barber in training might want to pick up a supply of styptic pencils; they help **staunch** this." The proper response, of course, was "What is bleeding?" "Staunch," however, is an adjective, while "stanch" was the correct verb. In spite of the occasional goof like that, the show is still my favorite.

Spooky!

J.H. (OK, daughter Judy) of Brooklyn Center, Minn., reads the only true gossip (oxymoron?) column in our local paper, the *Star Tribune*. It's written by Carol Johnson, who has secured C.J. as her byline, but we've all known her real name from the start. Anyway, C.J. wrote about a TV news situation thusly: "What's up at KSTP? Readers continue to be **exorcised** by the return of Cyndy Brucato to KSTP-TV ..." The word is "exercised" and the two letters are so far apart on the keyboard as to negate the possibility of this being a typo. The word is seldom used and the writer should not have tried it without checking, because both words would be accepted by her spell-checker. "Exorcise" means to chase out evil spirits, hardly the way to describe one's readers.

Another from the spirit world is this headline from the *Times-Republican*, donated by S.F. of Marshalltown, Iowa: "**Ethnics** remain dead in America." Well, I suppose some of them do, but lumping them all together like that is not nice. Oh? "Ethics"? Ahh, I see. Typo? No way.

Hurry, hurry

Sometimes something we see or hear makes us wonder whether there wasn't enough time for someone to look it over before it was printed or broadcast. Tight deadlines are faced by everyone in the communications industries every day, and quite often there is a scramble to get an ad or announcement to the paper or station just under the wire (I speak from experience). Such had to be the case with the newspaper ad placed for KSTP-TV, Channel 5's *Eyewitness News* program. In 68-point (almost one-inch high) white type on a solid red background were "EAT. SLEEP. **BREATH**. REPORT. (NOT NECESSARILY IN THAT ORDER.)" I really do hope they inhale more often than that. ("breathe")

I suspect that such deadlines occasionally create difficulties for game-show producers as well. As you already know, I am a devotee of *Jeopardy!*, what once was and may still be the most popular TV game show ever, although *Wheel of Fortune* also claims to be the most-watched. But although I enjoy matching my knowledge with that of the contestants, I am also delighted when I catch the production people in a gaffe. On occasion, things just don't work out right.

For example, during a "celebrity tournament," the Final Jeopardy category was "The presidency." The answer provided was "If a president is impeached, this official presides over the trial in the Senate." Well-known news reporter Bob Woodward and former presidential speech-writer Peggy Noonan both correctly responded with "Who is the chief justice of the U.S?" Talk-show host Tucker Carlson, however, wrote, "Who is the chief justice of the **Supreme Court**?" Carlson had it wrong, but his question was accepted on the grounds of common usage, and he won the day's game anyway. That's disappointing. The position is named in the U.S. Constitution and is rightly listed in most dictionaries as "chief justice of the United States." There is no such office as the one indicated by Carlson.

Same program, different day: The category was "Death of a President," and the answer was "His March 8, 1930 death occurred a month after he resigned as chief justice of the **Supreme Court** due to heart trouble." The question, of course, was "Who is Taft?" Again, the answer was wrong.

It's spreading like wildfire. The NBC-TV program *West Wing*, whose writing staff, of all people, should have known better, had character Josh saying, "Chief Justice of the **Supreme Court**," not once, but twice. Also, a local public TV program called *Almanac* gave us a printed graphic reading: "Historical – Warren Burger named Chief Justice of the U.S. **Supreme Court**." (Burger was from St. Paul.)

When?

Giving the devil his due, however, I must compliment the *Jeopardy!* folks once more, this time for knowing when the twentieth century ended and the twenty-first began. In spite of all the hoop-la in Times Square and elsewhere, the rolling over of 1999 into 2000 was not the "turn of the century" or the start of a new millennium. Even as far back as December 1993, a Final Jeopardy answer was "By our calendar, the First British East India Co. was founded on this date, the last day of the 16th century." Two contestants got it right, while the third erroneously said, "What is 12/31/1599?" The correct response, of course, was "What is 12/31/1600?" Host Alex Trebek then added that, annually the program tries to "teach people out there that centuries begin with year 1 [e.g., 2001] ... and they end with the year 100." What Trebek didn't say, although to those who know it didn't matter, was that the century does not end until the last day of that "100" year, and not on the first day of that "100" year. The same goes for decades that begin with 1 and end with 10, and millennia that begin with 1 (2001) and end with 1000 (2000, 3000, etc.).

The argument goes way back. In 1966 Arthur C. Clarke wrote an article In *Vogue* magazine titled "The World of 2001," in which he said, "On 1 January 2001, the second millennium ends and the third begins." Anyone care to argue with Arthur C. Clarke?

My favorite analogy is this: One dollar is 100 cents, so when you've saved up 99 cents, is your next – or one hundredth – penny the start of the next dollar? I realize that this really has little to do with the subject of this book, except as it regards fact-checking, but I had to get it off my chest. As a side note, In 1999 I had some bright-orange round stickers made up – the size of most pin-back buttons – with the statement, "It ain't the millennium, stupid." Unfortunately, the word came out as "millenium," but hardly anyone noticed it was wrong, including many who took them from me and stuck them on their chests. Onward! (So why didn't my spell-checker notice, either? It accepted both spellings. Spell-checker can be a great help, but it can also trick you.)

One last word on game shows: I think it would be really great if some-one – maybe Merv Griffin, the man responsible for creating *Jeopardy!* and *Wheel of Fortune* – invented a game show that was all about the kind of stuff in this book. Contestants would be asked to correct spelling and punctuation, to substitute proper words for erroneous ones, and solve problems dealing with goofy syntax and other gaffes. Wouldn't that be a riot? Unfortunately, it would probably never sell, more's the pity. Ah, well, I still think it's a good idea.

Strib

I'll have a lot more fun from other newspapers in due course, but this is as good a time as any to dump even more heavily on my daily *Star Tribune*, Newspaper of the Twin Cities (or whatever slogan it's currently using). It's the one delivered to my door, so it's the one I read the most.

Headline over Fixit advice column: "Instructions can help you **tie-die** shirts like '60s." ("tie-dye")

Front page headline in 1997: "McVeigh trial **underway**." Front page headline in 2002: "Early inquiry of police **underway**." There have been many such usages ever since, and no, I have not called or written to the paper's copy chief to ask why the decision was made to combine two words into one. My supersensitive gut feeling is that there is nothing I could say that would change anything, even in light of the research I have done. I went to our largest county library and ensconced myself in the dictionary section. In the many volumes there I found some agreement with the newspaper's policy, but there were more dictionaries that indi-cated opposition. My own feeling is that the usage simply doesn't make sense. Of the eight dictionaries I checked, seven of them had "under way" as two words, and the eighth volume was the *Canadian Oxford Dictionary*, which went the other way, not surprisingly (offense unintended).

At the same time, I examined those same books for the use of "fund-raising" or "fund-raiser." The *Star Tribune*'s style manual now recommends "fundraiser," but five of the eight dictionaries I checked gave the nod to the use of the hyphen. Besides, it makes for less confusion when the term is broken at the end of a line; without the hyphen it sometimes turns out to be "fun-draiser," especially in those small-town weeklies without copyeditors.

Apparently, however, the *Star Tribune* style is not engraved in stone. In an article in the Business section by former reader's representative Lou Gelfand were two "fund-raising" entries. Whether by accident or in deference to the emeritus status of the journalist, it caught my eye right away, even before I began reading the article. Isn't it remarkable that when we are used to seeing something wrong for a period of time, seeing it right somehow has an effect similar to that of seeing something wrong. Funny how the mind works.

Thou shalt not

It's not a big deal, but with all the fuss about the ten commandments being allowed or not allowed to be displayed on public property, one *Star Tribune* headline writer apparently failed spelling. The line read "No **Commandants**," although "commandments" was spelling correctly in the story itself.

Then there's the headline writer for the *Los Angeles Times* who also had a spelling problem with: "Kudos on Article by Conway That **Decifers** the Dress Code." Thanks go to R.M. of Rancho Santa Margarita, Calif., for supplying the clipping. ("deciphers")

Abigail Van Buren's Dear Abby column was one I read faithfully for years. She was also a language buff and occasionally would write about her pet peeves, many of which are embedded in this book. She did, however, miss the boat at least once when she chided some of her readers, even those in the jewelry business, who were inclined to pronounce the word as "JOOL-ree" instead of "**JOOL-uh-ree**." Correctly, it is pronounced JOO-wul-ree. I waited for her to print a correction, but none came.

For real?

If ever there was a word that got so badly trampled by the English-speaking world that it was in danger of losing its real meanings, it's "real." Everywhere we look and everywhere we listen, someone makes a mess of it. In those slick-paper coupon sections of our Sunday papers are innumerable mishandlings of the word. Egg Beaters is claimed to be "Real Eggs. (OK so far.) Real Cheese. (Also OK.) **Real good**." The alliteration is appealing, no question, but would it have been so bad to say "Really Good"? Here, once again, is a case of common speech threatening to bury logical speech. All right, my dictionaries all define "real" in the sense of "very" as informal or colloquial, and thus supposedly acceptable in certain circumstances, but that doesn't mean that dictionaries endorse the usage.

An ad for Hungry Jack Mashed Potatoes says, "Real Potatoes. **Real Fast. Real Good**." Where Egg Beaters got two out of three right, this one gets only one out of three. The contest-winner and current champion, though, was handed to me by D.W. of Minneapolis. Back Home, a service that delivers groceries direct to your door, prepared one of those large four-color, slick-paper newspaper inserts extolling these benefits: "**Real Easy. Real Convenient. Real Fast. Real Good**." Sorry, folks, but that's "Real Bad." What are our kids supposed to think? The word *real* means genuine, authentic, and is the opposite of false, fake, imitation, etc. The ad people could have substituted "really" for "real" without losing any of the ad's effectiveness and without taking up much additional space. They took such great care with the rest of the flyer and then messed it up with four words. Tsk, tsk.

I never heard him much myself, but Billy Graham has been extremely popular among those of religious persuasion beginning in the 1950s and even continuing to 2006 and maybe beyond. H.M. of Tyler, Texas, however, told me that he believes that the Rev. Graham was responsible for contributing to the increased use of "real" in place of the better words, and that country music folk merely added fuel to the linguistic fire. The preacher, H.M. says, always closed his radio and television programs with, "May the Lord bless you **real good**." And we wonder where the young'uns pick it up.

Incidentally, I puffed up a bit when I read the first paragraph of H.M.'s letter: "My copy of the *Bulletin* arrived today, and I enjoyed reading the SOTS column, as usual. It always gets scissored out and mailed to other family members elsewhere for their amusement." And that, dear reader, is exactly why I have been doing this for the past 30+ years. My thanks for the kind comments.

More? OK.

In a modest-size headline over the *Star Tribune* Fixit column was: "Manual lawn mowers are not **real** hard to find." I would have left "real" out entirely. Or I might have substituted "so" or "too" instead. I once had a reel-type mower, but that's another story.

In fairness and for balance, I'll insert a compliment here, to Sara Lee Foods for its Jimmy Dean hot-breakfast sandwiches. The ad says, "REAL EGGS, REAL MEAT, REAL CHEESE, REALLY, REALLY GOOD." So far, so good. But right at the bottom is "REAL, HOT BREAKFAST." It looks a little odd, but the comma saves the day. It therefore says that we get not a phony breakfast, but a real one, and a hot one at that. Hmm. What's wrong there? Nothing I can see. A "really hot breakfast" would scorch my palate; I don't know about yours.

With yet another twist on the word is D.S. of New London, Conn.:

> High on my hit list is the Hostess Pastry TV commercial that shows a delicious-looking pie while a female voice says, "I take care to use only **real** apples in my fruit pies." As opposed to what? Fake apples?

And not the least of this "real" conglomeration is the inch-high headline on the front page of – you guessed it – the *Star Tribune*. When 16 inches of snow fell on the Minneapolis-St. Paul area over March 8-10, 1999, the oh-so-clever banner read: "A **real** flaky storm." OK, so it wasn't a "fake" flaky storm, and a snow storm really is all about "flakes," but we know, don't we, that the line was intended to be cute and fell "real" short of the mark. What would the writer's English teacher say? That is, *if* the writer actually had an English teacher; there appear to be very few of them left.

But just when you think you've heard them all, up pop the publishers of *TIME* magazine introducing yet another periodical – as if we needed it – called ***REAL SIMPLE***. I've stared at the description and the coupon offer, and no matter how hard I stare and how hard I try to visualize a feasible excuse for it, I really and simply can't see any justification for the usage, which I will liken to the plop of manure on the floor of the stable of communication. Yes, I'm sure a large number of creative types sat around a conference table arguing, probably for several hours, and the sensible heads got outvoted. Those who held sway are not uneducated people, but they are so intent on being "so today" that they fail to realize the harm they do. None of them would hire a copywriter who says, "I write real good," but they themselves fearlessly proceed to write "real bad," and get paid handsomely for it. It's a crying shame, and the Time, Inc., staff should be hanging its collective head, because it does such a commendable job otherwise. Grammatically speaking, Time, Inc., has soiled itself.

Bowled over

S.W. of El Paso, Texas, got brought up short by this one:

> Here's another SOTS candidate from TV: "How long has it been since you had a big, **thick, steaming bowl** of Wolf Brand Chili?" My kitchen's just plumb full of big, thick, steaming bowls, isn't yours?

My only question is, do you keep your bowls steaming all the time, or only when you plan to put chili in them? If it's OK with you, I'll suggest "... a big bowl of thick, steaming Wolf Brand Chili." Makes a world of difference, doesn't it?

23

To whose ears?

Some things are grammatically correct but simply nonsensical. While traveling in Arizona I picked up a Music of Your Life radio station, one that plays the really old ballads and instrumentals from the '30s, '40s, and '50s. Remember Wink Martindale, the former game-show host? Here he was, coming out of my car radio, praising the music, saying that it "has touched a **nerve in the fabric** of our generation." Come again, Wink? Anything to do with warp and woofers? Sorry, I think I'm losing it.

Joining in the chorus was Paul Magers of KARE-TV in suburban Golden Valley, Minn, as heard by J.H. of Brooklyn Center, same state. During the O.J. Simpson trial Magers remarked that "Fred Goldman let the **epitaphs** fly once again at comments recently made by O.J. Simpson. ..." ("epithets") To be fair, we don't know whether Goldman said that or if Magers made the goof. Maybe either will let me know.

Slip fixed

Sometimes it's just a good story that deserves a place here. Such is one I tell about *Jeopardy!* and host Alex Trebek. At the opening of a 1992 program, Trebek said, "The reason no dollar figures were announced for any of the players on today's program is because yesterday we sent away a five-time undefeated champion." Immediately after introducing the first-round categories, he said, "Before we make our first selection, I want to clear up a grammatical error I made a few moments ago when I said 'the **reason is because**.' I should not have put in the word 'because.' That is wrong, and I have been taken to task by a number of viewers in the past. I'm sorry I made the mistake again. Darn! I never learn." It takes a big man, as they say. My admiration remains high.

E.M. of Placentia, Calif., felt compelled to report:

> "The only **reason** Congress can function is **because** the committee system provides private occasions for negotiation." The

writer is Irving Kristol in a *Reader's Digest* article. Can you
believe it?

One man's meat

The first time I saw a sign in a meat department for "boneless ribs," I
immediately pulled out a piece of paper to write the oxymoron down.
Including the name of the store in my speeches, I got two responses: (1)
laughter, and (2) one person asking what would be a better way of describing the product? After thinking about it for a moment, I had to admit
that there probably wasn't a better short way to say it. What is meant, of
course, is rib meat with the bones removed, and "boneless rib meat" might
be confusing to some, but I'm not sure why. So, "boneless ribs" it is, and
when they are prepared properly, they can be very tasty.

However, I'm not sure what to make of the sticker on the package of
meat labeled "English Roast." It read "SEMI BONELESS." It would seem
to me that the meat either had bones in it or it didn't. I'd guess that the
meaning was "not as many bones as usual," but … I think I just learned
not to try to look inside the mind of a butcher. Half of the bones, maybe?
Never mind.

Pronunciation pitfalls

If any part of this book can be said to deal heavily with pronunciation, this
will have to be it. Some examples of poor pronunciation are, of course,
liberally salted throughout, but there are words and phrases that won't
come up otherwise, so I'm adding them here.

How often do we hear a newscaster or narrator say OFF-ten, enunciating
the *t*? The usual and most accepted is OFF-'n, rhyming with soften.

Ki-LOM-uh-ter has raised its ugly head and threatens to bury its correct
form permanently. Jim McKay, when announcing the Olympic Games in
Calgary, Canada, invariably said KILL-uh-meter. I ask those who doubt
to follow my logic: A thousandth of a meter is a MILL-i-meter, right? A
hundredth of a meter is a CENT-i-meter, OK? A tenth of a meter is a
DEC-i-meter (dess-i-meter), all will agree, I'm sure. The same goes for
kiloliter. Would anyone say "ki-LOL-i-ter? Of course not. So why does
kilometer come out Ki-LOM-uh-eter? Because it rhymes so very nicely

with thermometer, barometer, odometer, speedometer, and sphygmoma-nometer. (That last is the thing the nurse uses to take your blood pressure.) But the difference is that all of those are the names of *measuring devices*, and those with the emphasis on the first syllable are *measures of distance* – two totally different criteria. In countries where the metric systems are in use, such as Canada and most of Europe, the pronunciation is KILL-o-meter, although even the BBC will occasionally have a news announcer say it the other way. That just tells us how pervasive something like that can be. Now then, repeat after me, KILL-o-meter. Class dismissed.

By the way, some American dictionaries, including those from the here-beleagured Merriam-Webster, are listing the wrong pronunciation of kilometer first. Ignore them. *Illegitimus non carborundum!* On the other hand, if you follow my lead and say KILL-o-meter, your friends may not take kindly to it. As always, when you speak, consider your audience.

How do you plead?

The world of broadcasting has become a helter-skelter, catch-as-catch-can one, with a mish-mash of ways to pronounce ordinary words or to sub-stitute different ones. The word *pled* has become *pleaded*. The defendant pleaded not guilty. Give Tom Jarriel of ABC-TV's *20/20* credit for saying *pled*. Would you say that the car *speeded* up? OK, so you heard that one recently, too. Doesn't make it right. How about the idea that the club president *leaded* the pledge of allegiance to the flag? Have you *readed* a good book lately? As for *pled*, I once heard John MacDougall on KSTP-AM radio say *pled* and *pleaded* in the same newscast, but fortunately not in the same sentence. Something for everyone, I suppose. Call me die-hard, if you like. But I sleep well most nights.

Jim King on WCCO-TV in 1996 said that the Take Back the Night parade "**weaved** its way" down the street. Dictionaries describe it as "rare" but acceptable. Better would be "wove." Perhaps that would be a bit *hoity-toity* for some. Too bad.

Harass. So is it huh-RASS or is it just like pronouncing the proper name Harris? We hear it both ways, don't we? Being a dictionary buff, I con-ducted a survey of my own volumes as well as those in my nearby public library. The consensus is that huh-RASS is much preferred. How the other got started, I have no clue, except that a friend once told me that huh-RASS sounded too much like a part of female anatomy. I don't buy it, but if anyone feels strongly about it, I wish you well. Incidentally, what about morass, (muh-RASS) meaning swamp? Would that come out sounding like Mr. Morris's name?

A while back I heard Ken Speake of KARE-TV reporting on "de-pants-ing," a rather nefarious activity in some local public schools. Interestingly, Speake spoke of HARRIS-ment, while those on the anchor desk indirectly contradicted his pronunciation by using the word correctly. And no, I'd rather not get started on "Uranus."

Toys are who?

Over-enthusiastic was the description writer for a Toys 'R Us newspaper insert ad: "LIFE-LIKE NASCAR HOT STOCKS RACEWAY – Set includes two Speed Wheelers™ that achieve over **500 mph**, flexicurves, banked loops, 90 turns, colorful graphics, more! Ages 5-up." Indoors? Wow! Stand back out there in the kitchen; we're lettin' her rip!

Chiron fun

Chiron is the name of the device that puts information across the bottom of your TV screen while a program is in progress. Sometimes it's related to the program and sometimes it's not, such as when a weather warning is in effect during a soap opera. The operators of chiron equipment should be well schooled in the use of English, but they occasionally give the appearance of having skipped a few classes. When our local KMSP-TV newscast was on the subject of a budget shortfall in our state government, the Chiron operator ran several words across the lower portion, one of them being "**bi-inium**," meaning, of course, "biennium."

Another chiron goof showed up on *CBS This Morning* in a story on real estate, with the REALTOR® being interviewed identified graphically as being from **Caldwell** Banker. Typo? No. ("Coldwell")

I have to give credit to the TV stations for their excellent attention to the weather. Years ago people died simply because there were no satellites and no radar to give us early warning of bad storms, etc. However, the chiron operator at WCCO-TV in 1994 overdid it by alerting us to "**deadly** lightning." Is there any other kind, maybe that which just makes us tingle a bit? It may not be grammatically incorrect, but it certainly is redundant.

Speak of the devil! The aforementioned Coldwell Banker had an ad running on TV in 1999 that asked, "Want to **replace** your sofa?" and showed it being moved to a different house. "Replace" means to throw out the old one and buy a new one. "Re-place" means to change location. That little-bitty hyphen alters the entire picture (copywriters, take note).

Its'?

Now I've seen everything. There's the substituting "it's" for "its," and vice versa, but the one that knocked me for a loop was in a two-color half-page newspaper ad for Home Life Furniture during the Going Out of Business Sale of its local store. The copy included: "CORPORATE DECISION TO CLOSE **ITS'** ONLY MINNESOTA STORE." I had never seen that use of the apostrophe before, nor have I seen it since.

C.Z. of Los Angeles, Calif., had to rub his eyes one day when he saw a most astonishing sight:

> In 1990 I wrote the following about three huge billboards to the president of Pacific Theatres: "I was startled to see, on the *FANTASIA* attraction board high above Sunset Boulevard, the misuse of 'it's' in the tag line 'See *FANTASIA* on **it's** 50th anniversary.'" About a month later I received a letter ... thanking me for my concern about something else I had written – and enclosing two free passes – but making no mention of my criticism of the display advertising. I had noticed earlier, however, when I was next in Hollywood, that the correction had been made on all three mammoth panels. I may not have been the deciding vote, but I'd like to think so.

It would appear that the top gun at Pacific Theatres was more sensitive to public opinion than most others in his position. My guess is that he understood that for every person who notices an error and calls it to the attention of the appropriate parties, there are many others who see it, too, but don't bother to say anything. This is a cardinal rule of advertising that is so very often overlooked. Advertisers and their agencies are used to charting demographics through the use of polls and surveys, from which they extrapolate the size and makeup of their audiences. Conducting polls and surveys requires approaching segments of the public and asking for opinions, whereas the opposite is true when members of the public complain or point out errors such as the one C.Z. identified. One would think that their experience would alert them to the even higher value of voluntary comments from the public, no matter how few. The SOTS hat is off to the parties just mentioned.

E.K. of North Miami, Fla., on the same infraction, may have the last word on it:

> *TV Guide*'s December 1979 full-page ad soliciting subscriptions as holiday gifts has right across the top, "**T'IS** THE SEASON."

Clearly the winner in the how-bad-can-it-get? competition. Now we've seen everything, on that score anyway. I do have one other bad one in that same regard, however, so before we get too far away from the subject, let's hear from B.H. of Whittier, Calif.:

> I will not be surprised if and when a new dictionary comes out that includes such punctuation as *your's, our's, their's,* etc. Then it won't matter that the GWC Development Corporation advertised a housing development, in *New Homes Magazine,* with the headline reading: "A VALUE IN **IT'S** OWN TIME."

More bad spelling

Several years ago, a University of Minnesota professor of engineering named Athelstan Spilhaus offered his opinion of elective courses being taught to students. He described them as "Typewriting, Tap Dancing, and Tomfoolery." He was not far off the mark. Today, fundamentals of English are taught only sketchily, partly because too many teachers never caught on to the basic principles and are now incapable of passing sufficient knowledge on to their pupils. Previously, I mentioned that the early grades, 1-6, made up what we once called grammar school, which was eventually changed to elementary school. We used to have spelling bees, and I understand that those events still take place in some schools, even leading to a national contest. I won several of those spelling bees in school, and I'm still not too bad at it, although some of the newer words particularly confound me. But I get by.

I bring this up in order to establish a "section" of this book devoted a little heavier to spelling and spelling errors perpetrated by professional writers, a great many of whom write advertising. Example: A half-page ad in our tabloid-size weekly *Sun-Sailor* for a home maintenance company included: "Ashco Exteriors Inc. will work with your Insurance Co. **HASTLE** FREE!" ("hassel") The misspelling was compounded by the odd use of capital letters, a missing comma (after "Exteriors"), and a missing hyphen in "HASTLE-FREE." The hassel with the insurance company is not free, as the usage suggests.

A mailed coupon flyer called *Coupon Messenger* contained one for Hobby-town USA, with local stores in both Minnetonka and Brooklyn Park, Minn. The heading, or slogan, read: "Where **Hobby's** Begin." ("hobbies") Need I say more about education? That's a two-fer, by the way; the apostrophe is extraneous.

Another two-fer comes from A.H. of North Grafton, Mass.:

> Enclosed is the front page of *The Evening Herald* [Worcester, Mass.] on which Inside Today's Gazette lists several news items. One reads: "**FIRINGS APPEALED** – A court appeal has been filed by three salesmen who were fired for refusing to answer questions on a company questionnaire they claim were **to personnel**. Page 5."

Again, of course, it was an unnamed "staff writer" who fumbled on the one-yard line. It should have read ". . . were too personal."

Apropos my previous mention of spelling bees, I watched the National Spelling Bee on TV, and was appalled to hear contest officials pronounce "antipyretic" incorrectly (ANT-eye). Later reports on radio and TV mostly were delivered correctly. Where they are now I have no idea, but the SOTS hat is off to Ray Sherwood (KLBB Radio) and Mark Suppelsa (KSTP-TV) especially, for saying it right. The word, which means "reducing fever," is pronounced ANT-ee-pie-RET-ik.

Screwball expressions?

I could not believe my ear (I have only the one) when I heard " We haven't had any rain as **of yet**" come out of the mouth of Dave Dahl, the weathercaster on KSTP-TV whom I praised near the beginning of this book. Then I heard Ken Barlow, on KARE-TV, use the same expression. Where the "of" came from I have no idea, but in this case it is an intruder. No rain "as yet" is sufficient unto the purpose, and let's not let this barbarism take hold. Also, just as acceptable would be "as of right now," "as of today," "as of this moment," etc. Let's not wander into superfluous muck.

Wife Celia pointed out another example of that same term going to pot. On the front page of the *Star Tribune* was an article by staff writer Mary Jane Smetanka about important changes expected to take place at the University of Minnesota. Included was "As **of** yet, no one is saying exactly what a new university will look like …" Catching, isn't it? Please, let it stop, right now!

Colloquialism in TV ads also offends E.B. of Syracuse, N.Y.:

> Then there is the advertisement [for] Liquid Plumr. A mechanic is talking about a certain job and says, "It's not too big **of** a job." I wrote to the advertising people, but they … sent me a stupid form letter. I asked them if that's how mechanics talk, if they are being patronizing to people who use mechanics, or do they just not know correct English, but they don't care one way or another.

Another hoity-toity term heard so often these days is the redundant "at this point **in time**." It appears to have begun in Washington, D.C., where government officials strive to outdo each other as "voices of authority." That is, each wants to let the others know that he or she is educated beyond the threshold of pain; that each one's spoken word carries more weight than the next person's. It's completely superfluous, this saying, in all its permutations, and all are nothing more than ways to say *now*, or *at present*. Certainly, no one needs to say more than "at this point," or "at this time," but to meld them together is unnecessary nonsense (as opposed, of course, to necessary nonsense). When next you hear a respected newscaster say "at this point in time," call, e-mail, or use a postage stamp to tell him or her to save his or her breath and knock off the double-talk. At least think about it.

24

Solution?

This may or may not be the best place to put this, but I'm going to do it anyway. I gave a speech to my Toastmasters club not long ago, and the response was mostly hilarious laughter, even though I was partly serious. In its slightly edited form, it began thusly:

> Mr. Toastmaster, fellow members, and honored guests. It's bad enough that we so often lose our messages in translation; it is worse that we do not speak the same language in the first place. There is, has been, and will continue to be much discussion about our decaying language. The problem, however, may be so far gone that nothing less than drastic, perhaps even radical, action be taken. Are you thinking what I am thinking?
>
> Distasteful as it may sound, and contrary to our entire way of life it may be, there is only one answer that makes truly logical sense. Ready? Governmental intervention.
>
> Emotionally, of course, we reject such a notion, but let us put our notions aside for a moment and give the idea some logical consideration.
>
> First, we must assume that there are some things that are logically in the federal domain. Libertarians, please bear with me, if you will. National security, the space program, interstate commerce, the Food and Drug Administration, these are but a few examples. Envision, then, a national Department of English, with a secretary of English, perhaps in the president's cabinet. This department would be charged with the responsibility of, first, creating and publishing a single, comprehensive dictionary, editing (for proper grammar, etc.) textbooks to be used at all grade levels, and examining all other auxiliary reference materials, such as those containing synonyms, antonyms, homonyms, and the rest.

These materials would be nonpolitical, nonreligious, and non-regional in nature. Disputes would be resolved by a panel of expert linguists. Use of the materials, of course, would be voluntary. They would serve only as recommended guidelines, with no penalties attached. And before anyone thinks how easy it would be to take the next logical step and make Official English mandatory, with appropriate penalties, consider how difficult that would be. Frankly, I'd say it would be impossible.

Prohibition of alcohol didn't work, and clandestine conversation would be easier to hide than booze.

But let us not forget what we are talking about here today. We are talking about the *professional* broadcasters and writers. They are the ones who would be directly affected. The United States Department of English would publish all necessary materials and establish a testing bureau for certification and licensing of professional communicators. It would also monitor and evaluate all of the communications media. Violators of "official" English usage would be subject to notification of their errors, with penalties administered in staged categories.

Depending on the frequency of violation, offenders would receive, in ascending order, reprimands, retraining, and, for the incorrigible, suspension, revocation, or permanent denial of license to publicly communicate.

An anchorperson, in such event, would then be said to have "cut the chain." A weathercaster would be "blown away." And imagine what could be said about sportscasters.

As unheard of as this may be, it does begin to make sense, if only in its own odd way. Public communicators have free reign to use the public prints and airwaves pretty much as they please. It may be just about time that they took responsibility right along with their privileges. Mr. Toastmaster.

OK, so it's goofy. It could have been better organized, and it ended rather abruptly. But if you look for that tiny grain of reason within it, it may not be as far-fetched as we think. And I ask you, does anyone have a better idea? I thought not. (Incidentally, I received a glowing evaluation.)

You're what?

On television several years ago, and long after I was out of the business, one of my former clients got carried away. Bob Fleming, owner and operator of a discount merchandiser called The Furniture Barn, ran a newspaper ad that announced a big sale. In one part of the ad were the words "**More** than ever before, we're going **all out**!" I almost called Bob to ask him when it was that he went "all out" less than before, but I was afraid he would hang up on me, as he had a couple of times in the past when I was "doctoring" his TV spots. But that's another story.

How perfect?

There once was a car named the Eagle Talon, and the Motoring section of the *Star Tribune* led off one day with the headline "Talon is **improvement** on perfection." Seems to me that a definition of perfection is "the highest degree of excellence, unable to be improved upon." And yes, we all know of the "imperfection" in the Preamble to the Constitution that says, "We the People of the United States, in order to form a more perfect union ..." Well, heck, nobody's perfect; even our founding fathers missed a step or two. But the end result was what mattered. Anyway, let's have no more of this trying to "improve" on perfection. Enough is too much.

Save off or on?

Have you been as confused as most people are about whether we "save off" or "save on" whatever it is we are buying? I had a pretty good idea of which was correct, but I decided to put my opinion to the test. I went through three full sections of those coupons that come with the Sunday paper, and here's what I found:

Save on: 105 mentions
Save x¢ when you buy: 11 mentions
x¢ off: 24 mentions
Save off: 2 mentions
x¢ off on: 6 mentions

My survey confirmed my original thought, that one cannot save anything
"off," but saving money "on" a purchase makes perfect sense. We can "get"
money off, or "take" so much off, but we can only "save on," or "save x¢ or
x$" when we buy. And I thought that those 6 mentions of saving so much
"off on" a purchase were a nice compromise, if such were needed. So now
you know. A scientific survey proves all.

Nowadays, however, we don't just save money, we "Save Big!" A.P. of
Victoria, B.C., Canada, was among many who wrote to air their ire at the
term. In her case it was a claim made by the makers of Magnavox television sets. Menard's, a chain of home maintenance stores in my area, has
for years advertised that we can "Save **big** money at Menard's." We can't
change the awful thing, but we can record it here for posterity. (Posterity
probably won't know the difference.)

Hic!

A.F. of Lincoln, Neb., sent me a thick envelope with several years' worth
of clippings she had saved, most from the local *Lincoln Journal Star*.
Among them was an AP story about a state employee arrested for driving under the influence. Get this: "The 46-year-old Lewellen man had a
blood alcohol level of **12** percent, according to the Nebraska State Patrol.
The legal limit in Nebraska [at the time] is 0.10." Mmmm ... maybe it
was a slip of a finger on the keyboard, and maybe not. Anyway, A.F. also
loaded me up with several more doozies of the less-than-literate variety
from that same paper: **Shear** for sheer, **flare** for flair [and we had the
opposite previously], **geneology** for genealogy, **sour** for soar [question-
able], and one I could never have made up, **super ventricular cardia** for
supraventricular tachycardia. A.F. worked most of her life as a medical
transcriptionist, so I didn't even have to look that one up. But, hey, have a
heart. Some poor slave probably worked far into the night trying to make
deadline and had no time to check such stuff. (Did I say that?)

No one is immune

Not everyone is going to see the error this time, but I'm leaving it
untouched as a challenge. Once again we hear from L.H. of Chicago, Ill.:

> Quote from Ann Marie Lipinski, the editor of the *Chicago
> Tribune*, in an article on replacing [advice columnist] Ann

Landers: "Her death created a void and we spent a great deal of time talking with readers about how to, or even if to, fill that void."

"Talking with readers about how to ... fill that void" is OK, but "talking with readers about ... or even if to, fill that void," or "talking with readers about ... if to fill that void," or any other permutation of the sentence simply does not work. I call it a strangling sentence because it leaves the reader hanging. There are, of course, several ways to fix it. My preference would be "talking with readers about how to fill that void, or indeed whether we should." Your turn.

L.H. also delivered a headline from that same paper: "2 BUILDINGS TAKE STEPS TO BECOME LANDMARKS." She says that "one of them is a school that was founded by St. Francis Xavier Cabrini, so perhaps it has miraculous powers." In the building trades, the area in square feet that a building occupies is known as its "footprint." Now we know there's a good reason for it, except that I always thought the "footprint" was permanent and immovable.

One more from L.H., who listens to WGN radio in Chicago, and heard that "a pair of frozen **embryos** have been **ordered** to remain in the freezer until the next hearing of the parents' custody case." L.H. adds, "Kids just don't get to make their own choices these days."

Common courtesy

M.J. of Punta Gorda, Fla., sent me a page from his local paper and included no comment except to locate the gaffe with a highlighter pen, most likely because it speaks for itself. It was in an article written by Gavin Off in *The Sun* about a pancake breakfast held at a local church, at which everyone had a great time. "It's a lot of work," [one woman] said. "The men **compliment** the women and the women **compliment** the men. I'm sure they bring in people for the pancake breakfast and we bring people for the **bizarre**. It's a two-way street." Yes. I'm sure they all held each other in high regard and voiced their admiration freely. ("complement," "bazaar")

Spam?

I never open spam. Boy, I really hate that word (I overdosed on canned SPAM in the army), as I am sure the folks at Hormel Foods in Albert Lea, Minnesota, do more than anyone else. But until someone comes up with a better one, we'll just have to accept it. However, M. DeW. of San Leandro, Calif., (maybe accidentally?) opened one of those mischievous missives and in large type the screen showed "As Seen On TV! America's #1 **Penal** Enlargement. Guaranteed to work or your money back." Our contributor comments: "This is one of the dumbest pieces of Spam I've yet received; I suppose Devil's Island was a "penile colony.""

I left "Spam" capitalized, but as it refers to "junk" e-mail, it should not be. In fact, not enough folks know that the meat product, SPAM, is trade-marked in all capital letters. Unfortunately, it will probably go the way of Xerox, Kleenex, etc., and be swallowed up by common usage.

Pow!

Here we go again with a noun becoming a verb. M.K. of Dorchester, Mass., offers this howler from *U.S. News & World Report*:

> Katherine Hobson grammatically but unfortunately wrote about women's clothing being "chic – and comfortable," while appropriately fitting each of four body types: "Mirrorless dress-ing rooms require customers to come out and be accessorized and **belted** by salespeople before catching sight of themselves."

Another case of battered women? All right, all right, I can't think of another way to say it, either. Unless I'm mistaken, however, a belt is an accessory, so it probably could have been left out of that sentence. Not an easy call.

Time out

By now you're probably wondering how much more damage is being done to the English language. How many more examples of profession-als mishandling our spoken and written words can there be? With almost no repetition so far, I have barely scratched the surface, and the variety of verbal infractions continues to amaze even me. So let's take a break about here before you and I become benumbed. If you're in a chair, get up and walk around a bit. If you're in bed, turn out the light and let the ministrations of Morpheus waft away the cares of the day and the daffy stuff you've been reading. Tomorrow's another day. On the other hand, if you are truly indefatigable, plunge on. I'm ready.

Such is fame

From F.Y. of Chillicothe, Ohio, comes this head-shaker:

> In the *Chillicothe Gazette* was the enclosed article about the legal intricacies of immigration, headlined: "Deportation **eminent** for Chillicothe woman." I just *had* to send this to you.

I just *knew* someone would come up with it, it was only a matter of time. The correct word, of course, is "imminent," as was the arrival of F.Y.'s missive. The woman, I suppose, was not "eminent" enough to avoid the reverse invitation. However, the fact is that the deportation was not imminent at all, considering the appeals process, so it was an altogether inappropriate choice of the word.

Hang in there

I suppose I could have combined all of my concerns with pronunciation into a single section, but it just seemed like too much work. Therefore, I will simply enter them as they emerge from my files and piles. Caveat: Have a dictionary handy in case you are inclined to disagree with my assessments.

Status. It's a short word and a simple one, but almost no one knows how to pronounce it anymore. It comes out "stattus," and rhymes with "lattice," and that is incorrect. The word derives from "state," meaning condition or standing. Some no doubt wonder why Dan Rather, once of CBS Television News, prefers STAY-tus. There are also those who have heard the same from Alex Trebek, the host of *Jeopardy!* In fact, there are those who are convinced that both Rather and Trebek are confused. Not so. They are among a small minority who say it right. Oh, sure, dictionaries will have both pronunciations, but the correct one is ordinarily listed first. Argue *that* one all you like, but it is nevertheless true, in most cases. We'll discuss that anomaly a bit farther on. Or did I mention it before?

Ration. This one fell into the disaster pit because it appears to be connected to "rational" or "rationale." Well, it is, because all are derived from "ratio," meaning reason. "Ratio" is pronounced RAY-shee-oh, so "ration" naturally follows with RAY-shun. The others have a similar root but take the short *a* in their pronunciation. Paul Harvey was once heard to say it correctly when he was talking about water shortages in California, and Marty McNeely of ABC Radio hit it squarely. Good for both of them. So far, no one has attempted to correct me when I say RAY-shun

Data. It is the plural of "datum," pronounced DAY-tum, and is a word that is almost lost to us. Not only is it too often said as DAT-uh, it is also used in the singular sense. A computer company that once flourished in Minnesota had been named Control Data, and any employee caught mispronouncing DAY-tuh was advised to cease the practice.

That word again?

The Minneapolis Board of Education owns its own radio station, KBEM-FM, and although it is known as the "jazz station" for the music it plays, it also gives school kids the chance to be announcers and reporters. One young lady from Tuttle Elementary School pronounced both "data" and "February" correctly. See? They're not all beyond hope.

On the air I have also heard it as Febby-rary, Febby-wary, Feb-you-rary, Feb-a-rary, and Feb-a wary. If I've missed any, it's not for lack of listening. If you know of any I missed, write it here _____.

(By the way, Alex Trebek is one among few who pronounce "February" correctly.)

And for those who think that mispronouncing February is no big deal, if any broadcaster should speak of Rodeo Drive in Los Angeles as ROE-dee-oh, he or she would be deluged with chastising mail.

A while back WCCO-TV on its 6:00 P.M. newscast had a large multicolored graphic reading "**TRIATHALON**." The sports guy, Ralph Jon Fritz, in his report, pronounced it the same way – "**tri-ATH-a-lon**." Later that night, on the same station, the graphic read "TRIATHLON," but RJ apparently wasn't told it had been fixed, so he pronounced it wrong again. Since then I've heard him say it right, much to his credit. Many other broadcasters, however, continue to say "**ATH-a-lete**," "**ath-a-LET-ics**," etc. The biathlons, pentathlons, and decathlons, especially during the Olympic Games, also continue to be abused, but not so much anymore on the networks. Someone must have put the word out.

In a CBS-TV news story about an older female triathlete, both reporter Jim Stewart and anchor Dan Rather said "**Tri-ath-a-lon**." This is why I keep a pad of paper and a pen next to my chair while watching the TV news.

I see you

Thanks to his scanner, J.J. of Alpena, Mich., was able to send along part of a page from his local paper, the *Alpena News*:

> Note the caption that mentions a soldier, "in the 2nd **Recognizance** Battalion, serving in Iraq." Is this the unit that checks IDs? I also know that I should have saved other examples of ignorance or carelessness, such as when the paper reported that a fire was **distinguished**. And then there was the time WHSB Radio announced that a man had stood **moot** before the judge.

How's that for a handful? In order, "reconnaissance," "extinguished," and "mute."

Whose walk?

A bit of controversy was stirred up when the University of Minnesota decided to dedicate a walkway to eminent university scholars and students. (Is there a difference? My guess is that scholars may be more studious than students.)   First it was the intention to call it Scholars' Walk. Then the leader of a fund-raising group disagreed and insisted that it be Scholars Walk. By way of an organization called The Wördos, I was invited to offer my opinion. Some respondents liked Scholar's Walk, as in Mother's Day, while many preferred to move the apostrophe outside in deference to the plural nature of Scholars'. In line with modern usage, such as Veterans Administration, I voted to go without the apostrophe in either position. My side won, in case you'd like to know, despite a two-thirds vote among 60 respondents in favor of the apostrophe.

"Scholars" and "Veterans" are both definitely plural, but neither the Walk nor the Administration "belongs" to the persons referred to, so a possessive apostrophe is not called for. "Mother's Day," however, implies a recognition of "Mother" in the singular sense, it being *her* day, so the apostrophe has its place.

As for the Wördos, it is a quasi-organization of individuals interested in maintaining understandable English among those making use of it, regardless of profession or persuasion. (The umlaut is in memory of the group's founder, whose name was Björn Björnson.) What's unusual is that there are no dues and no officers, just a couple of members who do what needs doing, including keeping order at the meetings. Even with such a loose construction, however, the group managed to publish a booklet, *92 (plus 57) abuses of English that drive curmudgeons crazy!* I attended only two meetings as of this writing, mainly because they meet at 10:00 A.M. and I'm a late-sleeping night owl. But I must say I'm tempted; rarely have I heard such pleasant bandying of words; I was in my element. Maybe again some day.

On the flip side

It made all the major sports reports across the nation, and left no doubt in anyone's mind that it was really a remarkable – nay, improbable – feat. A young basketball player on the Hopkins, Minnesota, high school team found himself flat on his back, holding the ball, with only 2.5 seconds left to play in the state championship game, and with his team behind by only two points. He had nothing to lose, so from that awkward position, just inside the 3-point circle, he gave the ball a heave, and sank the impossible shot from where he lay, throwing the game into overtime and eventually winning the title. Sam Barnes, editor of the Wednesday suburban section of the *Star Tribune*, commented in his Editor's Corner column about "the shooter's touch he put on the shot as he lofted it from his **prone** position …" Needless to say, Sam's grammar goof caught my eye.

As his phone number was listed right next to his column, I gave him a call. Startled that he answered in person, I managed to point out that a "prone" position has one on one's stomach, rather than on one's back. He paused a moment, then said words to the effect that "hardly anyone will know the difference, but thanks for calling it to my attention." That was it. There was nothing else for either of us to say. But I'm sure I wasn't the only one to notice. At least I think I wasn't alone. Hmmmm. The word that was called for was "supine," meaning lying on one's back.

Generally pretty good about corrections, the paper failed to post one about this error.

Tick, tock?

Ignorance, they say, is no excuse. Whom "they" are, I don't know, but usually they're right. As evidence I offer the following unattributed report, without naming a newspaper because it looks as if it came from a news service, and I won't guess about that either.

Headline: "**England:** *Time stands still briefly for Big Ben.*" (The boldface and italics are as they appeared.) "Big Ben, the landmark London **clock** renowned for its accuracy and chimes, stopped ticking Friday for 90 minutes, and officials don't know why." Well, now, I know why. It's because Big Ben *is not a clock!* Big Ben is that huge *bell* that hangs in the clock tower, blimey if it ain't! Ask any Londoner if you don't believe me.

An historic?

British English, revered as it is in its homeland, occasionally leads to what might be called a kind of "payback" for all the American words that have crept into Britain and many other countries. One example of this is the British use of "**an** historic occasion," or some such. I also hear "**an** Hispanic family" or "**an** hysterical patient." Over in Merrie Olde England is where, I suspect, visitors, military types perhaps, picked up the oh-so-easy-to-roll-off-the-tongue "an" in place of the article "a" (pronounced – remember? – as uh). Any English textbook or dictionary will support me when I say that *a* (uh) is a word; *a* (as in day) is a letter of the alphabet. Nothing more, nothing less.

Sorry, *Jeopardy!* folks, you had it wrong, too. The category was "Jolly Roger" for $200 and the clue was "He ran **an** historic 5,280 feet on May 6, 1954, later became a neurologist & was knighted in 1975." The question, of course, was "Who is Roger Bannister?"

Also, Tim Russell on WCCO-AM radio once referred to "**an** Geraldo Rivera thing," but I neglected to write down the context, so astonished was I at the blip. But he did it, yes he did. Ad lib? I'd guess so.

25

Applause

Never let it be said that SOTS missed an opportunity to praise. The *Star Tribune* once had on the front page of its Variety section an excellent feature called "Mixed Messages," or "mixed messages," as their trendy lack of capital letters delineated (but never mind that). I heartily applaud their courage – if that is the right word – in calling our attention to several of the language misuses I have already discussed on these pages. The only fly in the ointment was that the "team" led by Gail Rosenblum got two things wrong. Oh, for goodness sakes, you say? How can that be possible? In a carefully researched article about the English language, of all things? Yes, and I still have the evidence in my voluminous files.

In the form of a quiz, we were to provide the corrections to the listed examples. Number 4 read: "It was just a **fluke** (their boldface) that the car went off the road and hit that oak tree." The team determined that "purists reserve the use of 'fluke' for strokes of good luck, not acts of misfortune." *Au contraire, mon amis.* Although one definition is "the lucky pocketing of a ball in billiards (or pool), my dictionaries all agree that a fluke can be for either good or bad fortune, and none of mine is the *Webster's New World College Dictionary*, Fourth Edition, which is what the folks at the paper used. Strike one!

(Remember that smaller dictionaries are smaller because much of the content of larger dictionaries is left out. Duh! It's likely that this was the case here.)

In a follow-up listing of "Also mangled and misused" was "**Fortuitous**. Means accidental; not lucky, and not luckily accidental. To use it that way is a malapropism. Serendipitous is the word you need in those situations." Sorry, but again I must beg to differ, or at least my learned tomes do. "Fortunate" is a synonym for "fortuitous," according to my gang of Webster's. Their consensus is that it means "lucky, occurring by chance, accidental, fortunate." (And by the way, Webster's is a generic term that any dictionary publisher may use, hence the stacks of them in the bookstores and libraries, all with Webster's somewhere in the title. The Merriam-Webster Company does not have a hold on the name.)

Otherwise, I have nothing but good to say about the *Star Tribune* article's other offerings, and I can't reproduce it in its entirety without violating copyright laws, so you'll have to take my word for it that the article was, mostly, a wondrous thing for an old copyeditor like me to read. Needless to say, it confirmed many of the errors described in the book you hold in your hand. And that's good. (What's unfortunate, however, is that articles like that are about as rare as hen's teeth.)

Take a deep breath now, and – altogether – *however*, accolades usually don't last long, and now is no exception. In that same paper's Home section appeared an article by staff writer Jim Buchta about preparing one's home for sale. Among the recommendations was the suggestion that wood floors didn't necessarily need refinishing, but that it would be wise "to give them a good cleaning and then freshed [*sic*] them up by rubbing the scratches with wood stain and buffed [*sic*] them with **tongue** oil." Aside from the misspelling of "tung," the syntax left a lot to be desired, hence the [*sic*] interruptions.

Burgeon?

It's astonishing, sometimes, what can happen to a perfectly good word when an unlikely meaning becomes attached to it. In the case of "burgeon" or "burgeoning," for whatever odd reasons, it is now used with increasing regularity to indicate *erupting, mushrooming, ballooning, exploding, expanding rapidly*, or *growing by leaps and bounds*. With all of those proper words and terms available, why do things "burgeon"? I honestly don't know, but I do know that "burgeoning" means "budding," "just beginning to take shape," "peeping out of the ground in springtime," "sending out shoots or sprouts." Perhaps it's because of its resemblance to "burden," which carries the connotation of "big and heavy." Sorry if I've spoiled your day, but why do the professionals need to mistreat such a fine word when so many others will do?

I HATE TO CRITICIZE, BUT . . .

You who?

I don't know about you, but I always have trouble listening to broadcasters who make us wonder whom they are speaking to. On *Wheel of Fortune*, for example, announcer Charlie O'Donnell often says, "Pat [Sajak, host], tonight's Jackpot Round is being brought to **you** by ..." Why is it being brought to Pat Sajak, and not to us viewers, or even the studio audience? If he said, "... brought to *us*," I could accept that, but why not come clean completely and admit that the Jackpot Round is "sponsored" by the advertiser being mentioned?

Public radio, both local and national, tries to sneak by the sponsoring aspect by telling us that the current program is "supported by ..." Even worse, though, is public TV, which is supposed to be noncommercial, giving us "institutional" announcements on behalf of its program "supporters." Ad agency staffs everywhere are hard at work trying to come as close to selling products and services without actually doing so. No one is fooled, I hope. Extolling the attributes of a company is the same as pitching its product; after all, the company could not exist without sales of its products or services. Shouldn't the FCC or somebody be monitoring such behavior? Your tax dollars not at work.

Public radio's counterpart, PBS Television, also supposedly nonprofit and noncommercial, uses another dodge that says: "Major funding provided by ..." I guess it's supposed to indicate that the "funder" is footing the "major" or larger part of the particular program's production costs. No doubt many besides yours truly have wondered what percentage of the costs that means, never mind the breakdown of total costs, figures that would likely mean nothing to most of us.

Back to the misdirected exhortations, I also hear radio commercials of the "interview" type where the sponsor or its representative is supposedly in the studio (but is actually on a recording) chatting with your friendly announcer, who seems not too sure to whom he is speaking. After the two-way conversation, the announcer says something like, "We know you have the best (whatever) in town, so next time call (phone number) for (an estimate/appointment/what-have you) ..." Hey, you talkin' to me? Very confusing.

Acronyms?

It's time we talked about acronyms. Believe it or not, there are learned people in prestige institutions of learning who are convinced that any capital-letter abbreviation is an acronym. I have had arguments with individuals who are likewise convinced, and many of them will *never* be convinced. Without knowing the identity of the headline-writer at the *Star Tribune*, I must simply pooh-pooh the usage and stumble on. The headline I'm referring to read: "Long gone are the days of UHF and VHF. The **acronym** of today and beyond is **HDTV** – and that has shoppers coming up on a sharp learning curve." Nope! 'Tain't!

An acronym is an abbreviation, yes, but one that can be pronounced as a word, such as *snafu, radar, Anzac, NATO, COLA* (Cost-Of-Living Adjustment), *ESOP* (Employee Stock Option Program), etc. *FBI* is not an acronym because it cannot be pronounced as a word (try "fibbie"). *NFL* would come out "niffle," and many other abbreviations face the same difficulty. The technical term for a group of unpronounceable letters is "initialism." Unfortunately, there are those who say that it doesn't matter, that they are all acronyms. Bosh! Why are so many people intent on flushing another perfectly good distinction down the drain? Maybe one of them will tell us. Dictionaries I have checked have it right, but don't bother taking an Internet poll, because there lies madness and ignorance.

Part of my own learning curve has been getting accustomed to the Internet, and especially that Gargantua of information, Google. (The verb form "to Google" is now acceptable, even to me, as I obviously let on earlier, and it's only a matter of time before the capital *G* is dropped to lower case.) Entering "acronym" and clicking on "Search," I was directed to thousands of Web sites, several of them connected to colleges and universities. Although many of them agreed, far too many others failed to understand the difference between an acronym and an initialism. I can only shake my head wearily and wonder what this world is coming to. Sorry, but I'm not going into any further detail here. If you really want to know what others think, do what I did and Google the word "acronym." Have fun, and don't ever say I didn't warn you.

Did he?

My friend J.M. of St. Paul, Minn., had in interesting item he'd been saving for me:

> The *Wall Street Journal* article was headlined: "WorldCom's New Chief Thrives on Pressure and **He** Better."

That one illustrates an increasingly common colloquial form, which appears to be taking over. The correct word would be "He'd," for "he *had* better." It's similar to "**I bet it will happen** ...," instead of "I'll bet ..." or "I'd bet ..."

"I'll bet ... (I will bet ...)," means "I will now bet ..." or "I am now betting." It is the present tense.

"I'd bet (I would bet ...)" means "I would bet on such and such should the conditions warrant." It also implies certainty, as in "I'd stake my life on it!" It is the future tense.

"I bet" means that one has already bet, as in "I bet two dollars on that horse – and he ran last." It is the past tense. No, no, don't thank me. Well, OK, if you must. You're welcome.

How's that?

Reading the grocery ads for fun and profit, I came across a good price on "TUNA WATER" at Kenny's Markets. Would that be water that tuna swim in, or something else. I don't know. Oh? Tuna *in* water? I guess so. (Guessing is not the same as betting.)

I know I promised to take it easy on nonprofessionals outside the public sphere of communications, but someone got paid – I think – to prepare a newspaper flyer (not flier) for Roger's Petroleum Company, a "neighborhood gas, deli, and grocery store – open 24 hours a day." On this particular occasion, one of the deli specials was "50¢ OFF **Anti Pasta** Salad." ("antipasto") When I saw it I asked, to no one in particular, What is this hostility toward noodles? I never got an answer.

At the offices of our local suburban weekly, the *St. Louis Park Sun Sailor*, there was at one time a problem with the plumbing in their building. Deb

Schewe, writing about it later, said that the difficulty required that bottled water be "brought in by Glenwood **Inglenook**." Local folks got quite a laugh out of it, because the company is Glenwood Ingle*wood* and Inglenook is a wine. One wag asked whether it was red or white.

A little extra?

Back when I was watching altogether too much TV, I occasionally made notes on goofy stuff I saw and heard. An ad for Equal, the sugar substitute, advised that it was recommended by "B. SMITH, RESTAURANTEUR." The **N** does not belong. Correctly, it's "restaurateur," as I'm sure you know. I also saw and heard the same thing in a testimonial-type ad for Oil of Olay. Wrong again.

We've had billboards and matchcovers, but those ubiquitous little sugar packets are public targets, too, whether on restaurant tables or at home. Assisting is J.W. of Northlake, Ill.:

> This packet, packed for the Superior Tea & Coffee Co. of Chicago, Ill., has a trivia question on one side that asks: "**For** what role is Milburn Stone best known **for**?" The answer on the other side, of course, is "Doc" on "Gunsmoke."

The quotation marks around Doc and Gunsmoke are superfluous, which, along with the double "for" make me wonder whether the trivia writer's main job is answering the phone. (No, I'm not forgetting that TV show titles should be in italics. Everyone deserves a little slack now and then.)

Buy now!

For Be Kind to Animals Week, Snyder Drug stores once offered a "Geisler Large Bird **Cuddle** Bone," on sale at only 79¢. ("cuttle")

While we're in the store we can pick up some windshield-washer fluid. Ah, here's Splash, the "*Original* WINDSHIELD WASHER," from Fox Packaging Co. in St. Paul, Minn. It "PROTECTS TO –25° F BELOW ZERO." Just how low is that? Don't the "minus" and "below" mean the same thing? Yep. Sure do.

Also fighting cold weather is Trop-**Artic** Motor Oil from Phillips 66. Whoa, there! If you think that the boldfacing is proper and that the spelling is wrong, think again. OK, so "Arctic" *would* be the correct spelling, but there is a great difference of opinion among those who are aware of and/or use the product, which is still being sold. According to Google, there are 10,100 Web pages devoted to Trop-Artic, with or without the hyphen, and only 665 pages for Trop-Arctic, also sometimes hyphenated and sometimes not. I detect mass confusion here, but I can't argue against those numbers. Also, nowhere that I can find is an explanation about the actual name and whether it may have changed at some point. You may consider this as merely a report and not as a criticism. Sometimes you just have to step away and go on to something else. I'll have to remember to ask at my service station next time I'm there.

Google?

It is just not possible to keep up with this modern age. "Google," for example, gets that little squiggly red line under it on my word-processing program, when it's in lower case, but not when it's capped. Perhaps a later version will have that corrected, because Google is the world's largest search engine. Just about anything you want to know about is covered by this giant information resource. Interestingly, I Googled SOTS one day and found more than 20,000 Web pages (sites). Only a few referred to my endeavors, but some of the others were even more unusual. There was, for example, the Society for Old Testament Study, founded in 1917 in the British Isles. There was also a Sexual Offender Treatment Specialist, and something called Sounds of the Sixties.

The "Save Our Tongue Society" appeared three times on the first two pages of Google, accompanied by Symptomatic Orthostatic Tachycardia Syndrome, an element of chronic fatigue syndrome. It's really amazing what you can find, but the only hitch is that you can find way too much that you're not even looking for, some of which will catch and hold your attention. At least it has done so with mine, for longer than is good for me.

Speaking of Google, which do you think is preferred, "a pair of old pants" or "an old pair of pants"? It won't do any good to think about it, because either is perfectly correct, with Google giving 459 Web site citations to the former, and 577 to the latter. I apologize for the tangent into the nongermane.

Apropos of the same, though, is one "innocent *until* proven guilty" or "innocent *unless* proven guilty"? I cannot find either in the *Constitution* or *The Bill of Rights*, but I did check Google again, and got four variations: "Unless proven" got 10,600 pages, "until proven" got 194,000 pages, "until proved" netted 26,900, and bringing up the rear was "unless proved" with a mere 271 Web pages. I'd go with the big one, but you can take your choice, seeing as how there is no significant difference in meaning.

"Google" and "dependability" are two terms that are not mutually inclusive, so additional sources should always be consulted, or at least two or more Web sites on Google, in any case. Evidencing this is what I found concerning something out of my memorable past:

On *The Adventures of Sam Spade, Detective*, an excellent radio program starring Howard Duff as the title character, the part of Effie Perrine, the private eye's rather flappable secretary, was played by Lurene Tuttle. However, in a book I borrowed from the Museum of Broadcasting, which is located about three miles from my house, the actress's first name was spelled Lorene. Checking Google, I found 19,400 citings of "Lurene," but for whatever reasons, "Lorene" showed up 102 times. No, I don't recall the name of the book with the incorrect spelling, but it did serve to send me into a whole load of similar failures to pay attention. There's more of this kind of thing on Google than you might think.

More clips

I wonder how many different pairs of scissors have been used to lift goofs and gaffes from the nation's newspapers. One was in the hand of G.W. of Austin, Texas, whom we have heard from before:

> Note the ninth paragraph of business editor Kirk Ladendorf's article in the Austin *American Statesman*: "In a speech to the Alabama legislature last year, [3M chairman Lewis] Lehr spelled out some of his company's strong **tenants** about what makes a good corporate location." ["tenets"]

J.M. of Boca Raton, Fla., excised part of a theater review by Skip Shef-field in the *Boca Raton News* and sent it along. The play was *The Best Little Whorehouse in Texas,* and the write-up included: "Americans love to **play** lip service to the **tenants** of personal and religious freedom ..." There's a two-fer for you. The "play" *could* have been a typo, but I'm not so sure. ("pay" ... "tenets")

Ripped from the pages of the Westfield, N.J., *Suburban News* is this headline submitted by J.L. of Scotch Plains, N.J.: "Household Accidents Kill **Most** Children Each Year." So how come there are so many left? It was indeed an unfortunate choice of words. The writer meant to say that household accidents kill "more" children than are killed by childhood diseases, etc., but failed to hit the mark.

Another scissors-wielding clipper was W.L. of Glendale, N.Y., who attacked the *New York Daily News* with a vengeance, as they say. The victim was a television column by Kay Gardella, who reviewed a long-gone show about doctors, *Rafferty,* and the episode about the hero's "indifference to lawsuits, especially if they stand in the way of his saving a man's **life** who has been **stabbed** on the bus." This looks like another job for ... COPYEDI-TORMAN! (Or a female equivalent, but I can't come close, try as I might.) The "life" was not stabbed, the "man" was. Make it read: "... stand in the way of his saving the life of a man who has been stabbed on the bus."

In the Department of Bad Choices are two items found by S.K. of Port-land, Ore.:

> Headline in the *Oregonian*: "[District Attorney] Haas seeks grant to slow arsonists."

> Item in the *Sacramento Union*: "Pope John Paul II spent two and a half hours Sunday with 154 youths recovering from drug addiction, their parents, social workers and priests."

There are no names attached, but I have no doubt that the writers were working under the pressure of tight deadlines. Nevertheless, somebody should have scanned the material before it was indelibly printed and released upon the world.

If I had had a transom, this item would have been tossed over it. (Only really old buildings still have transoms above the office doors.) Bearing no name or return address, the envelope contained a clipping from the *Arizona Republic*. Written by Venita Hawthorne, the article told of the reunion of sweethearts separated for 32 years by war, a divorce, and the Atlantic Ocean. The man wrote to the woman in Poland. "Ten months later – on Nov. 1 – Kazimiera, who is **fluid** in three languages but unable to speak English, arrived in Phoenix." ("fluent")

B.S. of Santa Ana, Calif., has Orange County's *The Register* dead to rights for the headline over an article about the weather, notably a warming-up of the southern states: "N. California soaked; Southern states **unthaw**." How about that for having it both ways? ("thaw")

Long Island, N.Y.'s *Newsday* had F.B. of East Northport, N.Y., staring in wonder at the article by Jim O'Neill and Jim Scovel about a fire that killed four persons. Two men were charged and faced a possible "**maximum** sentence of **at least** 25 years in prison …" I'd have to say that there wasn't much leeway for the jury in that case. No more, no less, is the way I read it.

How can anyone not like a newspaper with a name like *The Daily Breeze*? Located in Torrance, Calif., it's read by S.N. of nearby Hawthorne, who spotted this sports double-header: "Briefly … The Washington High Generals snap the two-year **rein** of Marine League track and field champions by **garnishing** 55 points in 11 events." ("reign" – "garnering")

Back in the late '70s, J.R. of Philadelphia, Pa., sent me a clipping that I just now uncovered in one of my files. In the *Inquirer* a large double-deck headline read: "It appears there will be **more** love lost between Carter, labor." Unfortunately, extrapolating "*no* love lost" into "more" is mere nonsense. If it had said "*less* love lost," it would have gone unnoticed.

This one, from C.J. of Rapid City, So. Dak., appeared in her local paper but was datelined "FARGO, N.D." It was about the 1952 reawakening of a man declared dead and sent to a mortuary, and the unknown writer said that the man "told how the mortician who was preparing to embalm him found him to be alive on a Fargo radio station program Monday." Wow!

It's a good thing he was listening! Yes, there's another clever bit of word-play in it, but I'll let you figure out what it is.

G.W., our Austin, Texas, friend, adds this pair from his favorite paper, the *Austin American*:

> Business writer David Frink, mentioning the Garden Café, should have cleaned up the quotation from the spokesman for the group of owners: "W.A. McCormack said **seafood** will be the restaurant's primary **bill of fare** ..." The menu probably won't stand much handling.

> And in Liz Carpenter's column: "So my question for July is: Can 10 women, good and true (all of them thinner than **me**) lose weight and find happiness in Comfort, Texas?"

The first one should have read: "... seafood will be the restaurant's primary offering (category, kind of food, etc.) on its bill of fare." The bill of fare is that thing with all the choices and prices on it, otherwise known as the menu. If writer Frink were directly quoting the spokesman, that would have been a different "kettle of fish" (beg your pardon), and it wouldn't be appearing here. As for the second, the easiest way to tell "I" from "me" is to add "am," so that it becomes "thinner than I am." Also correct would be "thinner than I," but many would say that it sounded funny.

However, consider the old song "Bluebird of Happiness." The lyrics con-tained: "So be like I, hold your head up high, you will find the bluebird of happiness." Yes, language usage changes, but so many fine distinctions are falling by the wayside. It's a pity.

"Knock, knock." "Who's there?" "It's **me**." "Go away – send someone who speaks English." In my early days as editor of the *Mensa Bulletin* I was not as circumspect as I should have been, and I paid for my occa-sional lapse dearly. In one of the 1976 issues I used the phrase "Maybe it's only **me that** cares." Exigencies of deadlines being what they are, I made unfortunate haste and failed to avoid the trap of colloquialism; read-ers reacted sternly. I should have written, "Maybe it's only I who cares," which when paraphrased reads "It is only I who cares," or "I am the only one who cares," which would have been an even better choice. In any case, I blew it, and was "hoist by my own petard."

Now, before you take exception to that last remark about my petard, I will tell you that I know what a petard is, but perhaps some readers do not. A petard is a bomb used to break through a wall or door, and the phrase implies that one is caught in one's own trap or in a situation of one's own devising – supposedly from the idea of a bomb going off before the bomber can get out of the way. Anyway, I hope I have shown that I can take it as well as dish it out. Ouch!

I also confess to another shot from the hip by myself, except that I sometimes wish I had an evil twin I could blame. In an early column I said that I had once heard the phrase "immune from prosecution," implying that I thought it was wrong and should be "immune *to* prosecution." I later discovered, after being forced by several readers to look it up, that either "to" or "from" is correct, although in most cases, "from" is preferred. So my remark was hastily made and paid for at leisure, even though it wasn't totally incorrect. I've tried to be more careful since.

Upon further review, my Merriam-Webster *Second Unabridged* allows "immune from," "immune to," "immune against," and "immune of." The *Third Unabridged* says that "from" and "against" are the usual, while "to" refers primarily to medical usage. My 9th New Collegiate offers "from" and adds that "to" also indicates medical references. So "immune from prosecution" is agreed upon by all, and "immune to the black plague" would be the alternate incarnation. Rest easy – whatever you say is OK.

26

At sea

N.R. of Lompoc, Calif., discovered this triply redundant deep-sea treasure (in the SOTS sense of treasure, that is), in the *Lompoc Record*:

> A UPI (United Press International) article about deep-sea exploration for oil reported that an "**international** team of researchers from Canada, Mexico, and the United States" made a discovery of "superheated **hot** springs," using a "**submersible** submarine."

All three bold-faced words are superfluous. Not sure? Take your time.

From G.M. of Chicago, Ill., came news of a teachers' strike as reported in an unattributed *Chicago Tribune* article. It read, in part:

> "Negotiations in two junior-college teacher strikes are to resume Monday after **unsuccessful** weekend sessions between striking teachers and college administrators **failed**." Does this mean that successful sessions passed?

On the air

Ordinarily, I like to have names attached to language violations, but it is not always possible. And once in a while I just *have* to include a goodie without a name. M.L. of St. Louis, Mo., proved as much with this one:

> According to the 3:00 P.M. news broadcast on KMOX radio, the man who drove his auto into a Ku Klux Klan meeting in Plains, Ga., was found [to be] guilty of "**aggregated** assault," which only makes sense since his assault was against the whole aggregation. The exact same announcement was made later that same afternoon.

Makes sense to me. Or would you prefer "aggravated"? Also listening to the wireless was H.D. of Gastonia, N.C.:

283

From WEPR (a South Carolina *educational* radio station)
I heard, "The Columbia Lyric Opera Theatre will present
Madame Butterfly tonight. In honor of this anticipated event,
we'll [now] play the soprano aria from *Rigoletto*'s first act as
sung by Roberta **Peterson**." After playing "Cara Nome," the
announcer again called her Roberta **Peterson** and said that we
had just heard "the beautiful 'Cara **numb**.'" ["Peters"]

Another radio listener was D.T. of Medfield, Mass.:

Here's a compound fracture of the English language by Ron
Della Chiesa of WGBH-FM in Boston: "Stuart's trumpet has
a very unique sound, **like** Sweets Edison."

I'm not ignoring the "very unique," but I believe we've discussed that particular goof sufficiently. The "like," however, does not go unnoticed. What
was meant, of course, was that the sound of Stuart's trumpet was like that
of the trumpet of Sweets Edison. The concise version would have been
"Stuart's trumpet has a … sound, like Sweets Edison's," leaving the final
"trumpet" implied but left out. Anyway, the point is that a trumpet cannot sound like a man, although the reverse is occasionally true.

Tea, anyone?

SOTS folks have a special kind of pride in their fellow members who take
determined action against misusers of English, and who have provable
results. C.P. of San Leandro, Calif., is one such member:

Lipton Tea, made by Thomas J. Lipton, Inc., of Englewood
Cliffs, N.J., has an industrial product. The red and yellow box
differs from consumer packaging inasmuch as it carries a message, which, in 1978, stated: "**Exclusive** for hotels …" I wrote
their firm explaining that the term should be "exclusively." I
received a warm reply, thanking me for my advice and promising to reword the statement with the next printing. In 1979
the boxes read correctly.

Sympatico

Lowell Thomas, the famed world traveler and radio and television broadcaster, in his autobiographical *Good Evening Everybody: From Cripple
Creek to Samarkand*, tells of the time he was asked by the Jam Handy
Company, a Detroit, Mich., filmmaker, to appear in a film they were
producing for Frigidaire, a division of General Motors. Receiving a copy
of the script in advance, Thomas said that he had never seen anything like
it before. "It was full of verbal twists ... verbs wrenched into the form of
nouns, like 'freezability,' euphemisms in place of plain old reliable words,
like 'home food center' for 'kitchen,' and convoluted sentences endowing
inanimate objects with human characteristics and making sense only if
you didn't think about them."

Assured that the filmmakers would be "open to any suggestions for
change," he accepted the assignment. On arriving at the studio conference room he was introduced to several gentlemen and asked his opinion
of the script. He replied, "Well, first of all I'd like to know if there is any
reason why it shouldn't be in English?" When asked – including by the
scriptwriter – what he found so problematical, he told them that "English
was English and was almost always best understood when used according to the tried and true rules of orthography and grammar." Despite
the group's obvious opinion that Thomas was a greenhorn who "couldn't
understand the need for the specialized language of commercial movies,"
Thomas eventually ruled the day; his changes were accepted, "and we got
down to work."

Having worked in that same corporate-film industry, I could fully relate to
what Lowell Thomas was talking about. I too wrote commercial audio-
visual scripts of all kinds, and one challenge always facing me was trying
to get the client to put his words into forms better understandable by his
prospective viewers. Sometimes it was not difficult, but on other occasions the client was so entranced by the jargon he spoke daily that I could
not sway him. But at least I tried.

Rivals

K.M. of St. Paul regularly reads her local paper (once known as the *Pioneer Press Dispatch*, but now without *Dispatch*). On a full-page two-color

house ad (one advertising the newspaper itself) were a pair of those street-corner newspaper boxes, one red and one green. The red one contained the St. Paul paper and the green one the Minneapolis *Star Tribune*. Headlined "No wonder they're green with envy," the ad boasted that the *Pioneer Press Dispatch* had won two Pulitzer Prizes since 1985, compared to none for the other. The block of copy at the bottom of the page said, "Recently, Pioneer Press Dispatch [many newspapers refuse to use italics in names of publications] reporter Jacqui Banaszynski won a **Pultizer** Prize for her moving series on AIDS. It was our second Pulitzer Prize in the last three years. If you want to read this kind of thought-provoking writing **everyday**, pick up the Pioneer Press Dispatch. The newspaper of the twin **Pultizers**." ("every day," and one out of three ain't great – "Pulitzer")

I before E?

How about if we do serious damage to an old saw? The axiom of "I before E, except after C, or when sounded like A, as in neighbor and weigh," is not one to commit to memory. There are so many other variations, such as seize, weird, leisure, either and neither, height, sleight, their, caffeine, foreign, reveille, and names such as Eisenhower, Rubenstein, and Raleigh. There are, of course, many others. There are also others that sound like A, including vein, reign, rein, heinous, etc. And there are those that pull the switch after C, such as species, scientist, etc. Why did I put that here? I just felt like it.

Why communication matters

Some time ago, when I was still writing my columns for the *Mensa Bulletin*, I asked readers to give me examples of poor communication leading to actual difficulty. The response was hardly overwhelming, but what did arrive was more than I had expected, as evidenced by the following letter. The writer, a man, will remain anonymous for obvious reasons, but not a word is being changed:

> Dear Gordon: You requested real-life examples of losses
> through lack of communication. The end of a love affair in
> which there was mutual love, respect, and admiration should

qualify. This one fell apart for reasons no greater than and no less than the inability to use words to communicate.

As it was on the down-slide, I received a letter which stated:

"We've had talks about communication and words. I find that while I'm not sure I agree with everything on these pages, but it certainly is saying something of what I've tried to say to you. The last page I agree with – for sure."

Enclosed were portions from the book *Notes to Myself: My Struggle to Become a Person*, by Hugh Prather. The quoted sections included:

"My statements are requests.

"My questions are statements.

"My gossip is a plea: Please see me as incapable of that. Please respect me.

"My arguments insist: I want you to show respect for me by agreeing with me. This is the way I say it is.

"And my criticism informs you: You hurt my feelings a minute ago."

And the last magic page, with which she totally agreed, contained the following:

"I don't want to listen to just what you say. I want to feel what you mean.

"I won't hold you to your words. Deep emotions are often expressed in irrational words.

"I want you to be able to say anything. Even what you don't mean."

For a rough translation of all of the above, I arrive at the following:

> When she speaks, I should never take her words to mean what
> the words mean. I should always assume that she means some-
> thing other than what she is saying, and I should be under-
> standing enough (psychic enough?) to comprehend the true
> meaning and feelings.
>
> When I speak, she will always assume that my words do not
> mean what the words mean, but rather she will feel my true
> meaning and feelings.
>
> If we both totally discount everything that each of us says, we
> will be able to arrive at true emotional communication.
>
> I cannot handle that. I do not choose to attempt to learn how
> to handle that. And so, with great pain on the part of both of
> us, a love affair crumbled.

If ever there was an occasion to resurrect that old adage that admonishes
us to "say what we mean and mean what we say," that had to be it. Many
years have passed, but I saved that letter knowing it would appear somewhere in this book. I thought about ending the book with it, but soon
decided that it would better serve as a serious stopover in an otherwise
generally humorous linguistic adventure. I leave it to my readers to judge
the wisdom of my choice.

Good point

J.L. of Ossining, N.Y., who contributed earlier, also responded to my
request for communication failures, but did so in a rather different manner. He writes:

> First, I think that you should resoundingly dispute those corre-
> spondents who claim that technical correctness impedes creative
> expression. Some competent writers may have specific dis-
> abilities, but usually sloppy grammar is a strong indication that
> the associated work will be sloppy writing, just as a high body
> temperature usually indicates illness. Apologists for carelessness
> should not be allowed to dignify themselves as creators. ...

> Also, I suspect that if you receive examples of mishaps spe-
> cifically caused by misplaced commas and the like, then the
> examples, in sum, will have a slightly ludicrous air. I don't think
> you can persuade the Surgeon General that bad grammar can
> be dangerous to one's health.
>
> Rather, bad grammar, and the associated sloppy expression,
> slowly degrade the intellectual atmosphere until there occur
> disasters not specifically traceable to sloppy English, but prob-
> ably foreseeable, and preventable, through clear thinking. This,
> to me, is the true justification for SOTS. ...

I believe it's safe to say that we've avoided the "ludicrous air," but what was just said, as far as I am concerned, was right on the mark. There are no laws governing the use of language, but there are generally-agreed-upon rules, as I discussed in my introduction. We are in no way prohibited from breaking those rules and using our language in any way we choose, but we break those rules at our own risk. We always take the chance that we will be misunderstood, that we may lose credibility with those who are aware of our errors, and that we may even be laughed at, most often not even with our knowledge, and perhaps occasionally right to our faces. The effect of language misuse is a matter of degree, from little or none to total disaster, as in the previous lost-love case.

One last comment before we get back to taking our licks at the media:

In any communication situation, there is a sender and there is a receiver, except that in mass communications such as the public media there are many senders and many receivers. However, as far as the receivers are concerned, each receiver is an individual at the end of the communication trail, forming a single link among the many. Each is a unique hook-up.

The question then becomes, If, as in the movie *Cool Hand Luke*, we have a "failure to communicate," who is at fault, the sender or the receiver? Answer: In almost every instance, the onus is on the sender to formulate the message so that the receiver is "receptive" and able to understand what is being sent. The exception would be that whenever, and for whatever reason, a message fails to have the expected result, it is possible that an ill-prepared receiver has been assigned to receive the message. If the sender is in any way aware of this, it is the sender's responsibility either to adapt the message to the receiver, or to ask that someone better qualified take the receiver's place. In a business situation, the sender should "copy" the receiver's immediate supervisor, for obvious reasons.

When my wife and I decided in 1998 to take a trip to Norway for a family reunion, she decided to bone up on Norwegian, going so far as to buy books and tapes, even though she was not of Norwegian descent. The rest of us, of course, were impressed when she could read some of the signs and understand several words and phrases. On one occasion, we were aboard a commuter train, which had seating back-to-back and facing each other. Endeavoring to be friendly, my wife spoke some words to the woman across from her, who immediately responded with a torrent of Norwegian. My wife waved her off vigorously with "I don't speak Norwegian." The woman then said, "If you speak to me in English, I will respond in English." We all got a big laugh out of it. Those Norskies certainly do like to have fun.

Bogus?

In 1979 I was planning to have a little fun myself, and began a column thusly:

> SOTS has recently been the target of a modest barrage of criticism from a few readers who take issue with the purposes of our organization. In the interest of fairness, therefore, we have invited a representative of the opposition to serve as guest editor this month. He is Professor Blurt Froth, Chairman of the Department of Organic Linguistics at the Guano School of Journalism, Barren Lake, Minnesota. A recent recipient of the Casey Stengel Award for Special Achievement in Innovative Diction, Professor Froth is the author of the best-selling leaflet, "How to Get Attention on Citizens Band Radio."

> "You people make me laugh. This SOTS thing is just about the biggest waste of time I can think of. You have a lot of gall putting down writers and broadcasters who are doing nothing

more than try to communicate information to us in as interesting and imaginative a manner as they can. Just because they don't always conform to the dictates of so-called language experts and jerk dictionary-writers, you have no call to vilify them in print the way you do. Frankly, I don't think hardly anyone really cares, and those that do will be dead in a few years, anyway, and then it won't matter, will it?"

That's as far as I got, and it's probably just as well. Note that my imaginary professor was fairly adept at English, but I gave him just enough didoes to keep him believable, I think. Anyway, I had a bit of fun, and I'm including it here to show that I do not take myself totally seriously, any more than anyone should. Yes, of course I'm serious, but without a bit of humor it would be a grim task indeed. Sail on.

No hands?

Shaking his head in wonderment was G.T. of Florence, S.C.:

> Leading off the front page of *The Manchester* [Ky.] *Enterprise* was the story headlined: "Man Doing OK After Ax Attack." Under a large photo was the caption: "This small shack on remote Ephram Creek is the scene of the crime where Ray Finley was attacked **by an ax**." The text's fifth paragraph said that "Sometime on Tuesday night, May 31, Ray Finley was attacked **by an ax** and apparently left for dead. Then the seventh paragraph began: "The **ax** got him full in the face with the sharp side." How does one prosecute an ax?

27

The unheard

Allow me to take another break here to pay tribute to those who have written to me over these last 30+ years and who either have not appeared in my column or do not appear in this book, or both. Some of their missives were – quite frankly – full of more applause than I deserved. Aside from that, so many bolstered my own opinions that I hated to have to ignore them. I was reluctant to take the time or spend the postage to reply to many who had earned a reply, but there was nothing I could do about it.

There were the English teachers who told me about the silly things their students said; the mathematics instructor who was as passionate about English as he was about his own subject; the SOTS sympathizers who simply wanted to vent about their own pet peeves, even without specific examples; the like-minded who heard wildly-off-the-wall ad-libs they just had to share; and those who sent me some hilarious material I couldn't use because it wasn't public enough or specific enough or created by professionals. I could write another book about classified ads, and another about church bulletins, and yet another about things readers heard or saw somewhere but couldn't recall where. Maybe someday.

My special thanks have to go to those who offered to send money, to have "violations cards" printed up, some willing to do so at their own expense, and to those wanting only to help in general to get a formal organization started. Their support and encouragement is what kept me going all these years.

I would also like to thank those who wrote with varying intensity in disagreement with me. Some suggested that we accept professionals' use of slang as "more friendly," and be happy so long as we understand what they are saying. One correspondent said that since we hear the word "gonna" so often, we might as well adopt it in print, too. Such offerings may not have been of much appeal to me, but at least they made me think, and that alone I consider a contribution. So, to the unsung among you, my thanks for adding to the SOTS mix.

Convinced?

Although I may appear hard-nosed about English usage, I do not go around correcting people willy-nilly. In Toastmasters, of course, we correct each other frequently because we expect it as part of the program. But even there, we often let little things slide by. For example, here are a few that get less attention than others:

The *Washington Post* had a job-hunt article that included: "Maybe you have the skills to **convince** a camping-equipment manufacturer **to** hire you." More correctly, the word here is "persuade." Generally speaking (no pun intended), one *convinces* another *of* or *that*. One *persuades* another *to* take some sort of action. In Toastmasters we usually pay little attention to such minor infractions, especially with newer members whose skin has not been sufficiently thickened. Old-timers are fair game, naturally.

A *Minneapolis Star* headline over a story about contraceptives in 1978 proclaimed that "Options today hardly different **than** what they were in 1960." I mentioned this earlier, and the more correct word is "from." Things differ *from*, they do not differ *than*, although in some specific contexts, *than* turns out to be the acceptable choice if brevity is the requirement. If possible, though, skip brevity and go for the brass ring.

Tangentially

The following may give you the impression that I'm running out of material, but such is not the case. Although it is perfectly grammatical and has every word spelled correctly, I am including it simply because I think it is good for a laugh. It comes from P.M. of Cincinnati, Ohio:

The *Cincinnati Enquirer* sports page enclosed has an item which might intrigue you. The Tom Callahan1978 account of the [Muhammad] Ali-[Leon] Spinks rematch is spiced by the final paragraph: "World Boxing Association featherweight champion Indian Red Lopez got off the floor in the first round and flattened Juan Malvarez in the second; Mike Rossman upset Victor Galindez for the WBA light-heavyweight title; and a charmingly uninhibited woman named Edy Williams appeared in the middle of the ring and removed all her clothes. Guards took her away, two abreast."

Too public?

As early as 1979 I began to receive mail from people who were not readers of the *Mensa Bulletin*, but wanted to join SOTS anyway. Articles began to appear in publications all over the country, including *The Denver Post*. In that paper was a column called On The Air – unnecessarily capitalizing *the* – written by Clark Secrest. In one issue he took off after local broadcasters' pronunciations, and added that one of his readers (E.F. of Buena Vista, Colo.) was intending to send his column to me, which she did. I didn't mind that he spelled my name wrong, but he gave my mailing address and not much else, although he did include my leadoff disclaimer. Shortly afterward, mail began to come in from several places in Colorado asking for information. Not being organized, I was at a loss as to what to do for these nice folks, so I put together a short form letter that thanked them for their interest and apologized for being unable to do much else. Most embarrassing.

Secrest ended that by writing, "I'm sure glad I never make no mistakes in this column." Ohh-kay!

No one escapes

Back when there was heated debate about the Equal Rights Amendment, T.B. of Louisville, Ky., ran across a rather surprising gaffe by a prominent commentator:

> Syndicated columnist James J. Kilpatrick got into explaining the ERA and its effects on our society, particularly the amount of time needed for ratification. He writes: "Mrs. Phyllis Schlafly, head of the Stop ERA movement, and Ms. Eleanor Smeal, who heads the board of the National Organization of Women, came to town to fight the battle over extension [of that time needed for ratification]. In my own unbiased and objective view, ho-ho, Mrs. Schlafly had the better of it. She made the point, which seems to me almost unanswerable, that in terms of defining a period of 'contemporary' consensus, seven years **are** reasonable and 14 years **are** not."

When referring to periods of time, each is considered to be singular in tense, so the correct word is *is*. This is mainly because time periods are divisible into lesser lengths – years into months, minutes into seconds, etc. This also applies to weights, distance measures, and anything else that is divisible.

Nonglittering generalities

Although I am not loath to name names whenever possible, I hesitate to do so in certain areas of radio and television broadcasting that are so widespread that it would be unfair to single out only a few offenders. Instead I will point to errors that occur with overwhelming frequency, and let you listen for them as you catch the evening news, or whatever you watch.

Permit: This is both a noun and a verb, but each is pronounced differently. When you want to secure a permanent parking place, you usually have to apply for a PER-mit. The possession of that important piece of paper will per-MIT you to occupy that small but valuable plot of land.

Mischievous: It is pronounced MIS-chuh-vus, not mis-CHEE-vee-us.

Luxury: There are not many on the air nowadays who use the word, but some of those who do are pronouncing it LUGG-zhu-ree. Where the hell did those *G*s come from? It's LUCK-shu-ree. Easy. And never mind that many dictionaries list both. Go with what makes sense.

Apartheid: There are several inventive ways to handle this one. Correctly, it is a-PART-hate, not a-PART-hide. One broadcaster who got it right was Marty McNeely of ABC Radio.

Caribbean: James Michener, the author of many historical novels, including *Caribbean*, says that he prefers ca-RIB-bee-un. However, the people who are native to the region call themselves care-ri-BEE-uns. As I used to say to my kids during an argument, "Who knows better, you or me?" (OK, OK.) Those who live there should know, don't you think? The name comes from the Carib tribe of Indians, which is pronounced CARE-ib, so my vote goes to the people's choice. Care-rib-BEE-uns, it is, with the secondary emphasis on the first syllable.

To: This may come as a shock to many, but how such a tiny word is so badly treated is a sad tale indeed. There are two pronunciations, and *two* or *too* is one of them. The other is *tuh*. Although the first one, *too*, is ordinarily used before vowel sounds, we also hear the latter used the same way. Listen for the *w* sound in phrases like "She strove to (w)uplift her audience with her beautiful prose." So very many broadcasters will say, "She strove **tuh** uplift her audience ..." There comes that glottal stop again, the momentary interruption of breathing as the second vowel sound bursts forth in a grunt. Sometimes the pronunciation is the same, even without the glottal stop. Better it should sound like "too-wuplift," even though it can't be written that way.

But then, of course, you wouldn't say, "If I have **too** listen to the radio, I'd prefer smooth jazz." No, you'd say, "If I have **tuh** listen ..." The *to* is sort of tossed off, or elided, so as not to call attention to itself. Say it both ways to yourself and you'll see what I mean. Those old enough to remember "The moon belongs *too* (w)everyone, the best things in life are free" can't help pronouncing it right.

Going to: OK, two words this time, but when spoken together by a huge majority of the population, never mind the broadcast professionals, the replacement *gonna* is well on its way to the Department of Permanent Entrenchment. We all do it, and we hear it coming at us constantly from the radio and TV. Some attempts are made, however, to rescue the proper form, but I keep hearing the bouncing back and forth, especially from the weather people. "It's going to be a nice day tomorrow, but we're gonna see it cloud up a bit during the rest of the week." What ever happened to the word *will?* It will be nice ... we will see it cloud up ... there will be some sun, etc. It's a much more forceful word and greatly neglected. Go ahead, call your favorite station right now and suggest it. Maybe they will thank you. Or maybe not.

Temperature: Four syllables neatly packed into one word, and so easy to say when one is paying attention to what one is saying. Sadly, not many weather folk take the trouble. It comes out *temp-a-cher*, and drives viewers like me to distraction. Tem-per-a-chure, if you please. (This in no way excuses the advertising of the detergent as All Temp-a-Cheer, but that's one I haven't heard lately. Perhaps it's over and done with. One can hope.)

Calm, palm, balm, psalm, qualm: The *l* is silent in all of these words – *cahm, pahm, bahm, psahm, quahm* – but how often do we hear broadcasters add that unnecessary letter. Ken Barlow on KARE-TV has said it right, but I thought I detected a slip once or twice. For those in the South, it would be unthinkable to pronounce the *l* in DeKalb County, Georgia. (de-KAB)

Transport: The verb is trans-PORT, and the noun is TRANS-port.

Tryptophan or **Tryptophane:** It's not in the news much anymore, but every once in a while someone attempts it and fails. I have heard TRIP-tuh-fonn several times. Correctly, it is TRIP-tuh-fan or TRIP-tuh-fain.

Via: Meaning "by way of," the word is much too frequently spoken as VEE-uh. The Latin word is pronounced VYE-uh, as in viaduct, which means a bridge over a valley or roadway. The alternate pronunciation is listed secondarily in several dictionaries, obviously reflecting how common usage, however incorrect, eventually gets into the public communications arena. SOTS decries.

A.M., P.M.: How often do we hear that something is scheduled for "9:00 A.M. tomorrow morning"? But we never hear "9:00 A.M. tomorrow afternoon" or "9:00 A.M. tomorrow evening" or "9:00 A.M. tomorrow night." Of course not; there are no such things. Nine A.M. can occur *only* in the morning, so to mention A.M. in connection with morning is redundant. "Nine o'clock tomorrow morning" – or "nine tomorrow morning" – or "tomorrow at 9:00 A.M." – or "9:30 tomorrow morning," etc. – any of them will be just fine. (Note too that A.M. and P.M., whenever possible, should be in small capitals, but if they are not available, lower case is best.)

Aerate: Why this often comes out AIR-ee-ate is beyond me. Lawn services advertising on radio and TV sometimes offer air-ee-AY-shun at various times of the year. It's AIR-ate and air-AY-shun, pure and simple.

Economic, electric, election: ECK-uh-nom-ic, uh-LECK-trick, and uh-LECK-shun are all wrong. The initial *e* carries the long vowel sound, as in "eel," or "eek," if you prefer. It's in those big books, at least the good ones.

Immediately: It is not **um**-mediately, unless you are in a panic, in which case you are allowed to scream it at the top of your lungs. Otherwise, enunciate that first letter clearly, please, as in "impel" or "impressive."

Vice versa: The "vice" does not rhyme with lice; the Latin term is VYE-sa VER-sa.

Divisive: A former governor of New York once said that "abortion is an issue that is di-VISS-ive." Interviewing the governor on *60 Minutes*, Harry Reasoner immediately said that "although the issue of abortion is di-VICE-ive ..." Stick with Harry's way on this one.

Defense, offense: Sports guys have a lock on them. Originally, the emphasis was on the second syllable in both cases, but since they began to be almost inseparable, especially in an athletic setting, the pronunciation has fallen to emphasis on the first syllable, as in DEE-fence and OFF-ence. But – and this is a big but – in all other uses where they are used individually, the accent stays on the second syllable – dee-FENCE and off-FENCE, and don't let anyone else tell you differently. Oh, and if you don't believe me, look it up.

Insurance: In Texas, it's IN-shurnce; up north and on the air, it's in-SHUR-ance. Keep that dictionary handy.

Meaning what?

Warranty: This is a noun, dammit; one cannot "warranty" or "warrantee" something, one can only "warrant" against defect, etc. The word "warrantee" used as a verb is total nonsense, and I have heard it that way way too many times, it being a weasel word used in place of the verb "guarantee" to supposedly limit responsibility for poor quality in manufacture or service. A "warranty," however, is exactly the same as a "guarantee." Confused? Work on it.

Consensus of opinion: This is redundant. "Consensus" means "majority of opinion," or that the majority of those polled are in agreement, and stands quite well by itself, thank you.

Issue: What in the world ever happened to "subject," or "topic," or "problem," substituting "issue" for "problem" being the most pervasive of all. No longer do we have difficulties or questions or concerns or obstacles, we have "issues." Sometimes it's not even a problem; sometimes it's simply an item or topic for discussion, as in a meeting where we hear, "We now come to the issue of when and where we will hold the next meeting." Yechh! I have an issue with issue.

Into: "So what are you into?" "Oh, I'm into life and fun." Meaning "interested in" or the like, "into" has nudged its way into popular cant and jargon, and there is probably no way to fight it. But we can still make merry with it, as was the case of a series of women's sled-dog tours being promoted a while back. I don't recall how or where I heard it, but I swear I did, thusly: "But while she was living in Bemidji [Minnesota], Reuther said, she 'really got **into** the **outdoors**.'" She accomplished this, of course, by getting out of the indoors.

No, as far as English syntax is concerned, one cannot "be" into anything. One can "get" into all sorts of things, such as the soup. We can "get into the soup," "be in the soup," "be in (the) soup (business)," "get into soup," or "get soup into us," but that's about it.

As far as … : This is almost totally out of control. The term is supposed to have an object of some kind, such as "As far as we know," or "As far as this concerns you," or "As far as that goes." To say, "As far as apples, I prefer the Braeburn variety," is to throw all the rules aside. However, sometimes a particularly long sentence contains the term and it may be hard to tell where the actual object is. My personal solution to the difficulty is to substitute "As for … ," as in "As for candy, I'll take chocolate drops every time." Not only does it work, but it adds a truism in the bargain. I do like dark chocolate.

Max: "To the max," "maxed out," etc., have become bastardizations of "maximum," "maximized," etc., and are probably here to stay. I still hesitate to use them, although "maximize" is rather a handy way to condense "use to the maximum." I concede, but just this once.

OK, that's enough of my own ranting, at least for the time being. My linguiphilic scouts are out and about, and L.B. of Carmichael, Calif., reports:

Bill Conlin, writing his Track Turmoil sports column in the *Sacramento Bee*, tells about the difficulty of obtaining use of an artificial-surface track for the Buffalo Chips Running Club, a senior group of some 10 years' standing. I thought that was amusing. Conlin also began a sentence with "But an interesting controversy is developing for **we** watchers of California State University, Sacramento ..."

Aah, I get it! Running, standing, very clever. As for the other, "*we* watchers" is OK as the initiators of something, but on the receiving end it's "*us* watchers," in this case the object of the preposition "for." I thought everybody knew that, but I guess I was mistaken.

The sports pages of the Torrance, Calif., paper had M.S. of nearby Harbor City shaking his head:

> Staff writer Bob Cox wasted no time in committing his two faux pas in his first two paragraphs about skiing: "It's **extremely possible** that at least once – and **possibly** several times – in the next week, skiers will exceed the current capacity of Mammoth Mountain, America's leading ski area. The result? After driving 5½ to 6 hours, skiers will be forced to wait in **lift lines of 30 minutes and longer** ..."

How come only once is "extremely possible," but several outings a week are only "possible"? I'm used to "strongly possible" and "slightly possible," but "extremely" is a new one on me. A better word would be "likely," used almost anywhere in the sentence, possibly more than once. Also, a lift line cannot have a time, except for the hours it is in use, so the phrase makes no sense. Make it "wait in lift lines *for* 30 minutes *or* longer, etc."

I'm trying not to repeat goofs, but P.G. of Buffalo, N.Y., caught WKBW-TV in an indecisive and ambivalent posture that I could not let go by:

> A newspaper ad for a program about the Catholic Church declared: "Fewer people are attending Mass, and even **less** people are choosing to become priests and nuns."

I also saw a magazine ad for World MasterCard that offered "more living, **less** limits." Sure. (Do I really need to say "fewer"?)

More pronunciations

When TV's *Lifestyles Of the Rich and Famous* was rich and famous, an unidentified announcer proclaimed that Sally Jessy Raphael and her husband were off on a trip to Ireland in pursuit of a "**Seltic** adventure." "Celtic," of course, is pronounced "Keltic," except when referring to the Boston basketball team. No, the announcer was not Robin Leach.

Mushmouthed media mumblers have so much trouble with the simplest words and phrases. Translate, for example, this: "Y'gotta headache? Ummuna getcha an aspirin." It's not hard to decipher, but it surely does not belong in professional discourse. Often, in place of "Ummuna" we hear "Ungunna," which also means the same "I am going to ..."

Foreign words usually give broadcasters fits. They would be so much better off if they would avoid the pitfalls. Randy Shaver, on local KARE-TV, once said that "troops were **en rowt** to Somalia ..." He meant *en route*, a French term now part of English that is pronounced AHN ROOT.

Seldom-used words should always be checked. J.H. of Brooklyn Center, Minn., heard Frederika Freyberg on WCCO-TV in Minneapolis tell how Bobbi McCaughey, mother of septuplets, "**demures** at the idea that she is Super Mom." The word is "demurs," pronounced de-MURZ.

Apologizing for missing the poor fellow's name, but adding to our store of verbal stumbles, is R.M. of Maumee, Ohio:

> Perhaps some sort of damn-the-torpedoes award can be found for the inexperienced announcer on Toledo television station WTOL-TV. Undeterred by the fact that he was, somehow, unfamiliar with the word "misled," he drove on, pronouncing it "**mizzled**."

28

Thoughtful insertion

Something that looks odd, funny, or out of kilter to one pair of eyes may not appear the same to one or more other pairs of eyes. Over the years, I have received, metaphorically speaking, a virtual mountain of mail, most of a general nature and some of a more technical stripe that I am unable to handle. This is not meant to sound ungrateful, but is meant simply to explain why some of those generous contributions never made it either into my columns or into this book. Just so you know, I am sincerely grateful for everything I have received.

Keeping my mind open, however, I am seriously considering writing a second book, using some of the generic and unspecific material that has come to me, which is more than plentiful. A third book would then continue with a combination of both, if there is good enough reason to go that far. Believe me, I have more than enough to fill four or five books, all of some size. Let's see what develops.

I have said repeatedly that I am not a technician. My reason for doing what I do is that no one else has done it the way I thought it needed to be done. Also, with the exception of Safire, Kilpatrick, Newman, et al., few columnists have received as much contributed material as I have.

So just because I don't have every jot and tittle in a proper place is no reason for me to back off from the job. (A jot, in case you didn't know, is something insignificant, and comes from the Greek *iota*. A tittle is a mark over a letter, the most common being the dot over the *i*.) Onward!

Huh?

Some things are easier to understand than others. We hear now from J.C. of Alpine, Texas:

> According to television station KTPX (NBC) in Odessa, Texas, a high-ranking staff member of the Odessa parks department

was fired after being "charged with serious allegations." My
wife feels that if he was allegating, he should be fired, while I
believe that allegating among consenting adults in private, no
matter how serious, is not a matter of public concern. However,
if he was allegating in the parks, he should go to jail.

A little humor there. J.C. takes liberties by creating a back-formation of
"allegation," thus deriving "allegate" as a verb. None of my dictionaries
contains the word. Substitute "alleging" for "allegating" in the foregoing,
and although the syntax is now clear, there is still no explanation as to
what those "allegations" were. If the staff member was charged with some
sort of wrong-doing, that's one thing. But if he was charged with making
"serious allegations," as the report said, we have no clue as to whom those
allegations were directed. The story was unfinished. Is your headache
worse than mine?

R.F. of Kenosha, Wis., is back, and has been grocery shopping:

> Because of my interest in Egyptology, I picked up a beautifully
> decorated can containing Boston's Tea of Tut, purveyed by the
> Boston Tea Co. When I got my purchase home and had time
> to read the description on the can, I found that it read: "Bos-
> ton's Tea of Tut – From ancient **hieroglyphs** comes the secret
> blend of rare teas and natural berries. It's a treasure from the
> gods fit for a **Pharoah**."

Egyptology buff R.F. knows that hieroglyphs are the characters that make
up the hieroglyphics, which is the writing itself, which indeed may have
revealed a "recipe" for the blending of the teas. He also knows that the
rulers of Egypt were pharaohs, not pharoahs. Even my spell-checker
knows this.

Whether what R.M. of Dayton, Ohio, saw qualifies as professional is
open to question. However, let's see what he has:

> I thought you might appreciate the irony of this blunder, which
> was displayed for all the world to see on a large illuminated
> sign (with flashing light bulbs making up the letters) outside

of Riverfront Stadium in Cincinnati, Ohio: "Help Cincinnati Schools – Volunteer To **Tudor** a Student."

Someone needed to "tudor" the sign operator.

Rough draft?

G.S. of Ripley, Okla., sent me something I had never seen before, what appears to be a totally unedited editorial from the *Stillwater* (Okla.) *News Press*. I'll condense it and insert corrections, but see what you think of it:

> *"Sipper's Shuttle* – The tough **drunken-driving laws** [drunk-driving law] enacted in Colorado has led to the creation of a new business in Denver ... A former bar owner has established a 'Sipper Shuttle Service.' He **ferry's** [ferries] drinkers **berween** [between] bars and takes them home. ... Tavern owners, a taxi company spokesman, and law enforcement personnel believe the liquor consumption, **incrfeased** [increased] use of taxis and trimmed highway accidents [what?]. ... There's no doubt ... that a **marked reduction** in **drinking**[-]**driver**[-]**related** accidents and fatalities will show a **marked reduction**. ... It may be too early to tell[,] but judging from the effect Colorado's new tough **drunken**[-]**driving** law [same as before] has had. ... Maybe a Sipper Shuttle Service would go over well in Oklahoma? [That's not a question.] ..."

Once again I debated fixing the typos, but decided not to; they serve as additional indicators that the piece was rattled off rather quickly, it was not copyedited, and it appears as if no one looked at it before it landed on people's doorsteps. Now, if the writer had had more than a nip or two as well, and I'm not alleging anything, it would explain a lot.

Read all about it

From R.B. of Miami, Fla., comes this shocker:

> I thought you would be interested in [the enclosed] cover of *Forbes* magazine. The large-print headline, "THE COSMET-ICS GAME TODAY," has under it, "IF CHARLES REVSON WERE **ALIVE**, HE'D BE **SPINNING IN HIS GRAVE**."

It could, of course, have been intended as a joke, but I suspect not. Revson was the founder of the Revlon Corporation, and we'll just have to wonder what would make him spin. I tell you, friends, I never know what'll show up in the next day's mail. Until now, that is, as I discover this tidbit from P.A. of Vienna, Va.:

> *Washington Post* staff writer Molly Sinclair, in an item about unclaimed tax refunds, produced an interesting puzzler: In her penultimate paragraph, she says, "Unclaimed refunds represent **less than a fraction of one percent** of the refunds made, the IRS said."

Oh ho, I wonder if she was actually quoting someone from the IRS. Still, what could that amount be? Maybe $0.00? Tsk, tsk. Less than a fraction would still be a … ?

L.P. of Crystal, Minn., was looking at the availability of office space one day and found this in a newspaper ad: "7,500 sq. ft. in Tyrol Building. Attractive first floor offices with lovely reception room opening to main lobby. Newly decorated throughout in **sheik** grey and maroon color scheme. …" ("chic")

The *St. Petersburg Times* provided D.L. of Dunedin, Fla., with a laugh or two:

> David Finkel wrote a fine human-interest story about a woman living in a house that actually appeared to be abandoned, but wasn't. "Looking through one of the windows, the inside of the house seemed dark, muted, dusty …" In the same paper was a *New York Times* story by Suzanne Slesin about building a solar house. "They decided to **cite** the house on a pasture …" ["site"]

Cite for what, trespassing? As for the dangler, nuf sed. Well, maybe not. Taken literally, the inside of the house was looking at its dark, muted, dusty self through one of the windows. Here's another of that ilk from J.B. of St. Louis, Mo.:

> Advertising in *National Geographic*, Volcano Movies, whose mailing address is in Woodland, Wash., offered "Mount St.

Helens – the VOLCANO – Super 8 Color Action Movies ... **60 feet in length, you** will receive a piece of history ...” The film must share the properties of Alice's Wonderland mushrooms if it can cause one to attain the length of 60 feet!

My all-time favorite dangler is: “Almost immediately after lighting a cigarette, the bus rounded the corner and stopped to pick me up.” Danglers are certainly dumb, but they're also fun.

Turnabout?

What say we follow the lead of J.B. of Garden Grove, Calif., and pay another compliment?

> A *Consumer Reports* critique of the 1983 Buick Century ended with these words that I found quite amusing: “Those are the kinds of problems up with which one should not put in a car that costs more than $10,000.”

Aside from suggesting a comma after “put,” I, too, found it a rather pleasant change of pace, parodying as it does a famous quotation of Winston Churchill. Perhaps not in these exact words, he said, “Ending a sentence with a preposition is the sort of nonsense up with which I will not put.”

Snuck a what?

Ordinarily, I prefer some sort of context accompanying a submission, but even without one, this from K.E. of Oxnard, Calif., had me glassy-eyed on the third reading:

> Appearing in the *Oxnard Press-Courier* was the following unusual paragraph: “Mikel also told parishioners in 1952, the documents state, that he **snuck** a policeman into his house in a laundry bag while his family was being protected.”

Makes you want to know more, doesn't it? Well, you'll just have to guess what the policeman was doing in the laundry bag. “Snuck,” anyway, is unanimously considered by dictionaries to be “colloquial” or “dialectical.” In other words, not a good word for the educated eye. However, I can clearly recall bragging to my friends about how, as a teenager, I once *snuck* into a movie theater. But just because we kids all used the word, journalists should know better. ("sneaked")

Remember Freddie?

Sir Freddie, that is. R.M. of Los Angeles, Calif., caught *Business Week* magazine's crack copydesk napping:

> Sir Freddie Laker was an airline entrepreneur back in the '80s who gave lots of folks cheap rates across the Atlantic. Sadly, the report of the demise of his Skytrain in *Business Week* included the following: "Thinly capitalized from the beginning, Laker Airways' ratio of debt to equity **finely** ended up at 7 to 1."

A typo? No. Inattention? That would be my guess. No doubt that was also the case when the new Park Nicollet Health and Vascular Center, located not far from where I live, ran a full-page color ad in our suburban weekly paper, and also ran a same-size partial-page ad in the metropolitan daily. The heading read: "Excellence has a new address." There was just one thing amiss – the ad did not include an address. A few days later, it was corrected, but I have to wonder how many pairs of eyes checked it over before it went to press, and how many faces were red when the goof was discovered. My, my.

Undercover?

And how about this one, from A.M. of Decatur, Ala.?

> Sans comment, I submit the following from *The Decatur Daily*: "A boy turned over a bicycle to police he found in a wooded area near his home."

I agree; it needs no comment. And barely does this one from S.W. of Olney, Ill.:

> An advertising flyer for National Pen's Ledger Pens had the following: "NO STRINGS GUARANTEE – We're so sure you'll like our Ledger Pens that we make you this **unpresidented** guarantee.

If for any reason whatsoever you are not 100% satisfied, simply return them for a full refund anytime within two years."

Does that mean that everyone else in the company stands behind the guarantee, but the president demurs? OK, before we get silly, let's move on to D.B. of Tulsa, Okla.:

In the *Tulsa World*'s business section was an item in a column headed Of Local Interest: "In December, Vector Properties announced it would begin renovation of the building at Fourth Street and Boulder Avenue Dec. 21. However, a partnership agreement with a local oil company fell **threw**."

Just to keep things in perspective, the item appeared in January of 1982, well before computers had spell-checkers. A person blew it, and this is exactly why we will always need copyeditors, computers notwithstanding, although one fine day in the future there will likely be a grammar-check-ing program that *might* have caught this one. (Someone recently told me that grammar-checkers do indeed exist. It will be quite interesting to see how well they work.)

It's long gone now, but for some of us who remember, what follows got both laughs and groans. Providing the reminder is B.W. of Mountlake Terrace, Wash.:

Prime targets for SOTS are the ad people who wrote the copy for the public service announcement that ends, "A mind is a terrible thing to waste." The campaign was to raise money for the United Negro College Fund.

Most people always knew what was intended, but the word selection left a lot to be desired. As compelling as it is, it still slogs through a grammati-cal swamp we are unlikely to forget, and I'm not so sure they're not still using it.

Are they here?

This one is from S.D. of Tucson, Ariz., but I'm not sure what to make of it:

The following headline appeared in the *Arizona Daily Star*: "UFO reports hovering over Tucson."

As I read it, it makes sense in more ways than one, but none very clearly. Did the UFO provide a report on "hovering" by another aircraft or maybe even by itself? Were the UFO reports provided through skywriting, hovering up there in the sky? Once again, a headline writer creates his or her special form of mischief and moves on, leaving the rest of us mystified. All in a day's work.

More tortured prose

W.J. and J.J. of Berwyn, Ill., read the *Chicago Tribune*, also known as "The World's Greatest Newspaper," at least by the publishers:

> Headlined "Man plunges to death in refuse chute," the unattributed article said: "A short time before [Lee] Adams'[s] body was found in the ground floor garbage compactor, he was seen running through the lobby holding his head by a doorman."

Just in case you wondered, there is no possible way I could make up something like that. Besides, I have the clipping as evidence. Another of that same ilk came via K.A. of South Euclid, Ohio:

> The *Cleveland Press* headlined an article about real estate with: "Home sales **flower**, but **bloom** slowly." A subhead reads, "**Fertilized** by lower interest rates." What I don't understand is the difference between flowering and blooming.

There is none. Both words mean "to bring to blossom," which is yet another word meaning the same as flower and bloom. But I thought the "fertilized" reference was imaginative and in keeping with the headline, regardless of its nonsense. At least it wasn't one of those horrible headline puns we see so often.

Home, sweet home

A nicely prepared newspaper ad for Laurel Hill Condominiums in Golden Valley, Minn., quoted one of their purchasers as saying, "I like the

comaraderie with the other owners ..." Then in the block of copy was: "And with prices reduced by $30,000 to $40,000 **dollars,** now's the time to visit ..." ("camaraderie" – the word "dollars" is redundant)

Honk!

If there were a contest for Most Idiotic Advertising Slogan, a TV ad for Mazda automobiles would stand a good chance of winning with this one: "**We are** not **the car** for everyone." OK, so who is the car for everyone? *My Mother the Car* was a popular TV series, but it was nevertheless singular. The imaginary 1928 Porter would have said, "*I* am not the car for everyone," if the car was so inclined. "We," however, cannot possibly be a car.

Another Mazda TV ad caught my eye when the graphic across the bottom of the screen read: ("**Actual re-enactment**"). Is that more believable than a "Dramatized re-enactment"? Or would it be similar to an "Actual dramatization"? "Staged re-enactment" would be redundant, so nothing mentioned so far would work. I'd just use one word, either "re-enactment" or "dramatization." That was easy.

R.I.P.

So as not to be disrespectful, I'm changing the names, but the item was sent by R.H. of Linton, No.Dak.:

> From the *Emmons County Record*: "Our sympathy is extended to the Barney Phyffe family, who passed away Friday at the Bismarck hospital."

As Oliver Hardy used to say to Stan Laurel, I have nothing to say.

That same R.H. also read the Fargo-Moorhead *Forum* in 1980, which explains a lot:

> An AP article in the *Forum* about the U.S. money supply included: "Aubrey [G. Lanston & Co.] said that development would encourage banks to soon **reduce** their basic business loan rates **from** the current **11.25 to 11.50** percent rate currently charged." This must be why people don't understand that when the government reduces your taxes you pay more money.

OK, so now somebody is going to say that what was meant was the *range* between the two percentages makes up the current rate, which makes whoever points that out a heckuva lot smarter than the UPI writer, whoever that might have been. If that were true, however, it should have said "… 11.25 to 11.50 percent *rates* …" instead of "rate," except for which everything else was correct. R.H., of course, along with others, missed the specific point of the statement, not only because of the obvious "rate" error, but because of the tortured construction of the sentence. What was actually meant was that banks would be encouraged to reduce those 11.25-11.50 rates, perhaps to 11.00 or less. Need I explain further?

Oh, look!

C.C. of Daly City, Calif., was rather startled when he picked up his newspaper:

> Today's headline in the *San Francisco Examiner* – the original Hearst paper – proudly proclaims, "Climber **peaks** inside volcano." Apparently he achieved his life's highest goal, whatever it might have been. I would have liked to watch.

The volcano, of course, was Mount St. Helens, and from the edge of the crater it must have been all downhill from there. It had to be terrible knowing that life would never get any better for Fred R. Miller than at that special moment he spent peering into the smoldering cauldron. Well, maybe not, but if old William Randolph H. had been alive, he would have been tempted to fling his headline writer head first into those fires of hell. Obviously, no one could peak, peek, pique, or anything else while inside that bubbling vat of hot lava. (In case you are thinking of a caldera, that, I believe, is the depression left after a volcano has spent itself. Diamond Head on Oahu is an example of that. Mt. St. Helens was still active at the time of the foregoing report.)

29

Would you repeat that, please?

In spite of my stated intention to aim the SOTS shaming finger at named targets, I was so taken with the following from R.D. of Beaumont, Texas, that I decided to break my rule and include it almost intact:

> As a former broadcaster, I myself was the [deliverer] of a blooper or two. At my first radio job in McKenney, Texas, a local public service spot went something like this: "Collin County is planning to honor all of its deceased firefighters. All Collin County firemen are being asked to meet at the McKenney fire station, and then travel to the cemetery in a **body**."

Relax, R.D., you were just reading what they gave you. It happens. Moving right along, we catch another columnist with egg on his face. From E.R. of Waterville, Maine, comes this shocker:

> In his syndicated column appearing in 200 newspapers, Jeffrey Hart wrote a story about Eleanor Roosevelt's relationship with another woman that mentioned the woman's name: "Lorena – interesting, almost an **acronym** for 'Eleanor' ..." Whatever she was to Eleanor, an acronym she was not. ["anagram"]

What is particularly interesting about this item is that Jeffrey Hart was a distinguished professor of English at Dartmouth and an editor of the *National Review*. Knowing what we all know now about acronyms, it is perhaps not surprising that Professor Hart, as well as whatever copyeditors might have seen the piece, used a different definition of the word. Such is the all-too-common fate of the fine distinctions once reserved for so many of our time-honored words. What next?

Politics

A race in 1980 for a Senate nomination in New Haven, Conn., inspired R.C. of nearby Hamden to submit the following:

The New Haven Register had two staff reporters covering a
Republican primary election, the contestants being James
Buckley and Richard Bozzuto. Lynne Garnett wrote: "Buckley
was vibrant, and **delved** into the crowd of more than 300 supporters with enthusiasm ..." Not to be outdone, Mark Penders
said that the two contenders "have been in a race which appears
to have **aroused** the general public to **depths** of apathy."

Also, in an anonymously written editorial in the same paper
about school spending was a paragraph that began: "Teacher
unions **can be** of greater service to the communities if they
devoted their energies to rooting out wasteful or needless
expenditure of public funding."

"Delved" should have been "dived" or "dove," since "delved" means "to have
dug for information." As for "aroused" to the "depths," we have a split
oxymoron. And the unions "could" be of greater service if they "devoted"
their energies, or they "can be" if they "devote" their energies, etc. Editorials should be the most closely watched writings in any newspaper. Editorial writers should also be identified, as they are in some papers but not all.
My local rag is in the latter category, sad to say. The intention, of course,
is to give the reading public the impression that the entire staff agrees
with the editorial writers. Some of us are not so easily fooled.

Music?

We don't hear much about Muzak these days, and many have forgotten
that it once was the leading provider of what we now call elevator music,
and for all I know, it still is. D.S. of Reno, Nev., calls the tune:

I hope I'm the first to report on the following from a large ad
for Muzak in *The Wall Street Journal*. In bold inch-high type
was the headline: "WE MAKE PEOPLE HAPPY WITHOUT
THEM KNOWING IT."

Space in that newspaper does not come cheaply, which is why I left its
name there. The goof, of course, was the advertiser's. Without getting
technical about it, I and most others know that the word should be "their,"
rather than "them." I once got a call from Angela Astore, a news anchor

at our local KSTP-TV, wanting to know which was correct, "I appreciate *you* helping me," or "I appreciate *your* helping me." I thanked her for asking and told her the proper word was *your*, which she used on that night's 10:00 P.M. newscast. She didn't tell me how she got my number, but I suspect that someone on the station's staff heard me during a WCCO radio interview that same morning. Anyway, I was honored. Thanks, Angela, wherever you are.

Who?

Back in 1982 the local paper, which has had several permutations of its name, was known as the Minneapolis *Star and Tribune* (the *and* is now gone). A short item began: "Montevideo [Minn.]: Man jailed for taking soybeans from elevator to speak." The elevator was bankrupt, but he claimed that the contents belonged to him, and he just took them. The write-up doesn't say, but I suppose he was out on bail. Weird syntax, though.

Two years earlier and for many years prior, there were two papers, the *Minneapolis* (morning) *Tribune* and the *Minneapolis* (evening) *Star*. We took the *Star* because my dad had to leave for work very early and had no time to read any paper with his breakfast. When I had a family of my own, the evening habit continued, and it was in 1980 that the celebrity column (known as Personals, but not the classified kind) caught my eye. Henry Miller, the author and playwright, died at 88 "of clogged arteries and other **infirmaries** of old age." ("infirmities" – or am I explaining too much?)

It are?

Goodman Jewelers has been a long-time advertiser in the Twin Cities, and has used radio and television extensively, apparently to good effect because their ads have been with us for years. Eventually, they all fall into the SOTS trap, however, and this fine company was no exception. On both TV and radio, one of its slogans was, "The Beauty of Fine Diamonds **Are** Timeless." I spoke with the advertising manager, who told me he would fix it at the very first opportunity, but the cost of making commercials prevented him from pulling the offending ad until a new one could be made. He didn't lie, though; the error was fixed and has not recurred.

I see what?

As you've likely noticed, I've stayed away from books, mostly because they are not *as* public as TV, newspapers, etc., but since I gave Edwin Newman what-for earlier, I feel obligated to dole it out equally to those others who also write about the English language. In the prisoner's dock right now is John Simon, author of several books, including one called *Paradigms Lost*, an extremely thoughtful and erudite work. There was one flaw I found, however. He writes: "What we can see from Manhattan **as well as Brooklyn** is the Statue of Liberty." I'm sure that if he should see it here now he would quickly recognize his gaffe, which is that it is not at all clear what it is "we can see …" Adding the word "from" before "Brooklyn" makes it easy to tell. Without it, it would appear that from Manhattan we can see Brooklyn as well as we can see the statue.

Habituated?

On the telly, as the British refer to television, was an ad for *Woman's World* magazine that asked, "Is America Hooked on Addiction?" Now, I knew it was possible to get hooked on several things, but on addiction itself? Beats me. My doctor, by the way, is reluctant to use "hooked" or "addictive" or any other similar term, except for "habituated." Heck, I'm "addicted" to chocolate, ice cream, soft licorice, cashews, lots of things that may or may not be good for me. Call it "habituated" if you like, T.R. (my doc), but I really do believe I am solidly in the grasp, even of some rather helpful medications (note that we don't call them drugs anymore).

Oh yes, I almost forgot to mention popcorn. I love good popcorn, and I may be "habituated," so I try all kinds, including the microwave varieties. In our area, at least, Vic's Popcorn has been distributed under the authority of KLM Enterprises in Perham, Minn. On the very bottom of the back of the microwave package is the legend: "**Copywrite** KLM Enterprises." ("copyright," actually)

J.S. of Richford, N.Y., wrote to give the Pillsbury Company a "hard" time:

> Dear sirs: A notice appears on the back of your package of Hungry Jack Microwave Popcorn. The notice reads: IT IS NORMAL FOR UNPOPPED KERNELS TO REMAIN IN A

FULLY POPPED BAG. I cannot allow this illogical bit of careless writing to pass without comment.

First, it is my experience that the unpopped kernels do not remain in the bag, but fall out with the popped kernels. Second, the bag is not popped, but the contents of the bag is popped. Finally, if unpopped kernels exist, the bag is *not* fully popped, in spite of your claim.

Please rewrite the notice to read: SOME KERNELS MAY NOT POP – THIS IS NORMAL, or words to that effect.

Dental problems kept me from eating popcorn for almost 3 years a while back, so I haven't checked on that particular product and don't know whether J.S.'s complaint had any effect. (I've been spoiled, however, by Tom's Popcorn Shop's product, fresh-popped Brazilian White. None better anywhere.)

More bad news

Some things go way beyond the bounds of reason. In an ad in national magazines, Light 'n Tangy V8 vegetable juice supposedly has among its attributes, "And **its only got half the sodium**." There is so much wreckage here that I hardly know where to begin. The "its" needs the apostrophe, "only" belongs before "half," "it's … got" should be "it has," and the big question is: "half the sodium" of *what?* An equal amount of sea water, maybe? Or could it have been the same product as sold previously with twice the sodium as the newer product? Senseless advertising hyperbole, is what it is. But then, I suppose most folks don't care, so long as it tastes OK and gives them a good feeling about taking care of their health by drinking their veggies.

Fire!

In 1985 the Ohio Match Company of Wadsworth, Ohio, now no longer in business, put out a series of matchcovers with trivia questions on them. On the front of one of them was a drawing of a TV camera, and on the back was: "What was the occupation of Ralph **Cramden** on the TV comedy skit: 'The Honeymooners'"? The answer on the inside of the cover was "Bus driver." Ralph's last name, of course, was Kramden, but *The Honeymooners* was much more than a skit, it was an entire series of 39 programs. Also, what the heck was the purpose of that colon after "skit"? So, was the material public? Yes. Was it professional? I'd hesitate to call it that, but if the writer got paid, I guess it qualifies.

Barbeque?

Even the spell-checker won't accept that spelling, nor will any dictionary. But that won't stop Lloyd's **Barbeque** Co. from putting it on the labels of all its products. Since it is a local company, I called and talked to the advertising manager, who said he would ask the owner about the spelling, and that I should call again in a couple of weeks. I did call and the ad guy took my number, but neither he nor the owner returned my call. I'm guessing that they would claim that the spelling was a matter of "style," but I can't buy it. As for the reason(s), your guess is as good as mine.

Of the same ilk is Famous Dave's, a restaurant with several locations. One of its TV ads uses the slogan **"real honest barbeque."** Yeah, yeah, we know, we know – it's their "style," but that doesn't mean it's right. How in hell are kids supposed to learn any sort of decent grammar or spelling with this kind of stuff polluting the airwaves? **"Real"** as opposed to "fake"? **"Honest"** as opposed to "duplicitous"? And when you get the chance, tell a kid that there's no *q* in "barbecue." Really, there isn't.

AAWWKKK! Don't tell me! My new word-processing program now says that "barbeque" is OK. I'm afraid to look in my new dictionary, *Webster's Eleventh New Collegiate.* Frankly, my friends, I don't give a damn. I'm sticking to my guns. This is my book, and I'll cry if I want to!

Or what?

You knew, didn't you, that sooner or later I had to get around to "or what?" It pops up in so many variations and has become so ingrained, even among the educated, that it is probably beyond hope. However, I cannot finish this book without pointing out that IT IS A REALLY SILLY PHRASE! To ask, "Are we having a great time or what?" is nonsense.

"Are we having a great time, or are we not?" is what is meant, but the colloquialism prevails. "Are we having a great time, or, if not, what are we having?" also makes sense to a degree, but when MCI asked in a TV ad, "Is this a great time, or what?" I replied to no one in particular, "Or bananas, maybe?" Just between you and me, I think the phrase was given credence by its cleverness alone, and whoever started it will probably never be known, which is just as well. Am I right, or what?

Spelling for the birds

It may not be as widely distributed as the print and broadcast media, but the flyer for the Dakota County Fair, picked up by J.M. of St. Paul, Minn., certainly was prepared by an advertising agency. On Saturday, August 14, from 11:00 A.M. to 2:00 P.M., was the "**Rapture** Center" at the Children's Park & Barnyard. ("raptor")

J.M. also sent along a page from the weekly *South-West Review* containing an article about the production of a Hollywood movie (*Sugar and Spice*) on location in Minnesota. News editor Lori Carlson wrote, "Aside from about 10 Los Angeles-based actors, the entire cast is from Minnesota. 'That really works for the **voracity** of the movie, [co-producer Mike] Nelson added.'" What takes it out of the typo category is the call-out headline, the little blurb in bold-face italics in the middle of the article's text, that says "A primarily Minnesotan cast and crew 'really works for the **voracity** of the movie,' said co-producer Mike Nelson." We used to have a saying, "Monkey see, monkey do." Courageously, the paper published a letter to the editor the following week, pointing out the gaffe. Even "veracity" would not have served accurately, since veracity means truth or honesty. The word wanted was "believability."

The Miracle Mile Shopping Center in St. Louis Park was one of the first so-called strip malls in Minnesota, opening in 1949. Forty years later, the center ran an almost-three-quarter-page ad in the weekly St. Louis Park *Sailor* in celebration of its golden anniversary with this text in a round border: "WHAT DO THE **HOOLA HOOP** & MIRACLE MILE SHOPPING CENTER HAVE IN COMMON? Both originated in the **1950's**! Miracle Mile is having a hoop-di-do 'Back to the **50's**' style anniversary party, Sept. 22 & 23. We're celebrating with a **Hoola Hoop** contest ..." Do you suppose the ad was prepared by someone not old enough in 1989 to remember Hula Hoops? Shucks, those things are still being sold today. (By now, you should be able to spot several other errors, as well.)

More bad choices

In 1990 there were two events that warranted special attention by the media. One was the *Exxon Valdez* oil spill, which resulted in the headline: "[Ship's captain] Hazelwood sentenced to **clean beaches**." Actually, he was sentenced to help clean up the oily ones, so it was no picnic for him. He was sentenced to cleaning beaches, not spending time on clean ones.

And in another 1990 headline: "Turncoat swallows head for mansion, not mission." Have you figured it out yet? OK, think San Juan Capistrano. I knew you'd get it.

C.P. of Highland, Calif., sent along a clipping from the San Bernardino *Sun Telegram*, with a headline reading: "Chef killed **by** his home." Never mind the smart remarks about putting the building under "house arrest." Better, of course, would have been "Chef killed *near* his home," which would have taken up little more space. Actually, he was killed outside his home by thieves he accidentally surprised as they attempted to break into his car.

I've used Wilson Jones – or as they prefer it now, WilsonJones – products for years, but an ad for their 3-ring binders has me puzzled: "All WilsonJones traditional and contemporary colors are heavy duty suede grain **virgin vinyl** – for longer wear …" There are, of course, two hyphens missing, but what other kind of vinyl is there? As far as I know, vinyl is not recycled, so it all has to be "virgin." Doesn't it? Also, since when are "colors" made of "vinyl"? Not possible.

E.M. of Newtown, Conn., wrote to the Post Publishing Co., publishers of the *Bridgeport Post*, to say that he was a member of SOTS – with some details about us – and wanted them to know that their gaffe was likely to show up in my column. Unfortunately, it didn't, but here it is now:

> The rather large headline, four columns wide, read: "Yesterday's children are very reluctant to **having** today's children." ["have"]

Sooner or later

I don't know whether you've noticed, but I have tried to stay away from naming most of the publications that carry error-filled advertising. In the great majority of cases, it's the ad agencies that are the responsible parties, not the newspapers or the magazines, even though they do have a say about what's acceptable and what's not. However, an exception to my general rule was inevitable and for good reason. Oddly adjacent to Chuck Shepherd's News of the Weird column in the *Star Tribune* was a small 2-column-wide ad for a company specializing in wall systems called Atmospheres, Inc. In the largest type in the ad was the name "**Atmopsheres**." When I called the phone number listed, I was told by the owner that it was the *Star Tribune*'s advertising department that set the type in the ad, and that no tear-sheet (advance proof copy) had been sent. My gut tells me that the order was received late, that it was put together in a hurry at the last minute, and that no one even saw it before it went to press. I used to have to handle similar things at the TV station, so I know how easily errors can jump up and bite.

That much?

Once again I cannot single out any one writer or broadcaster because the usage is now of such epidemic proportions that it appears to be beyond our help. I'm referring to such statements as, "There won't be **that much** rain tomorrow," spoken without even a guess, let alone a specific amount being mentioned. "That much," it seems nowadays, means "more than is acceptable," as well as "very much," and in this case perhaps even "some." Another example would be "The Legislature didn't spend **all that much** time debating the issue." So, *how much* are we talking about here? Professional communicators should know better than to pick up jargon most likely originating with as yet uneducated teenagers, who, as a group, delight in playing games and inventing new jargon. "Much rain" or "much time" would certainly suffice, and even "very much rain" or "very much time" would work just as well. When I hear "all that much" coming from the mouth of a well-paid TV anchor or reporter, I quite often holler at the screen, "How much are we talking about here?" And I know I'm not alone, although I do occasionally hear an echo.

Punctuation

I've had surprisingly little to say about punctuation, at least so far, but the United States Postal Service has provided me with a multiple error on the selvage (edge paper torn off and thrown away) on its Winter Olympics issue of 1994. There were five different stamps, each illustrating a

particular Olympic event, one of which was the luge. Printed on the selvage was: "LUGE participants, known as 'sliders' careen down a course of
banked, and hair-pin turns at speeds up to 65 m.p.h." That comma after
"banked" is a long way from home. It belongs after 'sliders,' as I'm sure
you've already noticed.

Right next to the luge legend is one about ice-dancing: "Form and grace,
elaborate costumes and **charismatic** melodies combine to make ice dancing an Olympic favorite." I can't say I have ever heard of "charisma" being
used to describe music. Dictionaries apply it only to the special qualities
of people who are outstanding and compelling leaders. Someone at the
USPS was overly creative.

What a difference a comma can make. G.B. of Lombard, Ill., sent me a
full-page ad for a Marshall Field's mattress sale, with the following headline in huge letters:

25% TO 50% OFF
ALL OUR MATTRESSES
LAST 3 DAYS

Too fine a point? Nobody said you had to like 'em all. If there had been a
comma after "mattresses," or some sort of line or other mark between the
second and third lines, or if the third line had been printed in a different
color, the tee-heeing and tut-tutting that surely went on in some quarters
would have been prevented. OK, so everybody knows what was meant; that
does not get the advertiser off scot-free. If it had been done for some sort of
obvious effect, that would be different, but such was obviously not the case.
An old-line name like Marshall Field's surely deserved better treatment.

As I mentioned earlier, end-line hyphenation can be trouble, as in this
item from M.E. of St. Paul, Minn.:

> A fashion article in the *St. Paul Pioneer Press* was all about young
> women who wanted blue jeans that could be padded to give
> them a "shaplier, rounder, and firmer behind." Someone invented
> them and those testing them were interviewed. One tester said,
> "They're like control-top panty-hose. They slightly **rear-range**
> what you have ..." That hyphen was where the line ended.

The old double-letter break, is what it is. It's not incorrect, but it certainly looks funny.

How awful!

Another of that same stripe was the headline in the *St. Louis Park Sailor* that read: "**Catastrophic** insurance program airs on TV." The small article gave the program's actual title as "**Catastrophic** Insurance: The New Law." In both cases, it would have been a whole lot better to say, "Catastrophe insurance," don't you think? I thought you might. Describing a program as "catastrophic" is really going too far.

Which is it?

On May 13, 1981, Pope John Paul II was wounded by an assassin's bullet. News media worldwide described the incident as a "**papal attack**." A later speech by the same pope that was reportedly antagonist to gays was also described as a "papal attack." The former is an example of poor terminology, while the latter makes perfect sense. An attack *on* the pope is not the same as an attack *by* the pope.

Hello?

There's no way to tell whether the person who created and/or recorded the answering-machine message was a professional, but this is what I heard:

> Happy holidays and thank you for calling the Southdale Shopping Center. If you should need **further** information, please wait on the line and an operator will assist you at the completion of the general informational messages.

Callers did indeed get *no* information in the first place, before being asked if they wanted "further" information, that is, unless they considered "Happy holidays" to be informative. Also, if we wanted to talk to the operator, we had no choice but to listen to "further ... general informational messages."

Raising several questions was the slogan adopted by that same Southdale Shopping Center for the 1988 holiday season: "**One** gift doesn't fit all." This, of course, led to my only question: "Which gift is that?" It's also certain that there are *many* gifts that do not "fit" everyone. In sum, the slogan makes no sense whatever, and what was intended was "*No* gift fits all (everyone)."

Short but sour

Brevity, we hear, is the soul of wit. But abbreviations and word-clipping can be annoying, as in the case of a KSTP-AM radio newscast (person's name not noted) in which "nontraditional students" – especially mothers who have raised a family and have gone back to school – are referred to as "**nontrads**." It's sort of like the military "noncoms," but somehow it just doesn't ring right. Maybe it's me.

Back in the thirties and forties there were such oxymoronic things as Big Little Books, and if you've never seen one, take a walk around any flea market and you're quite likely to find some. Later, in 1991, Cray Research, manufacturers of supercomputers, not knowing how else to describe their latest product, dubbed it a "minisupercomputer." It was not quite as big and costly as a supercomputer, and I have to assume it was bigger and more expensive than a minicomputer, if there be such a thing. Seems to me that "mini" and "super" would cancel each other out, resulting in a plain old garden-variety computer. No doubt I would be told to "bite my tongue."

30

On the other hand

When I began this SOTS thing, I never expected that everyone would agree with me. In fact, I assumed from the start that some of the disagreements might make for some interesting exchanges. Because George Woods, an announcer with WBT-AM in Charlotte, N.C., was a public figure, I can use his name freely here. After describing a bit about his work and the reach of his station's signal, George had this to say about what I was doing:

> I hope that SOTS acknowledges the idea that *communication* is the most important part, or function, of language. Form and style have their place, but if someone understands the message, I say let the purists pick up whatever pieces please them.

> But your fun attitude is well-taken!

> In radio, the aim of most broadcasters I know in delivering a live commercial is to make it as conversational as possible, [leading] to easier interpretation by the listener, and indeed, a more communicative situation than a gaudy, blaring, cliched "spot." So in a case like this, you will hear bedroom "**soot**" and "if you're **gonna** go shopping …" or "details **comin'** up!" How many [people] always keep the final *g* in an "-ing"?

> Usually, it's the commercials from ad agencies that are the most insulting, and at the same time, the worst offenders to SOTS members. I used to work at an ad agency, and we produced, at the clients' requests, what we called "borax" commercials – ones that shouted at you, [using] the same old "FANTASTIC!" "REMARKABLE!" "UNBELIEVABLE!" "NEW AND IMPROVED!" lines it seems everyone uses in advertising. But it always worked, in terms of measurable sales results! But then again, [SOTS members] are a minority of the population, eh?

The most memorable event from my ad agency days was the suggestion an associate and I made in jest to the owner of a fast-food sandwich franchise. After picking our brains for several hours, I came up with the line "Makes a great meal, even if you're not hungry!" and the client seriously considered it until we poured enough alcohol [into] him to make him forget it.

Long live SOTS. Keep me (and my fellow broadcasters) on our toes!

Just so you know, that letter was dated May 29, 1976. Not much has changed in 30+ years.

My friend H.F. of Mequon, Wis., sent this note:

A Ms. Linda Sherman of local all-news radio station WRIT (Milwaukee) has been driving me (a serious SOTS member) crazy with her pronunciation of "afternoon." It comes out "**after-nyyoon**," ditto for "noon," of course. In no time, other announcers of that station followed suit [syyoot?]. I sent her a letter and a copy of your [column] from the [last] *Bulletin*, and I'm hoping for the best.

I never heard any more about that one, but I did catch holy heck myself for part of my final paragraph in October 1976. I wrote:

SOTS mail abounds and I now have enough material for a book … If things keep up this way, we may have to consider such a publication. I'll do what I can, though, to get as much of your contributions onto these pages as space allows …

As you can see, the forecast was correct, but at the time it gave the *real* nitpickers serious ammunition. Among them was V.P. of Maitland, Fla., who threw down the gauntlet with this:

Hmmm. As much of *my* contribution as space allows, you say. Does that mean you will print only half of each of my sentences if you do not have *much* space, and *more* of them if you have a lot of space? I am confused.

You couldn't possibly have meant to say "as *many* of your contributions ... as space allows," or "as much of your contribution ..." because you are in the business of saving tongues and wouldn't make a slip such as that, now would you?

I have to confess that I was over a barrel, but on later reflection, I saw V.P.'s point. No, I didn't mean "as many as," nor "as much of (a single) contribution." I was speaking about the overall mass of material I had, and I might have done better by saying, "... to get as much of the wonderful material you send to me onto these pages." (Hindsight is better, you know.) Some contributions were not usable at all (for various reasons), and a great many had several individual items, some of which were OK to use and some were outside the SOTS purview. Also, many things I received were too long or too involved to use in the column, but are now ensconced in this book, so whether "contributions" consisted of one item or several, I am still dealing with an overall mass as I try carefully to select from my readers' generous offerings.

Note too that there has been quite a lot of duplication of items in the contributions I received, so while everything readers have sent is gratefully appreciated, there is no way I could have included it all, either here or in my columns.

Take that, SOTS!

Pressed to the wall, I suppose I could go check my files, but I'll take the word of G.F. of Ajijic, Jalisco, Mexico, that I accepted someone's criticism of the word "sherbert," as it is so frequently used instead of "sherbet." Oh, heck. Hang on while I go look. ... Ah hah! G.F. is only partly correct: It's not in Merriam-Webster's Second Unabridged, but it is in the Third with a wishy-washy definition that says "also sherbet" and includes all possible ingredients. In M-W's Third, however, there are two separate listings, and only the "sherbert" has milk, egg-white, and gelatin. "Sherbet" does not. So where does that leave us? Apparently we cannot criticize the use of either form unless we know what the stuff was made of. As far as I have always believed, the flavored iced water is sherbet. Sherbert is new to me

Another shoulder-injuring recoil from the SOTS rifle came from L.W. of
South Gate, Calif.:

> Now, my English (American) grammar isn't perfect, but your
> entry on the Arrow shirt commercial bothered me a little bit
> with the "look good," "feel good," etc. According to my educa-
> tion, this use of the word "good" is correct in this situation and
> much preferable to the word "well," which would describe the
> preceding verb – look, fit, feel. "Well" would describe how the
> shirt "looks," but it is not the shirt that is looking, but a per-
> son looking *at* the shirt and sees that it "looks good" as stated.
> Now, if the shirt had eyes and did the looking, I feel that the
> expression "the shirt looks well" could apply if the shirt had
> excellent eyesight. But then, maybe that is what makes their
> shirts different from the others. My shirts can't see very well,
> but they do look good when I am wearing them. (Keep up the
> good work.)

What I actually wrote was:

> On radio, a commercial about Arrow shirts says that they
> "look good, fit good, and feel good." Let's send letters to the
> manufacturers of these products proclaiming a boycott of their
> merchandise unless and until they hire advertising agencies that
> use "good" English."

No doubt they look good (pleasing to the eye), and feel good (are comfortable to wear), but to say that they "**fit good**" is to depart from the
acceptable. It's obvious that the shirt has no eyes to see with, nor does it
have feelings of any sort, but neither does it assess its own physical characteristics, as "fit good" would imply. If it fits properly, it fits "well." For
many years I bought most of my clothes from the Fitwell Pants Store
(later renamed Fitwell Men's Store), and I cannot imagine that the business would have survived with the name Fitgood Men's Store. Also, my
guess is that if the agency copywriters had found a way to say that the
shirts "smell good" (which likely would be correct, but not much of a selling point) and "sound good" (hear that fresh crispness as you unfold and
unbutton it?), they would have done so, and in all respects they would

have been correct, save one – the inability of shirts to possess attributes of living things. They cannot fit "good." (Don't ask me about "taste good.")

Sign up!

The St. Paul Winter Carnival is a really big deal every year, and no expense is spared in the promotion of it far and wide. Even folks in Minneapolis deign to cross the river to attend, never mind the intercity rivalry. L.P. of the latter city happened across a poster in his travels, and tore it from wherever it had been placed; it still has a piece of duct tape attached. The specific event being touted was a broomball tournament, which, to the unschooled, is a form of ice hockey, except that no skates are used, a small ball replaces the puck, and modified house-brooms serve instead of hockey sticks.

Competition is fierce, as I recall from my own daughter's participation some years back, and teams signed up from far and near. There are strict rules; the entrance fees are not inconsiderable. But back to the poster: At the very bottom were the words "Tournament Rules, **Entree** Blank on Back Side." (My computer's grammar checker added an accent mark on the first *e*, which I removed, but it was not on the poster, which then makes it a variant of "entry," and that is what was on the reverse of the announcement.) In a technical sense, it should have been "entry," but the French version will do just as well, and aren't you surprised that this did not turn out to be a criticism? I am, as well.

Margot

Margot Seitelman was the executive director of American Mensa from 1961 to the day of her death in 1989. There is so much I could say about that "tough old broad," as she called herself, but I'll simply tell you that there are few human beings in this world for whom I had as much respect as I had for my friend Margot. Anyway, she was a great booster of SOTS and sent me tidbits now and then. Here's one of them:

> I am gnashing my teeth because on last night's CBS News the newscaster, in talking of the snows in Buffalo, said something about conservation being up to "you and **we**." I have written a nasty letter to CBS giving them my personal SOTS award of the day!

Could it have been "you and *me*," and she misheard? Not likely; she had a very sharp sense of hearing, to which I can attest. Once in a crowded and noisy hotel lobby I heard her react to an unkind comment made by someone quite a distance away. She said, loudly, "Put a cork in it … it's not true!" At any rate, I only wish that she had named the TV newsie so that I could give him his due right here.

Along those same lines, G.S. of Ridgecrest, Calif., heard a rather unusual example of an error in Olde English:

> In the Broadway cast-recording of *Man of La Mancha*, the song
> "Golden Helmet of Mambrino" contained the words "Thee and
> I now, ere I die now, will make golden history." I mentioned
> this to several people and my concern was not well received.
> But in the movie version, Don Quixote sang, "Thou and I now
> …" I felt a ridiculously personal elation when I heard the cor-
> rect version, and I want to gloat.

Nowadays we would say "You and I … ," but there is a difference between "thou" (the subject) and "thee" (the object). Think of "Of thee I sing …" or "A loaf of bread, a jug of wine, and thou beside me …" "Thou" does, while the action happens to "thee." I suppose this is a bit outside the SOTS purview, but it is public and it is on the professional level, so it stays.

He takes it all back

Newspaper editorials are difficult to deal with, mostly because they are written behind closed doors by anonymous drudges. I have seen very few papers that actually identify editorial writers by name, but none in a long time. However, I have the clipping from S.S. of Naperville, Ill., that made me chuckle:

> Imagine the delight of someone who shuns the *Chicago Tribune*
> because of its editorial policy and is shown this gem from it by
> less leftish friends: "Call it magic. Call it a special chemistry.
> But the unaffected camaraderie of cast and crew that evolved
> into *The Mary Tyler Moore Show* is something few have accom-
> plished and perhaps few will. With the very last show put to

bed, James L. Brooks, one of the series' creators, **recants** from the groundwork how it all began and why its end – on a high note of success – is such a downer."

No, not a typo, nor a spell-checker error – not in 1977. Just a simple loss of concentration, I would have to guess. The word he surely meant was "recounts."

A fine point

Here's an in-case-you-wondered item that may excite only those Latin-lovers – no, not Latin lovers – who care about word derivations and current linguistic practices. In an early column I agreed with a contributor, who shall remain unidentified, that the word "referendums" was inferior to the original "referenda," denoting the plural. Most dictionaries list both, but not in the same order. W.B. of El Dorado Hills, Calif., says, "A [person] who says 'referendums' is not necessarily illiterate, at least on that ground. He may own an unabridged Webster's, 2nd edition." Random House echoes that sentiment, as I suspect others will also, so I stand chastised and will never repeat *that* error.

An eager beaver

A.S. of Enfield, Conn., sent me a clipping from the *Hartford Courant* UPI story datelined MADRID, Spain. The story had to do with the wives of Spanish Communist Party leaders and how they got along with their husbands. One in particular said that hers was one who shared household duties:

> "On occasions Santiago went as far as making paella (a dish of yellow rice, chicken and seafood). But we were in a special situation. If he had worked eight hours like me, I would have told him 'Okay, let's share the housework.' But him, he sometimes worked up to 24 hours a day and **even more**."

Like, what?

It seems "like" a good time to remind readers once again that I am not perfect. Before I learned what I know now, I made some errors, and I usually caught holy hell for it. When you stick your neck out as (not like) I did, you have to expect your audience to hold you to account. J.R. of New York City did just that, and here's what transpired:

> Shame on you! How can you edit a column dedicated to SOTS when you let stand a sentence like, "It sounds **like** whoever wrote the story was just 'plumb wore out ...'"? I'm not referring to the 'plumb wore out,' either. Correct it yourself. [Then she helped me along.] The word "like" may not be followed by a clause. It may be followed by the objective case of a pronoun or noun or by a gerund (and their modifiers, if any).

She's right. And the way the word "like" is used today, in place of "ahs" and "ers" and "ums" and other crutches, supposedly to aid thinking and prevent being interrupted, makes it even more important for the educated to keep careful watch. I now do so, like, all the time. (Please forgive me.)

Prose-colored?

The Associated Press rolls on, providing its services to countless newspapers and magazines throughout the world. And just like those publications, the AP has its own staff of reporters and writers. As noted by K.C. of St. Cloud, Minn., an AP article written by Erin McClam, about the political division in the U.S. into red and blue states, included the following: "But 12 months have passed since [the 2004 elections]. We have had time to heal, to start listening to each other again. To become, in a word, purpler."

Writer McClam merely supplied the hook. Taking the bait was whoever was writing headlines that day for the *St. Cloud Times*, and who provided this 36-point masterpiece across five columns: "A year after red vs. blue, is America **more purpler**?" We're fighting a losing battle here, folks.

A classic?

From Tulsa, Okla., we hear from J.K.:

A film [name forgotten] was being locally promoted as having been "filmed entirely in ancient Greece." This is a good trick.

31

Grammar 101

This is as good a place as any to take some more lumps myself. In those early days of my *Mensa Bulletin* column, I bandied the words "grammar," "syntax," "usage," and "diction" with no real regard for their meanings. According to my dictionaries, the differences are:

Grammar: The means of indicating relationships [of words] to each other, and their functions and relations in the sentence [in] established usage. Originally meaning "skill in writing," the word's meaning has now come to include the features of [the] language, which are sounds, words, formations and arrangement of words, etc. It is a branch of linguistic science.

Syntax: That part of grammar that treats of word relations according to established usage. Also, patterns of the formation of words into sentences and phrases, as well as their study and description.

Usage: The way in which words and phrases are customarily used, regardless of prescriptions or proscriptions in such works as this book. No civil laws pertain.

Diction: Originally Latin for "delivery in public speaking," it has also come to mean "choice of words," as implied by the word "dictionary." Some purists decry the word's decidedly popular meaning of "enunciation, vocal expression, clarity, and distinctness of speech," preferring to hold "use of words" as being the primary definition. However, all dictionaries go along with the more prevalent usage, so there's no use fighting. It's unfortunate, though, that we can no longer use the word without defining it, either by the way it appears in context or by explanatory elaboration. How very sad.

There will, no doubt, be some who will tell me I'm all wet, and that my foregoing definitions are not totally accurate. Let's not get overly picky here. I am on just as safe ground as anyone when I use "syntax" to mean "grammar," and vice versa. If the former is a part of the latter, I have no problem equating one with the other in ordinary speech and writing. Most people have no idea that there is a difference anyway. Besides, I told you a long time ago that I was no technician. If what I write makes sense, that's good enough for me. (Are those puritanical screams I hear?)

Help what?

While we're all in the mood, let me take myself to the woodshed again, aided and assisted by three readers who would not let me get away with *anything*! Oh, sure, I have received compliments galore over the years, but it's my own errors that hang me out to dry. Here's G.G. of I know not where:

> I cannot describe the elation with which I discovered your column in the September *Mensa Bulletin*. I am a new member and had no idea that there was an organization featuring semantic "know-it-alls" such as myself (such as I?). What a revelation – to have found comrades in smugness.

> Conversely, what a tremendous disappointment to locate an error in your very own column. I would like to theorize that it was an error by a typist or proofreader, but alas I fear that it is simply an all-too-common usage error. Please consult your probably expensive library of reference books and learn that "cannot help but" is entirely *wrong*. The correct usage is "cannot help having a significant effect." Reprimandingly yours (is coining a word permissible?), [sig]

M.M. of Baton Rouge, La., and J.C. of New York, N.Y., also took me to task. What I originally wrote was, "If enough letters are written to offenders, we **cannot help but have** a significant effect." J.C. concluded by adding, "Redactor, redactus!" which means "Editor, edit thyself!" or some such. So now you know that I was once not fully educated (I first wrote "ignorant," but thought it too harsh). After many years of hearing and reading "cannot help but ... ," with no one to disabuse me, what else was I to do? OK, so now I know better, and so do we all. I am fully repentant and will henceforth recast as needed.

What's a preposition for?

There. I did it. I ended a sentence with a preposition, and I wanted to. Hah! I did it again! Just so we all know, it is no longer taboo to use a preposition to end a sentence with. (One more!) Yes, I was taught not to do it, but those days are gone forever. Never mind Winston Churchill's "… up with which I shall not put"; this is a classic case of popular usage attaining an unbreakable hold on our collective message-center. Some of us will end our lives unconvinced that the rule is gone, but most will neither care nor think much about it. *Que sera, sera.* I've already forgotten what the question was.

Peek-a-boo

Repetitively redundant is this from S.A. of Spokane, Wash.:

> Enclosed for your perusal is a copy of the [back of the] container of my favorite Maybelline eyelash glue. It says it "Holds firmly but peels away easily from eyelids and lashband. Creamy adhesive turns **invisibly transparent** when completely dry." It is my favorite because I don't like eyelash glue [that] is not transparent when it is invisible. Please send me two SOTS whistles – one for each hand.

What the heck is a "lashband"? It's not in any of my dictionaries. As for "invisibly transparent," could it mean that something might be "visibly transparent"? If a window pane is dirty, but one can still see through it, I suppose it *could* be called "visibly transparent," but then wouldn't it technically be "translucent"? I'll have to think more about it, or maybe not. In the meantime, there's this from L.T. of Framingham, Mass.:

> Here are some bloopers from the *Boston Globe*, one of the few papers fit to be read by intelligent people, although it has its share of functional illiterates among its writers, syndicated columnists, typesetters, and proofreaders:

> "High **heals**." Unlikely to be a typo.

> "**Observe**" and "**reserve**," referring to the two sides of a coin. (obverse and reverse)

"Lowering the **sites**," meaning "sights."

"**Whom** he said was being judged." (who)

"Shortly after that he was **nationalized**." (naturalized)

"**Bridal** path," referring to a horseback rider.

It would have been nice to have the offenders' names, but I thought they were worth including anyway. Next time, maybe?

Dear Sot

OK, so that is how P.B. of Marietta, Ohio, addressed his note, but if that is the worst I've been called, I can live with it. Here's what he sent:

> From a book critic writing in the *Boston Herald American*:
> "Readers will be amused for hours by what **amounts to** a selec-
> tion of **auditory slides** catching everybody at their worst verbal
> behavior." This also appears as a blurb just inside the front
> cover of Edwin Newman's *Strictly Speaking*, the Warner Books
> paperback first edition, of all places.

First printed in 1975, there were at least 11 subsequent printings, and I have a copy of the 12th, printed in 1977. Is that wording still there? Yes, it is, and I have been listening carefully to the book and have heard nary a peep. OK, so the "amounts to" qualifies the "auditory slides" tag, but it was a poor choice, as was the entire sentence. I'm sure we know what was intended, but I don't believe author Newman would have approved.

Quick, a dictionary!

J.P. of Westland, Mich., presented me with a clipping that I found hard to swallow (a beer chaser helped):

> Enclosed please find a Sydney J. Harris column from the
> *Detroit Free Press* and note the two items I have circled in red.
> Under an overall heading of "Thoughts at Large," he opines:
> "In most cases, when we are **abjured** to 'listen to reason,' we
> become busy thinking up ways to refute it." Immediately fol-
> lowing that disaster was: "The most self-contradictory phrase in

the language is '**prison reform**' – it is on a par with sending an infected person to a plague house in order to cure him."

To "abjure" means to renounce or repudiate. The word he was looking for was "adjured," although neither is very commonly used. Any of several others would have served better, such as "urged" or "asked" or "exhorted," etc. As for "prison reform," Harris missed his mark by a mile. "Prison reform" has to do with changing and/or improving the prison *system*, and has nothing to do with reforming or rehabilitating prisoners, as he implies. Where were the copyeditors on that big big-city newspaper?

Nap time?

How many copyeditors does it take to fix a word? In too many cases, the answer is "None. It doesn't get fixed." A story might originate with the Associated Press, as in the following 1977 example, but when it finally appears in a local newspaper, it suffers from mishandling somewhere along the line. R.H. of West Frankfort, Ill., found it:

> In yesterday's *Southern Illinoisan* I noticed an AP article datelined Qurna, Iraq. It told of Norwegian explorer Thor Heyerdahl's "voyage to the unknown," which was attempting to "see whether the ancient people of Mesopotamia were masters of distant sea travel.
>
> "Heyerdahls 30-foot *Tigris*, a replica of an ancient Sumerian reed boat, was safely moored after it was stuck in the mud for a short time Friday at the confluence of the **Tigress** and Euphrates rivers."

You'd think that *any* copyeditor who read it would have caught it, but none did. The two words being pronounced the same might indicate that they were spoken at some point, but that would have been unusual, considering that the item was most likely transmitted by teletype and recopied by a typesetter. (That's how it was done in 1977.)

An editorial, yet

Of all the varied material making up a newspaper, an editorial, one would think, would be the most likely to be scrutinized by one or more copyeditors. Arriving in my mailbox in a plain brown envelope, with no contributor's name evident anywhere, was an editorial clipped from the *Fort Lauderdale News* of that particular Florida city. The editorial dealt with charity drives and used a 6-year-old girl to illustrate the need for medical help for the economically disadvantaged (what we used to call "the poor"). Paying special tribute to an AMVETS post, the editorial writer noted: "Patty still needs help. And so **does** her parents. They would like to know [what happened to the money]." Inexcusable. But why did the contributor choose to be anonymous? Could he or she have been a staffer on the paper? Or might it have been someone from a *rival* paper? We were not meant to know, obviously. ("do")

Not inclusive

Here's one that really bugs me, and so too does it bug V.M. of South Paris, Maine:

> How about taking a crack at Western Electric for stating in
> its television commercials that it makes "more telephones than
> anybody"? Not "anyone else," but more than they make them-
> selves [as well].

Western Electric can, of course, no longer make that claim, as it could in 1980. China makes more telephones than anybody (else) nowadays, but the screwy locution is just as prevalent today as it was then. Western Electric was the wholly owned subsidiary of AT&T that made those great phones – mostly dial, however – that are still working as well as they ever did. I have one dial phone left, and someday I'll put it up on eBay and make a few bucks. Anyway, to say that anyone does something better than anyone is shy of the mark. (anyone else, or anybody else)

Down in flames

Here's a case of the horse following the cart, as discovered by J.W. of Palm Beach, Fla.:

> The headline in the *Palm Beach Post* reads: "**Arson Blamed on
> Fire** at Jupiter Bar." I'll bet you didn't know that things happen
> in reverse on the outer planets.

That's Jupiter, Florida, of course, and let's not blame the fire for the arson. Nice catch, J.W.

Mixed signals

R.K. of Chicago, Ill., sent me a very odd photograph from the *Conservative Digest* of February 1978. It shows a sign posted inside the W.T. Grant store in Olean, N.Y., in lettering easy to see at some distance, reading: "Entrance – Do Not Enter." There are neither pedestrians nor cars shown in the photo, but one can easily imagine the traffic jam just behind the photographer. If indeed the intent of the sign was to keep those exiting from doing so at an entrance, it should have read: "Do Not Exit Here," or "Not an Exit." Should the sign-maker have tried to fix it? No, a smart sign-maker never questions the customer's judgment. On the other hand, if the customer needs someone to blame, well, I guess that the sign-making business is not an easy one to be in.

Extra syllables

Newspapers are wont to save space and ink by eliminating the serial comma, but seem to have no qualms about adding unnecessary syllables. Two words come to mind, and there are others, I know. One was broadly displayed in a 1977 headline in the *Dallas Times Herald* that read: "Laetrile no cure or **preventative**, study shows." Remember laetrile? It was made from the pits of apricots and thought by some to be able to cure cancer. It wasn't. But that extra syllable added to the otherwise perfectly good "preventive" is still with us. Some dictionaries offer it as a variant, but then, we know dictionaries, don't we? As Yoda of *Star Wars* fame would say, "Grain of salt, take we."

The other word we see so often is "**orientated**," where "oriented" would do. "Orientation" is obviously where it comes from, and "orientated" and even "orientate" are known as back-formations of "orientation."

Punctuate this

Word people, such as I, love the linguistic peccadilloes of newswriters. A carefully turned phrase can backfire so quickly that hardly anyone sees it before taking a breath. Case in point: this from N.B. of Newark, N.J.:

GORDON K. ANDERSEN

"Pennsylvania plans cut in air pollution," reads the [1977] headline in *The New York Times*. The text of the article, written by
Donald Janson (Special to *The New York Times*), contains the
following: "Mr. Tasher [New Jersey deputy attorney general]
said in a telephone interview from Trenton today that two years
of 'exhaustive discussions' with Pennsylvania authorities had
failed to produce a satisfactory plan to reduce pollutants from
Philadelphia **smokestacks that drifted** across the Delaware
River into New Jersey."

Y'know, I would have thought that they would have those things pretty
well tied down. In fact, two commas would have done the job nicely; put
one each before and after "from Philadelphia smokestacks"; that way we
have pollutants drifting instead of smokestacks. Had a copyeditor done
so, we would have been deprived of a good laugh, so maybe we should be
grateful. OK, but not overly so.

Thin mints or samoas?

A word is a word is a word, to paraphrase Gertrude Stein's take on the rose.
D.G. of Boca Raton, Fla., sent me a piece of cardboard cut from a box.

I clipped the [enclosed] from a Girl Scouts cookie box. It says,
"Baked by **authority** of THE GIRL SCOUTS of the U.S.A." I
hope "authority" is a good cook.

Since it was the Girls Scouts organization that ordered the cookies to be
made, was it necessary to also "authorize" the baker to bake them? Somebody, apparently, wanted to make the baking of the cookies more of an
"official" event than it really was. The Girl Scouts order them, receive
them, and sell them, so what's the big deal? If I order a pizza over the
phone, will it be made by my "authority"? C'mon, folks, let's not make too
much of a cookie order. "Baked for the Girl Scouts of the U.S.A." would
have been sufficient. (An early baker in my general area was the Burry
Co., although various others did the baking in other parts of the country.)

Expensive misspelling

Billboards, road signs, nothing is more public than such displays. C.M. of
Nacogdoches, Texas, has this dilly for us:

On heavily traveled U.S. Highway 59, which runs between I-20 and Houston, is a pinball palace whose sign proclaims "THE GAME **ODDESSY**," in yellow lettering two feet tall, on a blue background. It is obviously a very nice custom-made sign and must have been quite costly.

It would be very interesting to know how many of those seeing it can recognize the gaffe. Not many, I dare to presume. Then there's another possibility: It was done deliberately, and anyone who points out the error to management gets a roll of quarters to plug into the pinball machines, and maybe a free package of beef jerky or a T-shirt. As an attention-getting stunt, however, it has to be a bust, since so few can spell ODYSSEY. Of course, if one gets it and tells some friends ... Ah, well, it's fun to speculate.

Since when?

Here's one that will drive you daffy if you think about it too much. Frequent contributor L.W. of South Gate, Calif., had his concentration come to a screeching halt:

> The full-page ad for The Lincoln Mint [in the Sunday newspaper supplement] offered small gold and silver bars with "Ten of the greatest locomotives that ever rode the rails" sculpted on them in bas-relief. I was amazed to learn that, according to the ad, "Silver and Gold have been precious metals since **before Biblical times**." Precious to whom? I ask. If the Genesis 1:1 report is to be believed, the heavens and the earth did not exist before "the creation," and there would have been no one around to mine the metals, let alone value them.

On *Fantasy Island?*

C.M. of Bloomingdale, N.J., enclosed an article clipped from the Hackensack, N.J., *Herald News*. Written about the difficulties senior citizens face finding suitable transportation for shopping, etc., the text was accompanied by a photo captioned: "Helen Vargo **de-buses**." C.M. supposes that it's no worse than "de-plane," but also wonders if "de-car" is next. In the article itself, staff writer Karen Grib notes that "For the most part, [the seniors] seem relaxed during the trips [by bus] and, **like** their driver says, 'They probably would stay home if they didn't feel secure.'" C.M. wasn't sure whether the driver smoked Winstons or not. ("as")

32

Typographical errors?

There are so many typos in publications that I decided early on to ignore them, but sometimes what may look like a typo is really not a typo. Case in point: K.M. of Houston, Texas, caught this 1978 headline in the *Houston Post*: "[President] Carter hosts college editors but Midge **steels** the show." (Midge is Midge Costanza, then assistant to the president for public liaison.) Aside from the left hand typing both "steels" and "steals," normally two separate fingers on that hand are involved, unless, of course, one is using the popular hunt-and-peck technique. There's no way to tell now how the goof occurred, but we can be reasonably certain it was not an accidental slip of the fingers.

From H.T. of Portland, Ore., comes another of the same ilk, although admittedly not as public:

> Please read the first line of the [enclosed] ticket aloud: "**24rd** Annual Ball." The ticket is for a yearly event to raise funds for our first-aid people and is sponsored by our local firemen's association.

Now, *that* one isn't a typo either. Typos are caused by typesetters, or keyboarders, as they are often known today, striking the wrong key(s) on a keyboard. In this case, however, someone likely said, "Just change the 3 to a 4, and let's get the job done and outta here." Whoever was striking the keys that day was probably just doing what had been ordered. But would you care to bet that, as with most printers, the job wasn't started until the day it was due to be delivered? Here's one that's even more mysterious, courtesy of C.F. of New York, N.Y.:

> Sometimes I wonder if writers and/or copyeditors and/or proofreaders know what the heck some words mean. In a *New York Post* book review (NEW YORK JEW, by Alfred Kazin) was this paragraph: "And if anyone finds irony in the fact that *New York Jew* Alfred Kazin became a major interpreter and force in

American literature, then it is still a necessary reminder that the day is long past when our national culture was a WASP **preservative**."

Oddly, for some reason I can't fathom, "preservative" makes sense in this use, even though it's unlikely it was the word the reviewer intended. For my money, the word should have been "preserve," somewhat better, although that would put it in the same sense as "game preserve" is used. But do you suppose it could be said that at one time our national culture served to preserve WASPs? Think about it. Or not.

Don't stay home without it

TV Guide is indispensable for many people. But lately it's been full of articles about shows I never watch, with characters and actors I never heard of. Nevertheless, many find it worthwhile, but most probably don't pay much attention to the spelling and punctuation mishaps. The afore-mentioned and sharp-eyed E.K. of North Miami, Fla., found mention of "Grisly *Grizzly Adams*," a very popular family show at one time, fol-lowed a couple of weeks later by an ad for local Miami Channel 7 for the movie *Secret Ceremony*, a now-forgotten Elizabeth Taylor epic. The blurb included: "Robert Mitchum also co-stars in this gripping, **grizzly** drama." (this time, "grisly")

E.K. also watched *The Wind and the Lion*, and was aghast to hear the actor portraying President Theodore Roosevelt speak of having a grizzly bear stuffed and displayed at the Smithsonian **Institute**. This gaffe is more common that we might think. The huge museum complex in Washing-ton, D.C., is the Smithsonian *Institution*; always has been, always will be.

Medium well, please

E.K. of Hardin, Mont. (no kin to the previous E.K.), is well traveled:

In North Carolina and Georgia my cousin and I stayed fre-quently at Days Inn motels. At most of them the dining room tables were topped with this dreadful little sign [enclosed]. In very large type is TRY OUR RIB **EYE'S**, which is followed by a list comprising "**Queens** Steak," "**Kings** Steak," and "Steak for Two," all in a very nice script. We think it was done by the same people who decided that Days Inn was not possessive, so the Queen's and King's steaks got the same treatment; but they also had a need to use an apostrophe somewhere, and there it is in EYE'S.

From N.R. of Kent, Ohio:

> Earl Nightingale, on his essay-type radio program [1978], talked about the Pilgrims coming over on the *Mayflower* amid all kinds of horrible deprivations, the food preparation being made difficult because all they had to cook on were small **brassieres** on deck. ["braziers," pronounced bray-zhurs]

> Also, on Akron radio station WAKR, a newscaster reported that a young lady charged with shooting somebody was being **"arranged"** in court. I could just see her sprawling while her attorneys put a leg here, an arm there, and her head back just a bit ... ["arraigned"]

Good heavens!

You'd think that the editors of *Scientific American* magazine would be especially mindful of what their writing staff produces, so it was some-what surprising to G.N. of Glen Cove, N.Y., to find the following:

> "The **radius** of some red supergiants **is** so **large** that the earth's entire **orbit** would fit easily inside it." A vague antecedent, trouble with plurals, and a topological impossibility, all in one independent clause, and it slipped right past the editors of *SA*. What's next?

Nope, I have never seen a radius, nor even any radii, described as "large," and an orbit fitting inside one is a mind-boggler. Would that be the length of the orbit, or the diameter, assuming that it's not an ellipse? The contorted syntax also leads us to presuppose that several, or at least more than one, supergiants have the same radius. There are vague clues to what the writer was talking about, but the result leaves some of us staring blankly into space, yours truly included.

Count 'em

B.W., an American consulate staff member in Sydney, Australia, sent along a clipping from the *Sydney Morning Herald*:

> The clipping is self-explanatory. Under the heading "Column 8" are announcements of local happenings here in Sydney, and this one caught my eye: "TODAY, at Ryde High, what may be the world's biggest display of tooth-brushing is being staged by 1,000 students under the guidance of the Dental Health Education and Research Foundation. ... Our invitation says 1,000 **pair** of teeth will be brushed simultaneously." (Incidentally, "pair of teeth" or its equivalent is the correct form of expression in the Hebrew language.) [In English it would be "sets" of teeth.]

An incredible gaffe

You'd think that, with audiences of millions, television producers and writers would pay careful attention to every aspect of their programs. This, however, is not the case, at least according to what J.K. of St. Petersburg, Fla., heard:

> On the 2-hour-long season-opener [1978] of *The Incredible Hulk*, a young woman, supposedly a brilliant research scientist, in explaining her use of self-hypnosis in the treatment of her own terminal illness, said that she was going down deep into her tissues and cells "to study my own **physiognomy**." Why did no one check on this?

My guess is that it sounded so "scientific" that the actors and crew never questioned it. By definition, "physiognomy" has nothing whatsoever to do with anything internal, and means, simply, "outward appearance," referring most commonly to the face of a person. What was actually meant was "physiology."

Quick! Call Research

I have had some really terrific contributors over the years, and if it seems that some of the more prolific ones are hogging a lot of space in this book, you cannot deny their eagle eyes. One such is E.K. of North Miami, Fla., who has supplied me with some of my best material, as you have probably noticed. Herewith, another gem:

> In a 1978 issue of *TV Guide* there was a three-quarter-page ad placed by WPTV, Channel 7, for an *NBC Theatre* offering called "Summer of My German Soldier." The ad's text described the program as "The compelling story of a **13-year-old** Jewish girl who falls in love with an escaped Nazi P.O.W. in a small **Georgia** town during World War II." On a nearby page was a ["Close-up"] item for the exact same program that read: "Set in an **Arkansas** town during World War II, the drama tells of a **14-year-old** Jewish girl ..." Actress Kristy McNichol was billed in both entries as the star of the show.

Comfy?

When Rockwell International, manufacturer of medium-size aircraft, advertised its Sabreliner 65 corporate jet in a magazine ad, J.D. of Allentown, Pa., was alert enough to spot it and send it along to me:

> "Sabreliner 65 is the only medium jet at its price to offer true transcontinental range against prevailing winds with IFR fuel reserves *plus* individual seating for six **comfortable** passengers." I would love to know what the definition of a "comfortable passenger" is.

So would I. "Uh, beg pardon, ma'am, but are you comfortable?" "No, not really." "Well then, you can't come aboard. We allow only comfortable passengers in our plane."

None? Are you sure?

Every once in a while someone will send me a clipping, but without identifying him- or herself – no return address or legible postmark either. But this one I cannot ignore: In the *Stockton Record*, published in Stockton, Calif., the front-page headline reads: **"Searchers Find No Radiation In Canada."** It leaves much to the imagination, I agree, but I doubt that the text of the report would help to make the banner look any less silly. Further, I suspect that several cancer patients would be disappointed to read it. I also suspect another tight deadline. Hey, you folks there at the *Record*, am I right?

You can't hit 'em if they keep moving

"When E.F. Hutton talks," we're supposed to listen. But when E.F. Hutton runs a magazine ad containing two cockeyed uses of the language, what do we do then? L.S. of Coon Rapids, Minn., sent the company a letter along with a copy of the ad, which he had highlighted in yellow:

> The headline read: "Eight New Year's Resolutions for an Investor," the first of which dealt with setting personal investment goals and which included: "A well-painted bull's-eye is **easier** hit." No. 7 stated: "I will **cooly** evaluate everything I hear."

As for the inappropriate adjective "easier," it should be the adverbial "more easily." And despite the Oxford tome (OED), "coolly" rules the day in all seven of my dictionaries. Responding to L.S.'s letter, William L. Clayton, a senior vice-president and director (in 1979), wrote, "Your grammatical correction did not go unnoticed, but colloquialism is allowed in our ads just to give a human touch to a stuffy subject. Now as far as 'cooly', [*sic*] I am attaching an excerpt from *Webster's Third Unabridged Dictionary* which indicates the **duel** spelling of this adverb." ("dual")

Well, now, let's examine it. In a paragraph previous to those I quoted, Mr. Clayton claimed he had "been given the ability to spot a spelling mistake from twenty paces." Granted, there are initials of a typist or secretary or stenographer at the end of the letter, so perhaps he didn't have time to check it before it was mailed. But that business of allowing colloquialisms in high-priced ads is a cop-out. It just isn't done, unless it is so obvious that it can't be mistaken for correct grammar. And why did I put that [*sic*] after "cooly"? Aside from missing a letter, two reasons: (1) He put the comma outside the quotation mark, and (2) he didn't finish his introductory phrase "as far as ..." "As far as" always calls for a subject and a verb of some kind, as in "As far as *that is concerned*," or "As far as *we know*," or "As far as *we have been able to determine*," etc. We do not say, "As far as bananas, I like them on vanilla ice cream and smothered with chocolate sauce." A much better way of beginning a sentence that will keep us out of trouble is to use a slight variation: "As *for* bananas, etc." If Mr. Clayton had said, "Now, *as for* 'cooly' … ," he wouldn't have gotten SOTS's attention. He is now immortalized, at least here, anyway.

(Just for the record, my dictionaries have "coolie," defined as an "offensive name for an unskilled Asian laborer." The word "cooly" does appear in *Webster's Third* as Mr. Clayton reports, but only as a variation of "coolie." We win. Incidentally, Mr. Clayton is not a professional writer, but in taking on the mantle of a language expert, he edges his way into qualifying for the SOTS treatment.)

It gets worse

There's been a TV show on weekends called *The George Michael Sports Machine*. I'm sorry I didn't get her name, but a reporter on March 27, 2006, so completely unhinged me that I neglected to write down the actual sentence in which she substituted *exasperated* for *exacerbated*. This is the first time I've heard anyone make a synonym for "made worse" worse, if I make myself clear.

Heal thyself?

You'd think newspapers would be more careful with their own material than with anything else. Not so, says R.D. of Sarasota, Fla. In a "disclaimer" box in the Sarasota *Northeast News* is the following: "Nothing that appears in *Northeast News* may be reproduced either wholly or in part without the written permission of the publishers discretion." There is no apostrophe to indicate whether "publishers" is singular, plural, or possessive, and I can't make head or tail of the "discretion" reference. We know what is meant, of course, but does that mean we shouldn't mock it. Hey, that's what we're here for.

33

Never assume!

"Never assume" has been one of my mottoes for many years, but by now you all know that there are times when assumptions are justified, nay, even necessary. I have so demonstrated with several examples in this book. However, there are also times when we are so sure of what we are saying or writing that we feel no need to check on a grammatical usage. Such was the case in 1998 as reported by D.M. of New York City:

> On ABC-TV, Regis Philbin called the nuisance birds "**Canadian** geese," a common error.

True. Nationality has nothing to do with the actual name of the bird, which is "Canada goose." Regis, of course, was not alone; more than a few others have made that same mistake, on the air and in print, but as of this writing, his was the only example of the goof I had.

The Internet

There is such a huge mass of information on the Internet that it is impossible to tell whether something is written by a professional writer. The obvious nonprofessionals often stand out clearly, having little or no grasp of the principles of grammar, and frequently having no conception of syntax and sentence structure. Therefore, I have taken it rather easy on most Web site gaffes, except, of course, for those emanating from educational institutions and other sources that should know better.

But how about the History Channel? Shouldn't it be held to the highest standards? If so, then C.S. of New Orleans, La., has a legitimate gripe:

> From www.historychannel.com, October 30, 2000: "1875 Missouri's Constitution Ratified. ... In 1861, when other slave states **succeeded**, Missouri chose to remain in the Union." (By the way, I loved your program in Philadelphia [July 2000 Mensa Annual Gathering].) ["seceded"]

Thanks for the kind words, C.S., and for the additional note about the Internet item, which also contained a fusillade of typographical errors (usable perhaps in my next book), one of which was that the "1875" was the first word in what I believe was a headline, whereas in a text sentence it would – or should – have been spelled out as "Eighteen seventy-five." Some of those typos, by the way, are real lulus.

(The program C.S. referred to was a seminar I conducted at that Mensa annual convention and that was one of many I held locally, regionally, and nationally over the years.)

I was once roundly reprimanded for a typo in my own *Mensa Bulletin* column, by D.R. of Heidelberg, Germany, who was reading my latest while waiting for the 747 he was on to land at Frankfurt. His criticism dealt with a missing comma, an off-setting one like the ones on either side of "Germany" in the preceding sentence. When I checked the document I originally submitted, I discovered that I had actually left out *both* commas off-setting the name and city of a contributor, a practice I have now adopted (especially in this book), but one I used consistently (almost) in every column. So I was wrong, but D.R. was only partly correct, but didn't know it. Whoever did the retyping erroneously added the first comma, but left off the second, so I suppose it could be called a "compounded error."

(This was in 1996, before I had a computer and the convenience of e-mail. Coupled with the amazing innovation we know as word-processing, e-mail gives one the attendant ability to attach complete documents that can be downloaded and transferred to the finished page without retyping, but with whatever editing is necessary. The word-processing computer and the Internet have created an entirely different way of writing and publishing, but as one can easily see, it is not possible to eliminate human error. Mine was a double one and the typesetter made it worse, by adding only the single comma.)

What next?

While I'm at it, I might as well take another swipe at myself and get it over with. (I'd like to see anyone change *that* prepositional ending to something better.) Many years ago I adopted the previously mentioned personal motto that has usually served me well; it is "Never Assume." However, as I said before, sometimes I do exactly that and sink myself into linguistic quicksand. Such was the case in 1997 when I "assumed" that *refractory* and *refractive* meant the same thing. It had to do with a classified ad that offered an "antique **refractory** table," the item having been sent to me by J.D. of Sherman Oaks, Calif. My comment was, "Personally, I'd rather have a refectory table, but, of course, it wouldn't bend light quite as well."

As I was soon to find out, via several pieces of mail, a refectory table is a table in a dining hall, which is itself also called a refectory. OK, so far. There is, however, no such thing as a refractory table. Refractory has several meanings, none of which have anything to do with the bending of light. The bending of light is *refraction*, especially in the eye, and the word also refers to the way we see things under water. The corresponding adjective is "refractive." The word refractory means – among other things nonoptical – unruly, intractable, etc., as it may be applied to a difficult child. As for a prism, it simply reflects light or disperses it into the color spectrum, but it does not "refract" light. Further study of all of the foregoing is available online and at your local library, and this is as dull as I expect this book to get.

Unless ...

Those who know the difference between transitive verbs and intransitive verbs will appreciate the following more than those who do not know the difference. But learning the difference is as close as the pages of this book. K.W.-D. of Kenosha, Wis., caught a fellow named Frank Cook – writing for something called Common Communications, Inc. – defying the rules of English in an article he wrote for one or more newspapers. It spoke to the practice of those home-sellers who take too much with them when they move out, usually things that are not totally tied down, but were assumed by the buyer to be part of the deal. Cook includes: "Less explainable are people who simply decide to **disappear** items from the house, knowing full well they should have stayed."

"Disappear" is, in all seven dictionaries I have, an intransitive verb, which means that it does not take an object, as does a transitive verb (*hit* the ball, etc.). One can make things disappear, but one cannot "disappear" any person, place, or thing. Even magicians do not have that ability. I like to think that "transitive" indicates a transition or connection between the verb and the object, whereas the "intransitive" type just goes and does what it does all by itself. Anyone have a better idea?

Picky? Hmmm ...

Up to this point, I haven't attempted to determine how far I can go before we're called "picky." There are, of course, those who label *me* with that adjective, often adding that I started out that way, but I know that there are others who are even more adept at "fly-specking" than I am. There are, however, some who maintain that being "too picky" is impossible. Daring a presumption, I offer the following from V.M. of South Paris, Maine:

> Companies [wishing] to advertise on TV pay thousands of dollars to the companies [that] produce the commercials, so it is understandable that they wish to use the same tape repeatedly. I dislike repetition, but could tolerate it better if the ad writers (1) could think straightly and (2) would stop underestimating the intelligence of their fellow humans.
>
> One of the irksome lines I hear almost nightly concerns Kellogg's corn flakes, wherein I am asked to "try them again for the first time." About as bad is a commercial for Dove. They don't tell us what Dove [really] is, but they say it "contains one-quarter moisturizing cream. It won't dry your face like soap." I would be reluctant to use anything other than soap to clean my face, so this ad would keep me from buying Dove. [I too wonder about the other three-quarters.]
>
> We are repeatedly told in another commercial that "only **one** prune tastes Sunsweet." [This] might incline an unsophisticated, gullible person to assume that much money is being spent to extol and publicize a single prune.
>
> More serious, however, is the error in a line spoken by [actor Karl Malden] who for years has admonished us not to leave home without American Express travelers checks. A while

back I heard him say on several occasions, "American Express has over a thousand offices to serve you. Don't leave home without them!" (Without 1,000+ offices?)

One commercial, which didn't last long, probably because of complaints, was the one that stated, "Man **invented** time, Seiko perfected it." Obviously, man didn't *invent* time; it is time-keeping that is being referred to.

See what I mean? Frankly, I don't think any of them is picky, but that's just my personal opinion, as is much, or maybe most, of this book. Pickiness, as far as I'm concerned, is in the eye or ear of the reader or listener, so when you are rolling your eyeballs or groaning at one thing or another, be generous enough to give your fellow language-lovers a bit of the tolerance you expect from them. Over the many years I have been writing and speaking about this stuff, I have yet to find anyone who doesn't have a gripe of one kind or another. Almost everyone who has argued with me about my unkindnesses toward my targets has sooner or later come up with a pet peeve of his or her own. It rarely fails. Audiences, when the door is opened to them, invariably spill out a flood of personal dislikes and examples of questionable grammar they've had bottled up, often for years. Apparently, it's a form of catharsis, because there are always those who say, "I've been wanting to talk to someone about (it) *forever*, but I've been afraid to, for fear of being laughed at."

SOTS and those who subscribe to its aims make up a largely silent and scattered group. We do not hold regular meetings, nor do we have a newsletter, and we are undoubtedly a minority among the population, but we nevertheless have every right to be heard, even if only on the pages of such books as this one. We may be like the god Neptune, trying to sweep back the tide, but whatever we can do to help stave off damage to our language we do with a sense of responsibility, along with a feeling of pride. Succeed or fail, often or seldom, or somewhere in between, we will always be able to say that we tried.

Now's the time

T.K. of Santa Rosa, Calif., is another of my correspondents whose contributions may have a bit of the off-beat to them, but are no less deserving of space here. They do, however, require a bit of tailoring, since T.K., or rather, t.k., disdains capital letters, *a la* e.e. cummings. I never understood why, but here, without any tailoring, is his offering:

you know how the spellings *orange, uncle, comptroller,* etc., and the common mispronunciations of *harassment, kilometer, kudos,* etc., and the misspoken phrases i-could-care-less, she-likes-me-going-to-bed-early, gladly,-the-cross-eyed-bear, all started with somebody's making a mistake, but thru the mistake's repetition, have all taken on a more or less aura of correctness, or at least respectability. i'm sure change, in former simple times, progressed along a curve something like this [draws a slowly rising line]. but now, with so many more people & better communications, the curve has probably gone into its more radical exponential pattern, thus [draws an abruptly rising line]. so, we are confronted with so many new mistakes that we can't combat them. as knowledge has exploded, so has ignorance.

i complained to *PEOPLE* magazine, when they wrote about a cheerleader waving her pompoms, that I hadn't seen any anti-aircraft guns in the picture. on the next sheet is their answer [attached].

"Dear Mr. [K.]: Thank you for writing in response to PEOPLE Weekly's August 17 Chatter item on Kristy Swanson.

"Regarding your comments concerning the distinction between *pompom* and *pompon, Webster's Third Edition's* second definition of *pompom* lists *pompon* as an alteration [*sic*]. Therefore, we are both correct.

"We appreciate your keeping us on our toes with your close attention to our editorial content and would like to thank you, again, for your interest in our magazine. Sincerely yours, (sig) Maureen Fulton."

[Even worse, *Merriam-Webster's Ninth New Collegiate* has "pompon" as meaning "pom-pom." Yikes! At least the hyphen was correct. Oh, how far we have strayed.]

[T.K. again] they admit that pompom is an alteration (read corruption), so *why do they use it?* it's wrong!

notice that they even misspelled pom-pom! when you make an error, and misspell it, where does that leave you? certainly not in a position to claim that we are *both* right!

i would like to quit butting my head against the stone wall, but it all still annoys me (as it does you, surely). i guess before long the country will just be one big mrs. malaprop sinking in a sea of ignorance, and *that's progress.* have fun – if possible. (sig)

Those who understand the Word word-processing program will sympathize with me for having to fight to get capital letters where they would normally appear. But I wanted to abide by T.K.'s preference, unusual though it may be. Also, this item would not have fit into my *Bulletin* column, so I'm glad I could get it in here. Frankly, I think it's a gem, warts and all.

More nonsense

L.W. of South Gate, Calif., is back with this one:

In an unattributed sports item in the *Los Angeles Times* was the news that "Center Ralph Drollinger of Athletes in Action has been sidelined with a **systematic** viral infection and will not play in the game ..." ["systemic"]

finis

So late?

So much of what has appeared here can be attributed to the unwillingness of communicators and their editors to pay attention to what they write and to double-check their work by using copyeditors. A perfect illustration is this from M.L. of Na'alehu, Hawai'i:

> No one wanted to take credit or blame for the article in the *Hawaii Tribune-Herald* about a railroad exhibit that told us that "Wailoa Center is located on Piopio Street in Hilo, and is open daily, Mondays, Tuesdays, Thursdays and Fridays from 8 A.M. to 4:30 P.M., and Wednesdays from noon to **closing**."

So how late is that? Speaking of "late," I've probably kept you up past your bedtime reading this nonsense, but I hope you had at least a little enjoyment in the process. I, of course, have had more than my share of fun, laughing and groaning all the way. So long as professional communicators continue to kick our beautiful language around, SOTS will be here to remind them that, "to those of us who know the difference, you will continue to stand out like sore thumbs, and your goofs will not go unnoticed."

I still have several hundred items that didn't quite meet the specifications for SOTS; that is, material prepared by professionals, and appearing in or on the public media. But because I hate to ignore the nonprofessional and nonpublic stuff, a big chunk of which is even funnier than what appears here, I'm going to tackle a second book. (But don't hold your breath; this one took 30 years.)

I continue to welcome contributions, and if you have something I might be able to use in the future, you can send it to me in care of the publisher, whose name and addresses appear on the copyright page up front. I can't promise to answer questions personally, but if you enclose an SASE, chances are good that I will send back a brief reply.

Nonprofessionals, of course, will not be identified in my writings in any way, nor will contributors except by initials and city. If you prefer, I'll even leave those off, but be sure to say so. And always remember,

(drum roll)

Abusing the English language is like picking your nose in public. It usually does little harm, but it certainly does nothing toward enhancing your image.

– 30 –

Index